The Salamanca Campaign

The Salamanca Campaign

Tim Saunders

Pen & Sword
MILITARY

First published in Great Britain in 2022 by
PEN & SWORD MILITARY
an imprint of
Pen & Sword Books Ltd
47 Church Street
Barnsley
South Yorkshire
S70 2AS

Copyright © Tim Saunders, 2022

ISBN 978-1-39900-136-6

The right of Tim Saunders to be identified as the author of this work has been asserted by him in accordance with the Copyright, Designs and Patents Act 1988.

A CIP catalogue record for this book is available from the British Library.

All rights reserved. No part of this book may be reproduced or transmitted in any form or by any means, electronic or mechanical including photocopying, recording or by any information storage and retrieval system, without permission from the Publisher in writing.

Typeset by Concept, Huddersfield HD4 5JL.
Printed and bound in England by CPI Group (UK) Ltd, Croydon CR0 4YY.

Pen & Sword Books Limited incorporates the imprints of Atlas, Archaeology, Aviation, Discovery, Family History, Fiction, History, Maritime, Military, Military Classics, Politics, Select, Transport, True Crime, Air World, Frontline Publishing, Leo Cooper, Remember When, Seaforth Publishing, The Praetorian Press, Wharncliffe Local History, Wharncliffe Transport, Wharncliffe True Crime and White Owl.

For a complete list of Pen & Sword titles please contact
PEN & SWORD BOOKS LIMITED
47 Church Street, Barnsley, South Yorkshire, S70 2AS, England
E-mail: enquiries@pen-and-sword.co.uk
Website: www.pen-and-sword.co.uk

Contents

Acknowledgements vi
Introduction vii
  1. The Situation in Spring 1812 1
  2. Plans and Preparations 21
  3. The Opening Moves 37
  4. To the Duero and Back 63
  5. The Approach to Battle 93
  6. Morning, 22 July 1812 107
  7. The Right Wing 135
  8. The Centre 169
  9. End of the Battle 187
 10. Pursuit and Garcihernández 211
Appendices
   I: Order of Battle: Salamanca 239
   II: Wellington's Salamanca Dispatch 243
Notes 251
Index 259

Acknowledgements

In writing this book during the lockdowns of the 2020 pandemic, the availability online of numerous articles, diaries and journals via Project Gutenberg, Google Books, etc. has been a godsend. Without them and those who have brought new or obscure memoires to print, the author would have struggled to adequately illustrate fresh insight into the Salamanca campaign.

Major William Napier famously described the battlefield as a 'vast cloud of smoke and dust that rolled along the basin'. This, of course, made it difficult for the combatants to know or subsequently describe exactly where they fought. A combination, however, of easy travel to Spain, four-wheel drive, modern maps, air photography, archaeology and more numerous and readily available accounts than ever before have allowed a greater focus on the substantial area of largely open rolling ground in the centre of the Salamanca battlefield. As a result, it is now possible with some greater certainty to locate the scene of the various actions. The almost fifty maps in this book are largely the product of this work.

I am most grateful to Major Rob Yuill and the living historians of the Napoleonic Association for answering my questions. They have also continued to play a significant part in recreating the drill, tactics and uniform of the regiments that fought in the Peninsular War. This has provided me with a far greater level of detail and understanding of the part played by those they portray in both battle and campaign. In this respect I am grateful to Paul Edwards for setting me straight on the use by British battalions of drum and bugle during battle.

There is, however, still a dearth of French material available on Salamanca but Marc Middleton, author of *School of the Soldier* has helped me with the complexities of the French column and tactics and provided me with diagrams to explain them.

Finally, to the team at Pen & Sword Books – Heather, Matt, Pamela and Noel – once again my thanks for their patience in nursing this project to fruition.

        Tim Saunders MBE
        Warminster, 2020

Introduction

The amount of new material and developments in the understanding of the detail of the Peninsular Army's tactics has made a reprisal of the Salamanca Campaign an essential part of the 'Peninsular War Battlefield Companion' series.

In 1812, another coalition against Napoleon's France, fuelled by English gold, saw the emperor turning east to take on Czar Alexander's Russia. Troops were stripped away from his armies in Spain and with the guerrillas tying down tens of thousands of French soldiers, the time was ripe for Wellington to take to the offensive. Several weeks of manoeuvre around Salamanca and east to the Rio Duero and back again were punctuated by a number of small but sharp actions including at the Salamanca forts and at Castrejón. By the third week of July, with French reinforcements for Marshal Marmont's Army of Portugal known to be on the way and both commanders unwilling to commit to battle without a clear advantage, it seemed that Wellington would be manoeuvred back to Portugal. Believing Wellington did not have the stomach for battle and, wishing to cut off the allies on the road back to Ciudad Rodrigo, Marmont made a mistake. The French army became over-extended and unable to support its divisions in a timely manner and Wellington pounced! In forty-five minutes the French were defeated, proving that Wellington's Peninsular Army could fight and win an offensive battle, marking an important point in the transformation of the allied army. It was, however, still a small army that had, as autumn set in, to withdraw back to the borders of Portugal in the face of the united French armies.

In this book I have continued my practice of letting the officers and soldiers of the respective armies tell their own stories of combats and battle in a campaign that took them from the borders of Portugal into the heart of Spain and the liberation of Madrid.

Chapter One

The Situation in Spring 1812

Following his advance into Spain that culminated at the Battle of Talavera, Wellington stood on the defensive for the remainder of 1809 through until the spring of 1812 with but a month of offensive operations. During this time a 65,000-strong French army under Marshal André Masséna invaded Portugal and though defeated at Buçaco, he continued to advance, expecting to be in Lisbon within weeks and as Napoleon said, to 'drive the leopard into the sea'. Masséna's ill-starred campaign, however, came to an abrupt halt before the Lines of Torres Vedras.

The lines were at the heart of Wellington's defensive strategy. He knew that the French could assemble armies in the peninsula that were much larger than anything the Anglo-Portuguese could field and that Lisbon was the political, economic and military heart of Portugal; he concluded 'deny it to the enemy and one is still in the game'. His plan set in train during the autumn of 1809 was to build a line of redoubts across the 25 miles of the Lisbon peninsula, from the Atlantic on the left to the Rio Tagus on the right, making use of the commanding ground of the Hills of Cintra. The Lisbon defences eventually developed into an embarkation area and two separate lines between 5 and 9 miles apart, which when Masséna arrived before them in mid-October 1810 consisted of 126 redoubts mounting 427 guns. With the salutary experience of attacking Wellington on Buçaco Ridge still firmly in mind and unexpectedly confronted by redoubts crowning every hill, the Army of Portugal's jealous, disloyal and warring corps commanders refused to attack.[1]

In support of the lines, the Portuguese Regency government agreed to Wellington's request for a policy of denial, which was essentially a 'scorched earth' policy with the removal of food stocks and anything else that could aid an enemy which when on campaign fed itself by foraging. Brutal though this policy was, the allies did not need to risk a general engagement while starvation did the job of reducing the enemy for him. The cost of drawing Masséna's army deep into Portugal was, however, the considerable suffering of the population, but militarily it saved the country. After a month before the lines, the French withdrew some 30 miles to country east of Santarém that had not been stripped bare of resources and awaited resupply and reinforcement. Very little of either reached Masséna and by March 1811 he had little choice but to withdraw his starving, disease-ridden army.

Initially the marshal intended to head north, cross the Rio Mondego and into northern Portugal, but without a bridging train, the Mondego running high and the bridge at Coimbra in the hands of Colonel Trant's *ordenanza* and militia, he

2 Salamanca Campaign, 1812

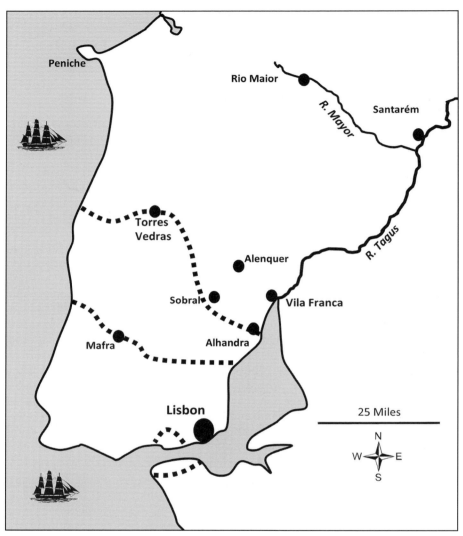

The Lines of Torres Vedras.

was effectively blocked. With subordinates who wished for nothing else but to march back to Spain, Masséna's commanders stand accused of not trying too hard to seize a crossing to facilitate their master's plan. Consequently, Masséna had no option but to march east to the succour of his magazines at Ciudad Rodrigo and Salamanca.

Wellington's pursuit was masterfully opposed by Marshal Ney and his VI Corps but with the Light Division on his tail, fighting a series of sharp actions, the marshal was manoeuvred out of every position he took up by a series of

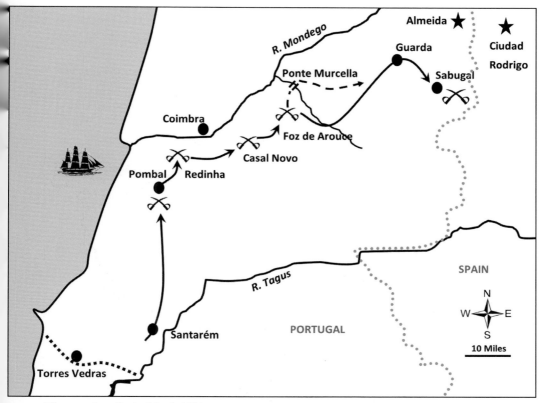

The pursuit to Spain: March 1811.

flanking marches by General Picton's 3rd Division. Lieutenant William Grattan summed up the experience for the 88th Connaught Rangers:

> The Light Division, so celebrated even at this early period of the war, was ever in advance; it had almost all the fighting as well as the fag, while ours (the Third) had plenty of fag but scarcely any fighting. The army, however, soon afterwards styled us 'The Fighting Division' ...[2]

Even though the French were bundled back to Spain, Wellington was far from satisfied with his army. After months remaining static before Santarém and the Rio Mayor, the commissariat was unable to form new magazines and feed the army as it advanced almost 200 miles to the Spanish frontier. This required halting several times to allow convoys to catch up and holding back more than half the divisions to provide the Light and 3rd divisions with sufficient supplies to remain on the march and in touch with the French. Supply was not the only issue that was revealed during the pursuit. Also found wanting was the synchronization of marches; that essential element of campaigning and successfully bringing the enemy to battle. On several occasions Wellington's plans failed or were only partly successful due to late arrival before Ney slipped away. He wrote:

> We certainly want practice in marching in large bodies, as at present no calculation can be made of the arrival of any troops at their station, much less

of their baggage. The order for the march yesterday was sent by Reynett ... the whole distance to be marched was not five miles, and yet the head of the column did not reach its ground till sunset ... In future I propose to order the period of departure and arrival of each division of the army, by which means I shall know exactly how all stands, and by degrees the troops will become more accustomed to march in large bodies on the same road.[3]

The Frontier Battles

With the Army of Portugal much reduced and with the allies having gained moral superiority following Buçaco, Torres Vedras and the pursuit, plus significant British reinforcement to create the 7th Division, Wellington was prepared to risk battle. At the beginning of May, General Reynier's II Corps was identified beyond the Rio Côa at Sabugal and out of immediate supporting distance of the rest of Masséna's army. General Merle's division was particularly vulnerable to attack and Wellington ordered the concentration of the allied army and prepared to cross the river to fall on the French. The day of 3 April 1811, however, dawned wet with fog in the river valley. The result was that while the 3rd and 5th divisions sought confirmation that they should continue with the attack, General Erskine, in temporary charge of the Light Division, pressed on across the river. The result was that when Beckwith's brigade emerged from the fog, it attacked Merle's division on its own as Erskine was yet to cross with the cavalry and on hearing gunfire, he forbade Brigadier Dunlop from taking his brigade across. Consequently, Beckwith was on his own with just the 43rd Light Infantry, a wing of the 95th Rifles[4] and the 3rd Caçadores facing a growing enemy force. The steadiness and fire-power of the musket-armed light infantrymen and the riflemen checked the French long enough to enable Dunlop to ignore Erskine's order and cross the Côa to join the action.

During the fighting that ebbed and flowed across a valley and a stone wall, a French howitzer was captured, but with Reynier appreciating the opportunity he had to overwhelm the Light Division, he marched Hudelet's divisions to support Merle. The Light Division was locked in combat and unable to withdraw without facing disaster, but the 3rd Division belatedly crossed the Côa and advanced on the French right flank and rear, coming into action just in time. With the 5th Division advancing through Sabugal, Reynier realized the peril he was in, disengaged and marched off at a speed that only the French could manage.

Wellington's pursuit of Reynier was circumspect, fearing being drawn too far forward and into a trap, but he occupied quarters that evening which Masséna had only vacated hours earlier as his army crossed the frontier into Spain. After a month of marching and privations, the allied army went into cantonments scattered around the border area, but they were all within mutual supporting distance of each other. While most of his divisions rested, Wellington ordered the Light Division and most of the cavalry into their familiar role of providing the army's outposts in the borderlands.

Marshal André Masséna, Prince d'Essling, commander of the Army of Portugal.

Napoleon had not properly resourced the invasion of Portugal and had insisted on attempting to control it from Paris, 800 miles away across mountainous, guerrilla-infested country. The result was failure, with the only piece of Portuguese territory held by the French being the lesser border fortress of Almeida, which was invested by General Cameron's 6th Division, covered by the 5th Division which was in bivouacs in Vale da Mula around Fort Concepción.

With the French back as far as Salamanca and Valladolid and assuming the Army of Portugal would be in no fit state to take to the field, Wellington rode south to join Marshal Beresford who was preparing to besiege Badajoz. This

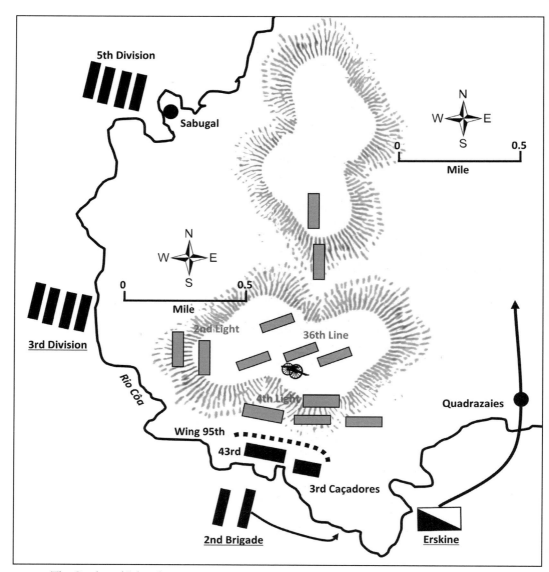

The Combat of Sabugal.

Spanish fortress had been lost to Marshal Soult in dubious circumstances as Beresford was marching to its relief during March 1811. Masséna incorrectly believed that Wellington had taken half the allied army with him and he put his rapidly reorganized army on the march back to Portugal. In his last chance to restore his fortune with a tangible success, he aimed to destroy General Spencer, who commanded in the peer's absence, and to relieve and resupply Almeida. Wellington, however, informed of French intentions, rode north and decided to fight.

Wellington's chosen position between Fuentes de Oñoro and Fort Concepción was not a commanding ridge like Buçaco but some gentle heights beyond the

Rio dos Casas. This stream to the north of the village of Fuentes ran in an increasingly deep gorge, while to the south it drained some marshy woods; at both ends of Wellington's position the Dos Casas represented an obstacle to movement. Behind this ridge of high ground was the Côa, with three widely dispersed and inadequate bridges. Wellington's decision to fight at Fuentes de Oñoro was a confident if not a brave one!

After a period of heavy rain, the Rio Azaba, which had separated the picquets of the two armies for several days, had by 2 May fallen enough for it to be forded by Masséna's divisions. The following day the French began their advance, with the Light Division and cavalry needing all their skill to withdraw to join the rest of the army without being fixed and overwhelmed.

The battle began as soon as the leading French arrived on the Dos Casas, with Reynier threatening the 5th and 6th divisions in the north and General Ferey vigorously attacking the village of Fuentes de Oñoro. The light companies of the 1st and 3rd divisions supported by companies of the 5th 60th Rifles and the Brunswick Oels were driven back to the top of the village, where a well-timed counter-attack by two battalions of the 1st Division drove the French down through the village and across the Dos Casas. Getting overextended, the two battalions were in turn driven back across the stream and the fighting ended with the French holding just a few houses at the foot of the village.

The following day, 4 May, was spent by the allies in barricading the village and entrenching on the heights and by Masséna in carrying out a reconnaissance of Wellington's right flank and it was on this flank that he was to attack on the 5th. Overnight the French assembled three infantry divisions and Montbrun's cavalry behind some higher ground east of Nave de Haver. At dawn they crossed the upper Dos Casas' web of wooded marshes and the cavalry fell on the unsuspecting Don Julián Sánchez's guerrillas, while the French infantry advanced on Poço Velho, where the outposts of the 7th Division had been established.

Seeing the French advance, Wellington dispatched the Light Division from reserve along with the remainder of Cotton's cavalry out onto the plain to aid the withdrawal of the 7th Division. Meanwhile, on the ridge the 1st and 3rd divisions were redeployed from facing east to the south and Masséna's outflanking moves. First in action were the cavalry in an unequal general melee on the plain between Poço Velho and Nave de Haver, which allowed the 7th Division to withdraw under pressure. Arriving behind the cavalry, the Light Division provided a shelter for the cavalry and Bull's troop to re-form. With the dragoons and guns assisting and the infantry alternating between column and square, the whole force withdrew, followed by Montbrun's cavalry. Over 2 miles they marched with the French horsemen circling around them just out of musket shot where they could only impotently swear and gesticulate at the columns while awaiting an opportunity to charge.

At a moment when additional troops could have swung events out on the plain in Masséna's favour, Marshal Bessières refused to commit his guard cavalry, which was on loan from his Army of the North. With his attack on Wellington's

8   *Salamanca Campaign, 1812*

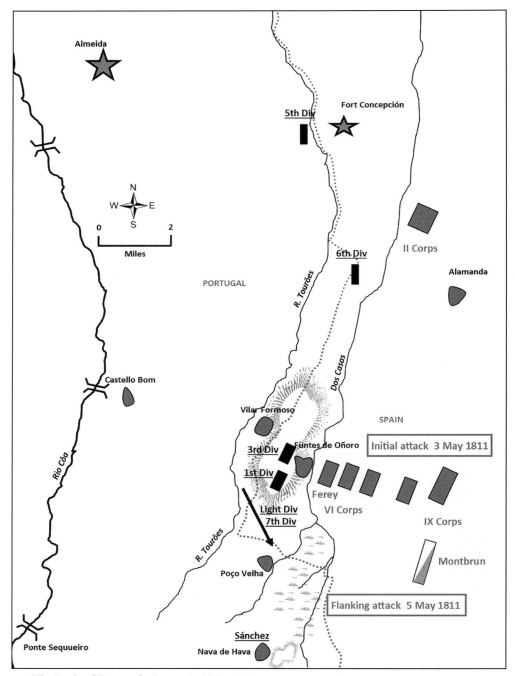

The Battle of Fuentes de Oñoro, 3–5 May 1811.

Don Julián Sánchez, otherwise known as 'El Charro', 'The Cowboy'.

Salamanca Campaign, 1812

right flank defeated, Masséna recast his plan for a sequenced attack on Wellington's main position starting with a resumption of the attack on Fuentes de Oñoro. As he was giving his orders, General Eblé rode up to report that the reserve of musket cartridges was all but expended and that the horse teams were already too exhausted to make the round trip to the magazine at Ciudad Rodrigo. Shouting that for a second time victory was being snatched from him, undeterred, the marshal ordered the attack to begin; the result was another epic ebb and flow of battle in Fuentes de Oñoro. Ferey's battalions were reinforced by grenadier battalions and regiments from Drouet's IX Corps,[5] while Wellington similarly fed fresh troops including the 88th Connaught Rangers into the village.[6] Lieutenant Grattan commanded a company:

> This battalion advanced with fixed bayonets in column of sections ... in double quick time, their firelocks at the trail. As it passed down the road leading to the chapel, it was warmly cheered by the troops that lay at each side of the wall, but the soldiers made no reply to this greeting – they were placed in a situation of great distinction, and they felt it ...
>
> The enemy were not idle spectators of this movement; they witnessed its commencement, and the regularity with which the advance was conducted made them fearful of the result. A battery of eight-pounders advanced at a gallop to an olive grove on the opposite bank of the river, hoping by the effects of its fire to annihilate the 88th Regiment ...

A French infantry attack.

On reaching the head of the village, the 88th Regiment was vigorously opposed by the 9th Regiment, supported by some 100 of the Imperial Guard,[7] but it soon closed in with them, and, aided by the brave fellows that had so gallantly fought in the town all the morning, drove the enemy through the different streets at the point of the bayonet, and at length forced them into the river that separated the two armies. Several of our men fell on the French side of the water.

The battle ground to a halt in the village as dusk fell, with lacklustre attacks by the French corps to the north and south of Fuentes failing to deliver any encouraging success. Having failed to reprovision Almeida and with Wellington barricading the village and entrenching the heights behind it, Masséna accepted defeat. The French, however, tarried for several days before withdrawing to Spain, while a message was got through the blockade to the garrison of Almeida.

On the night of 10 May General Brenier led a breakout through the loose blockade around the fortress and 8 miles across country to the Rio Águeda at Barba del Puerco and safety. Wellington was furious at the failure of the 6th Division to contain the French and with General Erskine who had failed to pass on orders for the 5th Division to extend its front to cover the Águeda at Barba del Puerco.

Badajoz and the South

Marshal Marmont was initially dispatched to replace Ney in command of VI Corps, but as he arrived fresh orders were received that he was to supersede Masséna in command of the Army of Portugal. Marmont set about reconstituting his army around Salamanca, while Wellington safely turned his mind to Badajoz where Marshal Beresford was besieging the city. He marched south with the 3rd and 7th divisions while the rest of the army remained in cantonments in villages between the Côa and the Azaba with the Light Division's outposts keeping an eye on activity at Ciudad Rodrigo. At the end of May Marmont with elements of his revived army launched a feint attack towards Almeida, at which General Craufurd, no doubt mindful of the situation he got himself into in 1810 by remaining in position too far forward, promptly withdrew behind the Côa. This feint had been designed to resupply Ciudad Rodrigo and cover the move south by Marmont's main force to join Marshal Soult in breaking the Second Siege of Badajoz following the French defeat at Albuhera.

Once Marmont retired on 6 June, the Light Division marched south, shadowing the French army. The division crossed the Tagus and on 23 June reached Arronches on the Rio Caia where Wellington was concentrated ready for battle, while Beresford's command besieged Badajoz. The combined armies of Soult and Marmont, however, did not give battle; in the aftermath of Fuentes de Oñoro and Albuhera they regarded the risk of attacking the allies as being too great; instead they raised of the siege of Badajoz. For almost a month the marshals, unable to fathom Wellington's dispositions and unnerved by their defeats at the

Lieutenant General Arthur Wellesley became the Earl of Wellington in the county of Somerset on 22 February 1812.

hands of the British, they still would not risk a general action. Despite French superiority of numbers, the allies had clearly gained the moral ascendency. Lieutenant Harry Smith of the 95th Rifles commented: 'Never did we spend a more inactive summer.'

With the French having broken the siege and reprovisioned Badajoz, Marmont and Soult argued, having failed to agree a course of action. Consequently, Marshal Marmont returned north to Salamanca with the allied army following suit, leaving Marshal Beresford in the south.

Blockade of Ciudad Rodrigo

With Soult having a large territory in Andalucía to the south to hold down, he moved off in that direction, leaving Marmont to return north to his fiefdom, which in turn became the focus of Wellington's operations for the remainder of the summer. To contemplate mounting an offensive from Portugal the allies would need to secure both of the 'Keys to Spain', Ciudad Rodrigo and Badajoz. His chosen objective was Ciudad Rodrigo and he ordered his battering train up the Rio Douro from Oporto, but this would take months and considerable labour to achieve. In the meantime, he would loosely blockade the fortress and look for any opportunity to seize it.

Once again, the Light Division was deployed forward in the army's outposts, this time in the hills east of the Águeda from where, if informed in time by Don Julián Sánchez's guerrillas, they could block the Ciudad Rodrigo to Salamanca road. In late September Marmont put most of his army in motion to reprovision Ciudad Rodrigo and, having achieved that, on 25 September the French advanced across the Rio Azaba beyond which they were checked at Espeja. Marmont's main force, however, struck south onto the plain where Picton's 3rd Division maintained the blockade. The result was a sharp cavalry action at El Bodón between a handful of squadrons of the 1st Hussars KGL and a mass of French cavalry, against which the 5th Regiment of Foot even mounted a bayonet charge! After two hours and with the French infantry arriving, Picton was ordered to retire 4 miles across the open plain to Fuenteguinaldo. The 3rd Division achieved this with admirable steadiness and little loss.

Wellington was, however, in a tight corner, with the Light Division on the far side of the Águeda and most of his other divisions in their dispersed cantonments, but he chose to stand his ground at the fortified camp at Fuenteguinaldo. This was a bluff, but Marmont couldn't believe that the allies were not fully assembled waiting on ground of their choice for him to attack. Overnight on 26/27 September Wellington withdrew some 9 miles to a strong position but Marmont again declined to attack and withdrew back to Salamanca.[8]

The Keys to Spain

As the autumn of 1811 turned to winter, Wellington started to receive intelligence that the Imperial Guard Division and Polish regiments were marching back towards France as the emperor prepared for a new campaign in the east. In addition, Marshal Suchet in Valencia, with the only successful French army, was being reinforced, drawing away several of Marmont's divisions in the resulting redeployment. By the end of December 1811, a window of opportunity to take Ciudad Rodrigo before the French could intervene presented itself and Wellington issued his orders on New Year's Day 1812.

Ciudad Rodrigo was invested on 4 January and after dark on the 8th, the outlying Fort Renaud was captured and the Light Division broke ground, beginning to dig the first parallel that night. Under heavy fire from the defenders, the

14 *Salamanca Campaign, 1812*

A well-dressed representation of Sánchez's cavalry; the reality was very different.

divisions took it in turns to extend the parallels and the first three batteries, initially consisting of twenty 24-pounders and two 18-pounders, started battering the walls before sunset on 14 January.[9]

The Greater Breach, created at the point where the French had attacked the previous year and where the rock and soil had yet to compact, was declared practicable on 17 January. Wellington, however, aware of the approach of

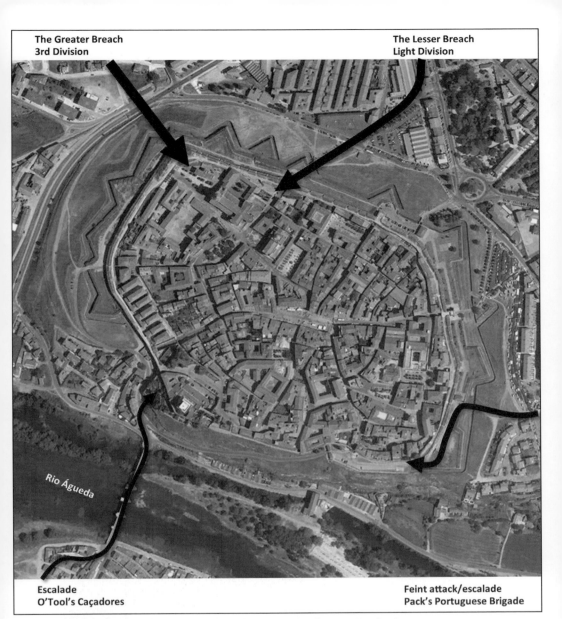

The Defences of Ciudad Rodrigo and Wellington's plan for storming the fortress.

Marmont's relief force knew that he had just two days in hand and ordered a second or lesser breach to be created at a weak part of the northern walls. As Marmont closed on Ciudad Rodrigo, Wellington ordered the assault on the fortress to take place on the evening of 19 January.

The 3rd Division stormed the Greater Breach while the Light Division climbed the steeper and narrower Lesser Breach. Both divisions were quickly up on the city walls and within an hour General Barrie proffered his sword in surrender. Ciudad Rodrigo had fallen after a lightning eleven-day siege, but at a

A miniature of General Robert Craufurd painted for his wife.

cost. Casualties included General Craufurd of the Light Division and General Mackinnon, one of Picton's brigade commanders. In the aftermath of the assault those 100 or so scoundrels to be found in every regiment were bent on finding drink and loot, but after a night of great disorder the regiments marched out of the city.

The army's expectations that they would be promptly marching to Badajoz were not realized and they went into winter quarters for six weeks before, one by one, the divisions marched off to the south. Badajoz was to be an altogether sterner test, with two previous British sieges having failed to reduce the larger and more up-to-date defences. In addition the French, under the direction of General Philippon, had used the year since the fortress's capture to strengthen the walls.

On this occasion Wellington chose to attack from the south-east, with the immediate problems being Fort Picurina and the San Roque lunette. Ground was broken under cover of wind and rain on 17 March. The siege works were not only more extensive but working the hard rocky ground was slow; however, eventually the first batteries opened fire on Fort Picurina and the city walls on the 25th. That night the fort was stormed by General Kempt's brigade of the 3rd Division supported by marksmen of the Light Division. Over the following days the trenches and parallels were dug ever closer to the defences, in which the guns breached the walls of La Trinidad and Santa Maria bastions. Informed that there was a weak stretch of wall between the two bastions, he concentrated the fire of his guns to create a third 'flying' breach.

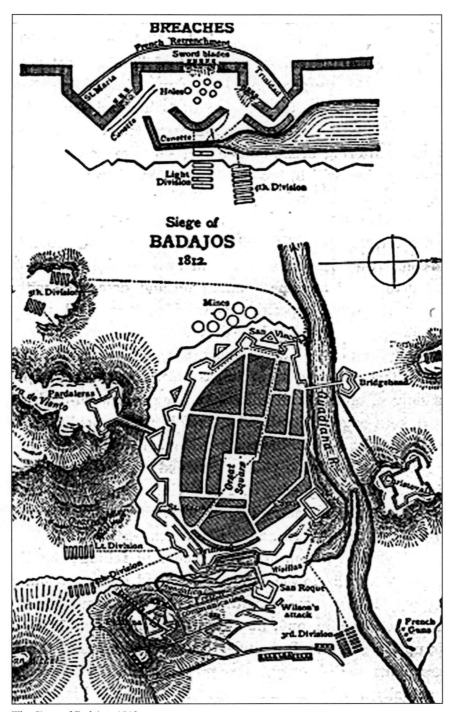

The Siege of Badajoz, 1812.

With Soult only four or five days' march away, Wellington was again under time pressure and the storm of Badajoz was ordered for the night of 4 April 1812. The 4th Division was to assault the Greater Breach and the Light Division the Lesser Breach in the walls of the Santa Maria bastion. With a difficult approach due to inundations and the moat full of every conceivable obstacle and trap, the stormers were in difficulty from the outset. The French were expecting them and concentrated fire from the walls, exploding mines and shells all illuminated by fireballs thrown down into the moat repeatedly checked the assaults. The breaches were covered with the dead and dying. After two hours, Wellington called off the assault; the prospect of a third failure loomed!

Elsewhere, diversionary and speculative attacks unexpectedly succeeded. The 3rd Division at Picton's insistence attempted an escalade of the old Moorish castle, which eventually succeeded when the division's 3rd Brigade was brought forward. There was no way out of the castle which was barricaded, but it contained the French reserves of ammunition and food. Around the other side of the city the 5th Division's attack which had been intended as a diversion succeeded when they found a lightly-defended section of wall that was low enough for their ladders. With the enemy in the city behind them, the defenders, who had been concentrated around the breaches, knew that the game was up and withdrew into one of the outworks where they surrendered the following morning.

The cost of taking Badajoz had been very high and the soldiers felt they had earned the spoils of war. If the aftermath of the storm of Ciudad Rodrigo had been bad, the eighteen hours of drunkenness, looting, rape and murder at Badajoz were terrible and remain a stain on the reputation of the Peninsular Army. Order was re-established when the provost marshals were ordered into the city and a gallows was set up in the Plaza Mayor.

With both the 'Keys to Spain' in his hands and the number and quality of French troops in Spain reduced by the needs of Napoleon's 1812 Russian adventure, Wellington could prepare to advance into Spain.

The French Army in Spain

Over the winter of 1811/12, Napoleon had stripped some of his best troops from the armies in the peninsula in preparation for renewed war with Russia. The Imperial Guard cavalry and infantry, along with Polish units and some of the other veterans of the *Grande Armée* had marched across the Pyrenees into France, but they were replaced. Coming in the other direction from regimental depots were the hastily-raised 4th and 5th battalions of infantry and additional squadrons of cavalry, but these troops and other replacements were not of the same quality as years of war were telling on the population from which men were conscripted. Also mitigating against quality was the fact that officers who could avoid the unpopular war in Iberia in favour of marching with the emperor did so without hesitation.

Even though the French armies in Spain during 1812 numbered around 300,000 men, having occupied far too great an area of the country they were both thinly

French *Ligne* infantry on the march.

spread and organized in a manner that limited King Joseph's military options. Firstly, with most of the country in seething revolt, the usual garrisons and picquets on lines of communications were necessarily significantly larger than in other theatres of war. Secondly, convoys and even ADCs with messages needed substantial escorts if they were to resist attack from guerrillas. It is said that the French only controlled the country within a musket shot of where they stood. Thirdly, French commanders tended to regard their area of responsibility as their personal fiefdom, with Soult, for instance, being notoriously reluctant to leave the wealth of Andalucía. In short, strategic consumption and a lack of co-operation greatly reduced the effect of French numerical superiority in the peninsula.

The chain of command in Spain, along with the jealous marshals, also mitigated against effective operations against the allied armies. Napoleon had the autocratic ruler's concern about creating a powerful subordinate who could become a competitor. Consequently, he ensured that there was no overall commander-in-chief in Spain, which gave Joseph limited control over the Peninsular armies. To make matters worse, Napoleon insisted on personally controlling events and in doing so he had fatally undermined Masséna's 1810 invasion of Portugal with instructions that were based on supposition, not facts, and were weeks out of date by the time they arrived. Even when the emperor marched east to join his army in May 1812, the Ministry of War in Paris continued to attempt to control events in Spain.

Although there were many factors working against French commanders, the one thing they had was ability. When the *Ancien Régime* was swept away by the revolution, generalship in the army became a meritocracy based on success in battle rather than seniority, patronage and social standing. On top of this, with years of campaigning at scale under their belts, the majority of French generals knew the business of war inside out.

One of Napoleon's secrets of success was the mobility of his armies, based on a much-reduced reliance on a secure line of communication and slow-moving convoys of rations for his soldiers. This had, of course, worked well in prosperous central Europe and Italy where French soldiers could effectively live off the land, but in the harsh impoverished peninsula, large armies famously starved. Consequently, availability of rations for the various French armies and formations was a seriously limiting factor in planning operations, with the time of year and a country already denuded of food being among the considerations. Consequently, French armies had an increased reliance on magazines and convoys of rations, which would in ideal circumstances have been confined to providing ammunition and small amounts of replacement weapons, clothing and equipment.

Marshal Jourdan, King Joseph's chief of staff.

Chapter Two

Plans and Preparations

In the aftermath of the siege of Badajoz, Wellington had considered turning on Marshal Soult but with the news of the fall of the fortress, the marshal, realizing his vulnerability, had marched quickly back towards Andalucía. While the allied army had been concentrated in the south at Badajoz, Marshal Marmont's Army of Portugal had taken the opportunity to advance to Ciudad Rodrigo, which had been only partly repaired and restocked by its new Spanish garrison. Without a siege train there was, however, little that he could do other than blockade the city and hope that Wellington and his army would not return north before Ciudad was starved into submission. At the same time four divisions of Marmont's army made an incursion into Portugal as far as Celorico and Guarda, but on hearing that Badajoz had fallen and that Wellington's advanced guard had recrossed the Tagus, they pulled back to Sabugal. Wellington did his best to conceal the movement of his 40,000 men, hoping to catch and overwhelm Marmont's 20,000 but a predictable dearth of food forced the French back to Spain just before the trap could be sprung.

With the 'Keys to Spain' in his hands and the decision made to campaign against Marmont in Castile, Wellington needed to be sure that there would be no undue interference from Soult while he was occupied in the north.[1] To achieve this, the French bridge of boats over the east/west-flowing Rio Tagus at Almaraz needed to be destroyed. With Soult's bridging train captured in Badajoz, this bridge was the only link directly across a river barrier that divided Marmont and Soult. Wellington concluded that 'unless the enemy have another bridge, they can no longer pass the Tagus as an army, excepting at Toledo', which was 50 miles upstream. The destruction of the bridge at Almaraz would prevent any sudden French advance across the river.[2]

General Sir Rowland Hill duly mounted an audacious raid into enemy territory to attack the well-defended bridge at Almaraz on 19 May. In his report to Wellington, Hill described the enemy's fortifications:

> The bridge was, as your Lordship knows, protected by strong works, thrown up by the French on both sides of the river, and farther covered on the southern side by the castle and redoubts of Miravete, about a league off, commanding the pass of that name, through which runs the road to Madrid, being the only one passable for carriages of any description, by which the bridge can be approached. The works on the left [southern] bank of the river were a *tête de pont*, built of masonry, and strongly intrenched [*sic*]; and on the high ground above it, a large and well-constructed fort, called Napoleon,

St Clair's 1812 picture of British ferrying operations on the Tagus.

with an interior intrenchment [sic] and loop-holed tower in its centre. This fort contained nine pieces of cannon, with a garrison of between 400 and 500 men, there being also on the opposite side of the river, on a height immediately above the bridge, a very complete fort [Ragusa], recently constructed, which flanked and added much to its defence.

General Hill advanced across country without his artillery, via an undefended pass, to attack the fort from the rear. Meanwhile, he used his guns to distract the enemy with a bombard of their defences that covered the route over the Pass of Miravete. The allied troops stormed Fort Napoleon on the southern bank of the river and took it by escalade. Hill's accompanying gunners immediately turned the fort's captured guns on Fort Ragusa on the northern side of the river and its surprised garrison, with the British infantry heading for the bridge panicked and fled. The whole action was over within forty minutes and Wellington was able to report that 'Hill's operation has deranged Soult's, as well as Marmont's plans.'

At the same time as Almaraz was denied to the French, in order to shorten his own lines of communication, Wellington ordered the Trajan bridge at Alcântara to be repaired. Lieutenant Colonel Sturgeon of the Staff Corps created a remarkable suspension bridge of ropes and planks across the 90ft gap blown in it during 1809. The resulting structure could bear the weight of artillery and its horse teams.[3]

Wellington, however, also needed to keep the other French marshals in the peninsula and their armies tied down. If one or more combined with Marmont's, they would significantly outnumber the allies on the Salamanca front. Conse-

The Roman bridge at Alcântara.

quently, Wellington put in place a policy of distraction in which the sundry Spanish armies in unconquered corners of the country were urged into action. This was, however, more in hope than expectation; he wrote: 'But I am apprehensive that I can place no reliance on the effect to be produced by these troops.' The guerrillas, of course, continued to absorb the attentions of an increasing number of French troops, but could only take on relatively small enemy detachments. In addition, Home Popham's Royal Navy squadron would make landings of Marines on the Biscay coast of Spain, while the Mediterranean fleet with General Bentinck's troops from Sicily and Gibraltar posed a similar threat to the south.

With his right flank secure and distractions under way, in May Wellington could proceed with planning and preparations for the coming campaign. It would, however, be another month before the 1st and 6th divisions rejoined him from the south and all would be ready for the advance into Spain.

Spanish Volunteers

To make up for the paucity of replacements and the steady attrition caused by the sieges and continuing operations, Wellington negotiated with the Junta a formalization and expansion of what had become a low-level practice of enlisting Spanish volunteers. The problem was that the regular army had only managed to recruit 26,000 British and Irish volunteers during 1811 to make up for the army's losses worldwide, with those in the Peninsular Army alone totalling 21,000 that year. On top of that, losing 10 per cent of his British strength in the two sieges reduced the head count of units in some cases by as much as 30 per cent before the main campaign opened.[4]

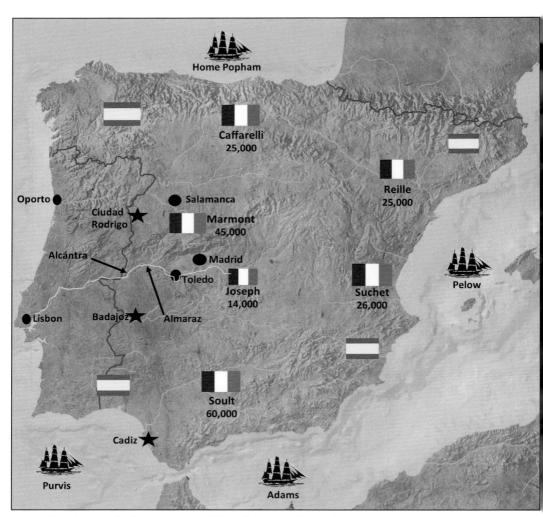

French armies in the peninsula in 1812 and the naval 'distractions'.

An agreement was reached that the hardest-hit regiments could enlist a share of 5,000 Spaniards in exchange for a million pounds, plus arms and clothing for 100,000 men. Wellington wrote to his commanders:

> The Spanish Government having been pleased to allow a limited number of natives of Spain to serve His Majesty in the British regiments composing this army, I have to request that you will authorize the regiments named in the margin to enlist and bear on their strength 100 Spanish volunteers, on the following conditions:
> First; the men must not be under five feet six inches high, strongly made, and not under nineteen years of age, nor older than twenty-seven.
> Secondly; they are to be attested according to the following form by the commanding officer of the regiment to serve during the present war; but in case the regiment into which they shall enlist should be ordered from the

Peninsula the Spanish volunteers are to be discharged, and each of them is to receive one month's full pay to carry him to his home.

After laying down sundry terms and conditions of service, he concluded:

> In communicating this arrangement to the several regiments, I request you to point out to the commanding officers how desirable it is that these volunteers should be treated with utmost kindness and indulgence and brought by degrees to the system of discipline of the Army.[5]

The numbers authorized were up to 100 per battalion, which was theoretically between 6 and 10 per company of infantry, but it seems that these quotas were seldom realized. Rifleman Costello of the 95th wrote:

> Our regiments, by constant collision with the French, were getting exceedingly thinned, and recruits from England came but very slowly, until we found it necessary at last to incorporate some of the Spaniards; for this purpose several non-commissioned officers and men were sent into the adjacent villages recruiting. In the course of a short time, and to our surprise, we were joined by a sufficient number of Spaniards to give ten or twelve men to each company in the battalion. But the mystery was soon unravelled, and by the recruits themselves, who on joining gave us to understand, by a significant twist of the neck, and a 'Carajo' (much like the breaking of one), that they had but three alternatives to choose from, to enter either the British, or Don Julian's service, or be hanged! The despotic sway of Sanchez, and his threat in the bargain, so disjointed their inclination for the guerrillas that they hastily fled their native 'woods' and 'threshold' for fear of really finding themselves noosed up to them and gladly joined the British regiments.[6]

Even though Spanish volunteers served in the Light Division until the end of the war in 1814, overall the policy was not a great success.

Intelligence

Though it must not be supposed that the French did not have an intelligence system of their own, by 1812 Wellington's system was well-developed and rarely left him in doubt for long as to the movement, numbers and intentions of the French. The guerrillas intercepted orders, often in a cipher, while correspondents, including Doctor Patrick Curtis, aka Don Patricio Cortés, dean of the Irish College in Salamanca, regularly wrote to Wellington keeping him informed of activity in his area.[7] In addition, exploring officers and deserters all furnished information, which once assembled by intelligence officers such as Major George Scovell provided an insight into French intent that gave Wellington a significant advantage. During preparation for the coming campaign, however, Wellington received a number of intelligence setbacks.

The first was the capture of one of his exploring officers, Major Grant of the 11th Foot, who Napier described in glowing terms: 'That gentleman, in whom

Rifleman Costello as an officer in later life.

the utmost daring was so mixed with subtlety of genius, and both so tempered by discretion, that it is hard to say which quality predominated ...'

The army's Surgeon General Doctor McGrigor wrote of Grant that

> He was as fluent as any native was in the different dialects of at least three provinces of Spain. He knew all their customs, songs and their music and even their particular prejudices. He was widely read in Spanish literature and joined in their local dances with such perfection of footwork that they might have been highland reels. Sensing his interest in all that was Spanish, the local people loved him in return. Among his many friends were the peasant farmers, and priests who, while welcoming him into their houses, were always forthcoming with news.

Grant, always wearing uniform to avoid being shot as a spy, was known by the French to slip between their outposts into the Army of Portugal's cantonments.

Major Colquhoun Grant of the 11th North Devon Regiment was Wellington's leading exploring officer. He is depicted here wearing a staff officer's uniform rather than his regimentals.

With the aid of his Spanish guide Leon and local people, he would ride around their camps and routes of march on a fine well-fed horse, counting numbers of troops and identifying regiments and their formations while collecting information from sympathizers. During the French incursion Grant's luck ran out when they trapped and captured him, denying Wellington the services of his most able intelligence officer for four months until he escaped from Paris.[8]

The second setback was the capture of one of his correspondents in Tordesillas 'through his own imprudence'. The loss of this source of information was serious and had wider implications than just intelligence, as Wellington explained to General Graham:

> I am apprehensive that some traces may have been found of my letters to different guerrilla chiefs to urge them to intercept Grant and offer a reward to the party which should take him and that Marmont will take care that he shall have a sufficient escort. This was the person with whom all correspondence with the north was carried on.[9]

Although these were reverses, such was the extent of Wellington's intelligence network that he maintained a good picture of Marmont's capability and intentions. As we will see, Scovell broke a ciphered message at a crucial point in the campaign.

As far as the French were concerned, even though they had their own spies, sympathizers and deserters who provided them with information, operating in a hostile country they were at a distinct disadvantage. The capture of one of King Joseph's dispatches revealed that they had some success. On 7 June 1812 Wellington wrote:

> I can see, however, that the King and Marmont have discovered that I intend to carry on operations on this side [i.e. north of the Tagus]; and the King had already given orders to Soult on the 7th of May, which he has repeated on the 26th of May, to take a position with a view to those operations. I conclude that the object of those orders is to distract my attention from Marmont by an attack upon Hill. This, I think, will be made; but if Morillo and Penne Villemur stay with Hill, and there is any garrison for Badajoz besides Morillo's troops, Hill will be in tolerable strength; and they will all be disappointed in their expectations of finding a very weak corps in that part of the country.

Despite knowing Wellington's intent, Soult in particular believed that he was going to be the object of the allied offensive, which was a further disincentive for him to co-operate and send troops to other commands.

Logistics

As ever in the peninsula, logistics were at the heart of what was operationally possible for both sides. For Wellington it was the time needed for the commissary to form and stock magazines in the border lands, along with assembling sufficient transport to sustain the coming campaign in Spain. Major Napier highlighted the problem of operating from bases 200 miles away on the coast: 'He had drawn so largely upon Portugal for means of transport, that agriculture was seriously embarrassed, and yet his subsistence was not secured for more than a few marches beyond the Agueda.'[10]

To solve this problem Wellington intensified work to make both the Tagus and the Douro navigable from the ports of Lisbon and Oporto to the Spanish frontier. With the Douro navigable almost to Almeida and Ciudad Rodrigo where magazines were established, Wellington wrote on 22 May to General Graham, stating that 'We are nearly all ready with our magazines here; and it is obvious that this must be our operating flank; and I intend to put the troops in march as soon as Hill should return.'

While the majority of biscuit, grain and fodder could be imported and brought up to the magazines by boat, in convoys of mules and ox waggons, the army's perennial shortage of cash was a logistical problem, as well as a problem for paying the army.[11] Treasury promissory notes for the purchase of meat and stocks from the concealed granaries were known to be unacceptable in Spain. With the government unable to supply sufficient silver, Wellington had to report that he had a 'dread that if his operations led him far into Spain, the subsistence of his army would be insecure'.

Even though the burden on the Portuguese to provide transport had been eased significantly, advancing 100 miles from the magazines in the border area to the Douro between Toro and Tordesillas would require some 15,000 mules plus ox carts to maintain supply and meet the daily demand for food alone, which totalled 200,000lb.

The scale of the logistic effort is hard to visualize, but Major Broughton described the scene:

> The concourse of mules, carrying the baggage of the army, and the various camp followers, occupied more than treble the space of the army itself, and presented a moving scene so far as the eye could reach on all sides.

Mules were not only required to supply the army but move its impedimenta as well. Infantry battalions and cavalry regiments had thirteen and fourteen mules respectively, plus officers' baggage animals. These figures seem modest in comparison with Colonel Dixon's calculation that a single howitzer battery required 770 mules to carry its equipment, baggage and 180 rounds of ammunition per gun. In addition to the battery's mules, one commissariat forage mule was required for every two horses and four mules. Further mules were needed for food, which in turn required more forage mules![12]

Every day colourful convoys of hundreds of hired Portuguese and Spanish mules, with each group led by an animal with a bell around its neck, would set out from the magazines to the army's divisions. It was a slow business, with the ox carts moving at just 2 miles an hour. The allied army's tail extending back to Ciudad Rodrigo was akin to columns of ants.

The vehicles of the Royal Waggon Train heavily laden with stores proved unequal to the terrible roads in the peninsula and were primarily used for evacuation of the sick and wounded.

The French were by 1812 only too aware of the limitations in Iberia of their preferred policy of attempting to live off the land. Consequently, for Marmont his logistic issue was waiting for Spanish crops to ripen and the moment to seize grain with which to make sufficient biscuit to concentrate his army for operations against the allies. Wellington was aware of this factor and explained that 'Our first object must certainly be now to get the better of Marmont's army, of which we have a chance in the two months which will elapse between this time and the period of reaping the harvest in Castille [late July].'

Plans and Orders

In a letter to Lord Liverpool, Wellington spelled out his campaign aims and timing:

> I propose, therefore, as soon as ever the magazines of the army are brought forward, which work is now in progress (the troops continuing in dispersed cantonments for that purpose), to move forward into Castille, and to endeavour, if possible, to bring Marmont to a general action. I think I can make this movement with safety, excepting always the risk of the general action. I am of opinion also that I shall have the advantage in the action, and that this is the period of all others in which such a measure should be tried.[13,14]

A miniature of Lieutenant Browne painted in 1805 when he was serving with the 23rd Fusiliers.

When Wellington advanced into Spain from Ciudad Rodrigo towards Salamanca, General Hill with the 2nd Division and the Portuguese Division would remain in the south to watch for any intervention by Marshal Soult. As explained by Lieutenant Thomas Browne, who was a staff officer in the Adjutant General's Department in Wellington's headquarters, the plan was to advance in three columns:

> The right column of the army composed of the 1st, 6th & 7th divisions was commanded by Sir Thomas Graham. The centre was formed of the 4th, 5th & Light divisions under General Leith. With this column moved headquarters. The left column consisted of the 3rd Division with the Portuguese brigades of Generals Pack & Bradford was commanded by General Picton. Sir Stapleton Cotton commanded the cavalry, the greater part of which moved with headquarters. The total strength of this part of the army moving under the immediate orders of Ld. Wellington was about 45,000 men.[15]

The Light Division led the army as its advance guard and the 3,000 Spanish troops under General Don Carlos de España were to follow several days' march behind the Anglo-Portuguese columns.

The Army of Portugal

Wellington's estimate of Marmont's situation was set out in a long letter to Lord Liverpool:

> Strong as the enemy are at present, there is no doubt that they are weaker than they have been during the war, or than they are likely to be again, as they will certainly be in some degree reinforced after the harvest, and very largely so, after Buonaparte's projects in the North shall have been brought to a conclusion. We have a better chance of success now, therefore, than we have ever had; and success obtained now would produce results not to be expected from any success over any single French army in the Peninsula upon any other occasion.

He concluded: 'The certainty of the loss in every action, and the risk which always attends such an operation, ought not, therefore, in my opinion, to prevent its being tried at present.'

With Napoleon having stripped away both quality troops and quantity from the peninsula for the invasion of Russia, King Joseph's orders were essentially to remain on the defensive and continue to suppress the guerrillas while awaiting the return of the victorious *Grande Armée*. The king's exhortations to the various marshals and generals commanding armies in Spain to co-operate produced open disobedience. Napoleon had failed to establish a clear chain of command, as this would have put too much power in any one marshal's hands. In addition, he continued to issue detailed orders from Paris, which were either given in ignorance of the true situation in the peninsula or were way out of date by the time they arrived in Spain.

On the ground in Spain, with the lack of accurate intelligence thanks to Wellington's measures, the king's ability to react to developing events was heavily circumscribed. His chief of staff Marshal Jourdan penned a reply to Marmont with a clear degree of frustration!

> Your letter of June 6th says that Wellington will soon fall upon you. But we have similar letters from Soult, declaring that the blow is to be delivered against him: he encloses two notes of June 2nd and 5th from General Daricau in Estremadura, declaring that 60,000 of the allies are just about to begin an invasion of Andalucía. We are too far off from the scene of operations to determine whether it is you or the Duke of Dalmatia who is deceived. We can only tell you, meanwhile, not to be misled by demonstrations.

Finally, all was ready and, having issued his orders, Wellington wrote to General Hill from his headquarters at Fuenteguinaldo on 11 June:

> The army is collected on the Águeda, and I intend to move forward on the 13th.[16] I am almost certain, from what I have seen of the intercepted letters from Joseph to Soult, and from Marmont to Joseph, that Soult will move upon you with a part at least of his force ...

British Infantry Swords

Swords were carried by officers and most sergeants both as their personal weapon and as a traditional symbol of rank and status. The design and utility of a particular sword was, however, always the subject of debate in the infantry no less than among cavalrymen, based on opinion as much as experience. Most swords owed their design as much to look and fashion as they did to functionality on campaign or on the battlefield.

The most common infantry sword was the 1796 Pattern. A General Order of 4 May 1796 reads: 'The sword to have a brass guard, pommel and shell, gilt with gold, with gripe or handle, of silver twisted wire. The blade to be straight and made to cut and thrust; to be 1 inch at least broad at the shoulder and 32 inches in length, conformably to former orders given out in April 1786.' The sword was worn by dismounted junior regimental officers in a cross belt and, despite regulations, in a conventional waist belt by mounted officers. The shell guard was uncomfortable and caused wear on uniforms and equipment when worn on the hip and a version was produced with the shell on the right folding down when not being carried.

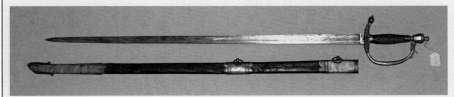

The 1796 Pattern infantry officer's sword.

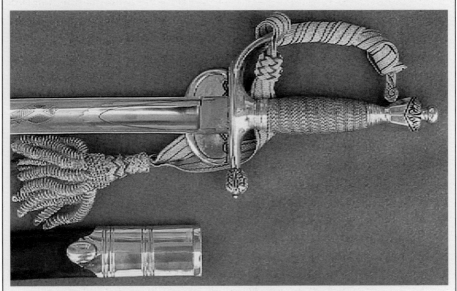

The 1796 Pattern showing the folding guard and gold wire sword knot.

The sergeant's version was of a similar appearance but with the hilt made of plain brass and lacking the blueing and etching on the blade of the officer's version. It was worn in a bayonet cross belt.

The hilt of the sergeant's version of the 1796 sword.

As a fighting weapon the sword was a slight improvement on its predecessor. The shell guard provided slightly better protection to the hand but in practice they were fragile and, along with the quillon, were easily broken off. Captain Mercer was one of the 1796 Pattern's critics: 'Nothing could be more useless or more ridiculous than the old Infantry regulation [sword]; it was good neither for cut nor thrust and was a perfect encumbrance. In the foot artillery, when away from headquarters, we generally wore dirks instead of it.'

By the turn of the century it was fashionable for flank company officers, light infantry in particular, to carry a curved sabre that emulated that of the light cavalry and in 1799 the Horse Guards gave in to this practice and authorized the carrying of sabres but no pattern was specified. The 1803 pattern regulated the fashion sword for grenadier, light company and light infantry officers. It was a fairly elaborate sword of 30in to 31.5in with many regimental variations to the detail.

An example of the 1803 Pattern flank company officer's sabre. Note the 'blueing' of the blade.

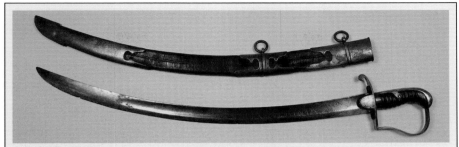

An unusual sabre with '51st LIGHT INF^y REGT' etched on the blade.

The example of the 51st Light Infantry sword is post-1809 (51st Foot converted to light infantry in the spring of 1809) and is essentially of a shortened 1796 light cavalry sabre design. With the regimental etching on the blade, it was clearly not a campaign expedient, but possibly reflects a desire by regiments or individual officers to wield a more substantial weapon for use on campaign and in battle. The 51st Light Infantry joined the 7th Division in the peninsula during early 1811.

The hilt of the 95th (Rifle) Regiment's version of the 1803 Pattern sword.

Every British regiment in the Light Division had its own version of the 1803 Pattern sabre. That of the 43rd Light Infantry is noticeably ornate, while the 52nd Light Infantry's simplicity reflected Sir John Moore's maxim: 'Everything that is necessary, nothing that is not'. The 95th Rifles' version was of a simple design, with a light cavalry-style guard and reflects the regiment's colours of silver and black; the hilt is chromed and has a black leather sword knot. Sergeants of the Rifles did not carry swords, but like their soldiers they carried a rifle and sword bayonet.

A French *Ligne* infantryman.

Chapter Three

The Opening Moves

After six weeks during which the 'cracked bones of the sieges' were repaired, the main body of the allied army numbering some 48,000 men crossed the Águeda before dawn on 13 June 1812 in order to avoid the heat of the day. They marched the 60 miles to Salamanca in three columns each preceded by a light cavalry brigade and for three days they did so without contacting the enemy. Marshal Marmont had been caught with his eight divisions dispersed, with the furthest away, Bonet's, more than ten days distant.

Most diarists barely mention this initial advance through the wooded country but Lieutenant Cooke of the 43rd Light Infantry marched with the advance guard of the centre column:

> The march of the Light Division was worthy of notice. The men were not tormented by unnecessary parades – the march was their parade; that over, the soldiers (except those on duty) made themselves happy, while those with sore feet, by such a system, had rest, which enabled them to be with their comrades, when, by a mistaken notion of discipline, it would have been otherwise: their equipment was not regularly examined, nor were the men on any pretence permitted to overload themselves – one of the most serious afflictions to an army.[1]
>
> The baggage followed the line of march in succession. The mules of each company were tied together, and conducted by two batmen in rotation, right or left in front, according to the order of march.[2] Each regiment found an officer and each brigade a captain to superintend. The alarm-post for them in camp was on the reverse flank of respective regiments. When the enemy were at hand, the baggage was ordered to the rear – the distance according to circumstances.
>
> The army was four days clearing the forest, which was clothed with verdure, and supplied the most delightful bivouacs. The Sierra de Gata lay on the right hand, covered with snow, while a cloudless sky formed our canopy, and the sunshine of hope and happiness was beaming on every countenance, not excepting those of the growling surly batmen, who were seen to smile at finding forage at hand for their animals. On the fourth day the division encamped within two leagues of Salamanca, and quite clear of the wood.

Cavalry Action

The French were finally encountered on the Rivera de Valmusa approximately 6 miles from Salamanca on 16 June, when General Victor Alten's light cavalry

Lieutenant Cooke of the 43rd Light Infantry.

brigade, which habitually worked with the Light Division, clashed with picquets provided by two squadrons of General Curto's division of chasseurs à cheval. That day Alten's brigade was led by the duty squadron of the 1st Hussars of the King's German Legion (KGL). Captain Leith Hay, ADC to his uncle General Leith (5th Division), had ridden forward with the leading horsemen. He wrote: 'The enemy stood firm and exchanged shots with the hussars, only retiring when the main body of that regiment debouched from the wood.' Lieutenant Cooke reported that 'The officers of hussars described it [the action] to us', and

> related the conversation that took place between them and the French dragoons [sic] stationed on picquet in front of Salamanca. The enemy requested the Germans not to charge; the hussars replied, while advancing, that if the French fired, they would. The enemy then fired their carbines to stop their progress. The hussars charged and cut most of them down.

There was to be no live and let live in the first action of the campaign and being strongly pressed by the hussars, the chasseurs fell back towards Salamanca from

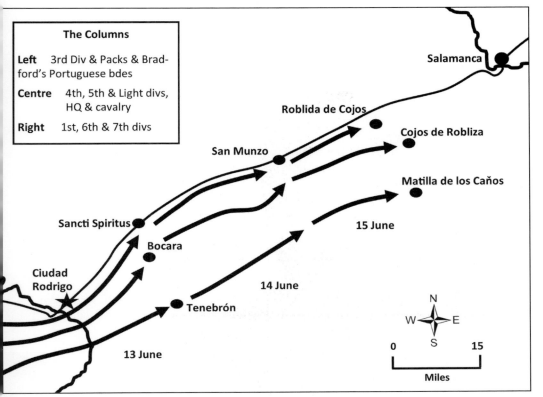

The initial advance into Spain.

the hills above the Rivera de Valmusa. Lieutenant Tomkinson, an officer on General Cotton's staff, added:[3]

> They pushed them within a league of Salamanca,[4] and the 11th Light Dragoons coming up from the left column and the 14th from the right, advanced on the plain ... Major Bull's guns came up and cannonaded their cavalry, and the Hussars, with a detachment of the 14th, charged a small advanced party of three squadrons. The affair was nothing, and contrary to the orders of Lord Wellington.[5]

The leading regiments of all three columns which were converging on Salamanca were now in what was developing into a significant action. Captain Leith Hay witnessed the fight:

> On ascending the heights, which rise gradually from the right bank of the Valmusa, several squadrons of the enemy's cavalry were perceived formed on the extensive plain reaching to the banks of the Tormes. Small detached parties occupied the several eminences immediately on the flanks of the main body, and it appeared their intention to dispute the ground until outnumbered or driven back. The scene now became very animated and interesting. Parties were observed firing or charging in all directions. Repeated attacks were made by either force, as circumstances warranted, or as they

became most numerous at the particular points. In one direction was to be seen a troop or squadron charging half their number of opponents, who, by a precipitate retreat, fell back on others, until their strength became superior, when, in turn, they for a time carried with them the successful tide of battle. The plain was covered with officers and scattered cavalry soldiers; carbines and pistols were discharged without intermission; frequent personal conflicts took place. On one occasion, Major Brotherton of the 14th Light Dragoons, mounted upon a very small Spanish horse, crossed swords with a French officer of chasseurs, and continued cutting and parrying until the mêlée broke up the encounter ... During the progress of this protracted skirmish, although occasionally successful, the enemy was losing ground, and was finally driven within two miles of Salamanca; orders were there received to desist from farther pursuit; I then returned to General Leith, who had encamped his division on the bank of the Valmusa.[6]

The following morning, as recorded by Tomkinson in his diary for 17 June, 'We moved forward at daylight, the whole assembling on the plain near Salamanca.

The cavalry action of 16 June.

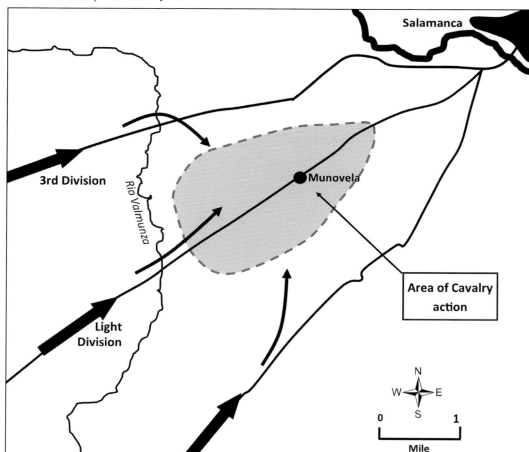

The enemy left the place last night about 12.' The allied army was able to enter the city, but not by the single standing bridge over the Tormes as it was covered by a pair of guns mounted at Fort Merced, one of three convents the French had converted into forts. Crossing the river above and below Salamanca, the leading elements of the army entered the city at about 0800 hours. They were followed, as recalled by Captain Leith Hay, by

> Lord Wellington at about ten o'clock in the forenoon: the avenues to it were filled with people clamorous in their expressions of joy; nothing could be more animating than the scene. The day was brilliant, presenting all the glowing luxuriance of a southern climate. Upwards of fifty staff officers accompanied the British General; they were immediately followed by the 14th Dragoons and a brigade of artillery; the streets were crowded to excess; signals of enthusiasm and friendship waved from the balconies; the entrance to the Plaza was similar to a triumph; every window and balcony was filled with persons welcoming the distinguished officer to whom they looked for liberation and permanent relief ... At the same time, the 6th Division of British infantry entered the south-west angle of the square. It is impossible to describe the electric effect produced under these circumstances by the music; as the bands of the regiments burst in full tones on the ear of the people, a shout of enthusiastic feeling escaped from the crowd, all ranks seeming perfectly inebriated with exultation.

The French in the forts were much annoyed by this celebration of liberation and duly opened fire on anyone, civilian or military, who came within range of the forts!

The Salamanca Forts

As already mentioned, three of Salamanca's numerous convents in the south-west quarter of the city, overlooking the Tormes, had been converted into forts mounting more than thirty cannon. During the three years of occupation the French had rebuilt the convents using the dressed stone to produce proper fortifications. They were sited on high ground, astride a gully, with the largest of the three, Fort San Vincente, sited to the west and the two smaller forts to the east. Lieutenant Browne recorded in his diary some additional detail: 'These works ... of solid masonry were loopholed, palisaded, & stockaded, & had two ditches round them.' Wooden beams taken from demolished buildings roofed much of the fort and had been covered with a thick layer of earth and rubble to absorb the detonation of howitzer shells. The forts were held by a garrison of some 800 men made up of the voltigeurs detached from Maucune and Montrand's divisions, plus artillerymen.

Not only did the forts cover the river and approaches from the west, but the French had also cleared fields of fire of 250 yards towards the city by demolishing a considerable number of buildings.

The view looking across the old Tormes bridge from the south to the city of Salamanca.

Even though Wellington was well aware of the presence of the three forts and had made provision for heavy guns and howitzers to be brought up, it will be seen from the course of the siege operations that his correspondents had underestimated the strength of the forts' construction and defences. Major Jones of the Royal Engineers described them as '... formidable works, which also served as a citadel to keep the inhabitants in subjection'.

While the rest of the army marched around the city to take up positions below the heights of San Cristóbal to the north-east, General Clinton (6th Division) prepared to invest the forts. Major Jones reported:

> On reconnoitring the works from the cathedral and other high buildings, they were found to be far more respectable than had been supposed; the information regarding them on commencing the march having been only to the extent that some convents had been fortified, and a confused sketch of the buildings by a Spaniard, not a military man. They consisted of a fort on the north-west of the city, formed out of the large convent of St. Vicente, which stands in the centre of an angle of the old town wall, which is there very lofty, and built on a perpendicular cliff over the river. The windows of the convent had been closed up with masonry and loopholed, and its exterior connected on both sides with the town wall, by lines of works, with masonry scarps and counterscarps loopholed, and the embrasures arched over ... and the whole was constructed to be well flanked in every part.[7]

Of the guns assembled for the reduction of the fort, six 24-pounder howitzers had been ordered to march from Elvas on 31 May, along with 1,000 shells. In addition to the howitzers, artillery officer Lieutenant Colonel May of Wellington's

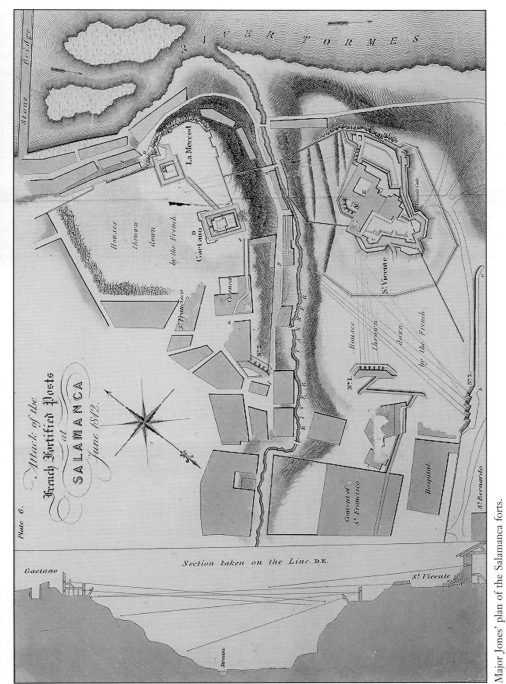

Major Jones' plan of the Salamanca forts.

An engraving of Major John Jones's memorial in St Paul's Cathedral.

headquarters had a considerable amount of ammunition, stores and guns to move:

> Four iron 18-pounders, drawn by 10 pair of bullocks each. Six hundred 24-pounder shot, in 20 bullock cars, being intended for the howitzers from Elvas. Four hundred 18-pounder shot, in 10 bullock cars. Sixty barrels of powder, in 10 bullock cars, for the howitzers from Elvas. Thirty barrels of powder, in 5 bullock cars, for the 18-pounders. Spare stores in 5 carts. Twenty ladders on a transporting carriage drawn by 5 pair of bullocks.[8]

The entrenching on the night of the 17th did not start well. The working party of 400 men of Hulse's brigade found the stony, rubble-infested ground hard going and they were under musket fire. The 11th North Devon Regiment, for example, lost two killed and five wounded during the night. The 6th Division had no previous experience of siege works and after a short night their knee-deep trenches offered scant cover. Beamish, in his history of the King's German Legion, recorded that

> on the morning of the 18th, the light brigade of the legion, having been ordered at the particular request of General Clinton, to take the duties of the picquets and firing parties, three hundred men, under the command of captains Rautenberg and Holtzermann, were posted among the ruins, and these by a continued and well-directed fire, kept up throughout the night, nearly silenced the defenders by the following morning.

These 300 marksmen were the rifle-armed element of Halket's brigade, which were detached from the 7th Division to aid the 6th Division's single company of the 5th 60th Rifles in suppressing enemy fire. Despite the success, it was not possible to work on the battery during daylight hours. Consequently, two 6-pounder field guns were mounted in the San Bernardo convent and opened fire at 1700 hours with shot and spherical case.[9]

The subsequent night's work, overseen by three engineer officers and nine military artificers, was more successful as Major Jones recorded:

> Night between 18th and 19th June. – Battery No. 1 was completed and armed with four 18-pounders, and three 24-pounder howitzers. A battery No. 2, for the two remaining iron howitzers of the field-brigade, was thrown up in a good situation for assisting to breach the convent of St. Vicente; and cover was also made for two brass field-howitzers on a small height to the right of St. Bernardo, favourable to enfilade the side of the fort opposed to the breaching batteries.

Fire was opened by the heavy guns at daylight on the 19th and the upper parts of San Vicente were brought down, but nothing like a breach was created. Flaming carcase projectiles were also fired into the fort, but were extinguished by the garrison before the resulting fires took hold.[10] The day's battering, however, revealed that the amount of ammunition brought up with the guns was based on

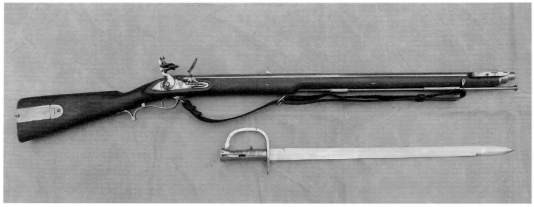

The Short infantry rifle and its sword, aka the 'Baker rifle'.

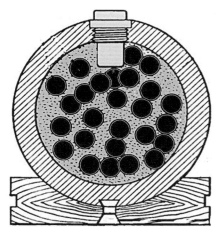

Spherical case shot or shrapnel. If the fuse was cut to the correct length it would burst above the target and lead balls beat down on anyone below.

faulty intelligence reports and that to have the necessary effect on the fort's walls more was required.

On the 20th results were better, but with Marmont's appearance before San Cristóbal Bowe's brigade was summoned to join the main army. With Marmont's strength increasing and battle seeming imminent, Hulse's brigade also marched off to San Cristóbal at 0300 hours, leaving the Portuguese brigade to invest the forts. As there was a danger of the army falling back, during the 21st the siege guns were withdrawn from the batteries, while the 24-pounder howitzers were sent to join the army on the heights.

When it became apparent that Marmont, rather than attack Wellington in a defensive position, was content to watch and wait, Hulse's brigade returned to the forts. On their return, in a change of plan, they laboured to throw up a third battery. Jones explains the new intent:

> As possession of the Gaetano redoubt would give great facility for establishing a lodgement close to St. Vicente, from which a mine might be carried under it, or the convent set on fire, it was proposed to expend the remaining 220 rounds of ammunition in an attempt to breach the gorge of that work. At night, battery No. 3, for four guns, was thrown up with these views, at a spot from which the gorge of Gaetano could be seen obliquely at 450 yards distance.

During 24 June the remaining ammunition was expended and it was decided that the division's light companies would attempt to capture the two smaller forts by escalade. General Bowes' men were to storm San Gaetano and Hulse's brigades were ordered to storm the largely intact walls of Fort la Merced. Captain Leith Hay was again an onlooker:

> Exactly at ten o'clock, Generals Hulse and Bowes proceeded on this service. From the spire of the cathedral I witnessed the scene that ensued, certainly one of a very brilliant description: the enemy was on the alert; the moon shone bright, rendering the slightest movement discernible. The moment the British troops debouched, an uninterrupted and vigorous fire burst forth from the artillery of the forts, accompanied by incessant discharges of musketry: the valley presented one continued blaze of light.

Captain Alexander Leith Hay in later life.

In this poorly-planned and executed attack, General Bowes had ignored engineer advice to use a covered approach and led his men straight up the open glacis slope into the teeth of heavy fire from the forts. During the advance most of the ladders made of green wood fell apart and the two that reached the wall of San Gaetano were 6ft too short. Bowes was killed and within the hour the escalade had failed. The 11th's Light Company alone had five killed and ten wounded, including in the latter Captain Teale, the company commander.

Lieutenant Colonel Bingham of the 53rd wrote home criticizing General Clinton's part or lack of it in the storm: 'He goes poking around the church steeple, and I am sure will do anything else than head his division; time will show; if he fails, I will never trust a martinet again.'

On 26 June a resupply of ammunition arrived from Ciudad Rodrigo and this time red-hot shot was used. Major Jones wrote:

> At day-break the fire of hot shot was accelerated, and the breaching battery No. 3 resumed its fire. About 10 A.M. the breach in the gorge of Gaetano became perfectly practicable, and about the same time, a tremendous fire broke out in the roof of the convent of St. Vicente, which proved beyond the efforts of the garrison to extinguish, and the whole building was soon in flames. The troops were formed in the trenches in the ravine [between the forts] ready for the assault of Gaetano, when a white flag was displayed, and the commanding officer proposed to surrender it and La Merced in two hours; which time he wished to have to represent his situation to the superior commandant in San Vicente.
>
> The Earl of Wellington offered him five minutes to march out, in which case he should preserve his baggage; but after trying many evasions, he said he could not comply with such terms, and was ordered to take down his white flag. In the meantime, the commandant of San Vicente sent out a flag of truce and offered to surrender in three hours. Lord Wellington, however, being determined not to lose the favourable moment of the convent being in flames, limited him also to five minutes, during which time he might march out with the honours of war and preserve his baggage. The five minutes having passed, and no appearance of the garrisons quitting the forts, the fire of the batteries was renewed, and shortly after the assaulting party advanced and carried Gaetano by the gorge, the garrison making little or no resistance. Some of the [9th] Portuguese Caçadores from the adjacent houses entered San Vicente also at the fascine battery without opposition, and the besiegers became masters of the whole.

Taking the Salamanca forts cost Wellington approximately 375 all-ranks casualties. The French suffered 190 casualties but about 600 prisoners were taken and 36 cannon were captured. The 6th Division's reputation had not been enhanced by the poor leadership and tactics, but on the other hand the proximity of Marmont's army had led to the suspension of siege operations on two occasions. Wellington also shouldered some of the blame, writing: 'I was mistaken in my

A chosen man of the 5th Battalion, 60th Rifles.

estimate of the extent of the means which would be necessary to subdue these forts; and I was obliged to send to the rear for fresh supply of ammunition. This necessity occasioned a delay of six days.'

The Heights of San Cristóbal

'Marmont will not risk an action unless he should have an advantage; and I shall not risk one unless I should have an advantage; and matters therefore do not appear likely to be brought to that criterion very soon.' [Wellington]

While the 6th Division tackled the Salamanca forts, during 17 June the rest of the army marched to the north-east of the city to bivouac in sites below the heights of San Cristóbal. This low ridge of high ground, 100ft above the surrounding open country, stands between the villages of Monterrubio de Armuña and Moriscos, with the village of San Cristóbal at its foot as a forward bastion. It offered Wellington his preferred reverse slope position, but there was seemingly little to prevent a French outflanking movement to north or south. Closer observation, however, revealed that there were a number of dry water courses, particularly on the right flank. Some were little more than ditches, but the combined effect would have been to disrupt manoeuvre around this flank.

The allied divisions bivouacked on the arid plain during 18 and 19 June, under the burning summer sun without shelter and little water. Cavalry patrols reported on the 18th that the French rearguard was 15 miles away, having fallen back on the road to Toro. Wellington's men were, however, not inactive during this time, as Private Green of the 68th Light Infantry recorded:[11] 'While in this camp we had working parties making a fort of a farmhouse and garden about two miles from our camp-ground.'

After several days Marmont concentrated five of his eight divisions and marched to the relief of the significant garrison he had abandoned in the Salamanca forts. Lieutenant Tomkinson of the 16th Light Dragoons reported that 'At 3 p.m. the enemy moved forward in three columns. The brigade turned out, General Alten's on the right, as before, and Colonel Ponsonby's on the left.' After an initial thrust around the left the action developed on the right. Lieutenant Cooke of the 43rd Light Infantry recorded:

On the 20th a staff officer rode up to a group of us, and said, 'The enemy are advancing.' I rode up the side of the position of San Cristóbal and discerned them afar off in the vast plain. The Division fell in and were ordered to crown the heights. At the same time, some Spanish regiments came in our rear with two pieces of cannon ... The different divisions of the army were now ascending the heights of San Cristóbal at many points.

The French army continued to advance and began to debouch from the different roads in order of battle. The country was level, covered with a sheet of corn as far as the eye could reach. To those fond of military evolutions, the scene was bold. To those of more tranquil habits, time was given to pray for the good of their own souls and, if charitably inclined, for the rest of the

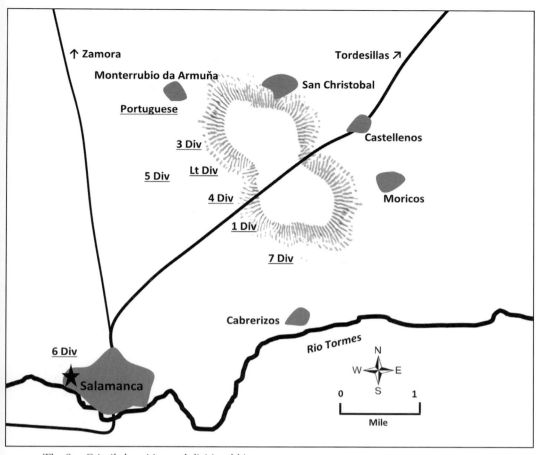

The San Cristóbal position and divisional bivouacs.

The view from the ridge looking north-east over San Cristóbal and the plains beyond across which the French advanced.

army present, which consisted of seven divisions, besides cavalry, artillery, the Spaniards and some Portuguese infantry.

The army was deployed in two lines to oppose the enemy. At first our Division was deployed on the left of the front line, then moved and took post in the centre of the second line. The cavalry were to the right, and some detached on the left to scour the plain between us and Salamanca, where part of the 6th Division remained to cover the forts.

The French, although outnumbered by the British, advanced on Wellington's San Cristóbal position and skirmished vigorously at the foot of the ridge. Tomkinson wrote:

> By 5, the whole had arrived and taken up their ground, and about the same time the enemy's cavalry marched through Castalliano, forming in its front. They drove back our skirmishers rather quickly, and fired with their artillery on the whole advance, to warn the fort of their approach. From a hill close to Castalliano, we were within 800 yards of their cavalry; and on the light guns from the 7th Division coming up, they did not long keep their ground.[12] The cannonade on both sides was sharp, but from our holding the commanding ground they suffered much more than we did.

It would appear that Marmont was testing the resolve of Wellington and his allied troops to stand and fight: 'Their light infantry pushed close to the position and had an affair with ours from the 1st Division. There was a considerable fire on both sides, but at so long a range that nothing of consequence was done by either party.'

The most severe fighting of the day was, however, on the allied army's right flank.

Action at Moriscos

The 68th Light Infantry had recently arrived in the peninsula and joined the 7th Division, where out on the army's right flank, they were to fight their first action of the war. Private Green described it in detail:

> Just as orders came for the division to march, our men were going to receive their wine, but was obliged to leave it with the Quarter-Master and move off as fast as possible. We had no sooner reached the top of a rising ground, than we saw the different divisions and brigades taking their position. We halted a moment or two ... but in vain; for we were ordered forward and continued to advance until we reached the edge of the plain. We then saw the whole of the French army encamped about one mile below us, the ground forming a gradual descent.

Skirmishing and exchanges of artillery fire broke out along nearly the whole front, but the French could only see the allied light companies, gunners and ADCs on the ridge, raising doubts about Wellington's deployment and the

A depiction of the uniform of the 68th Light Infantry.

spectre of Buçaco. On the 7th Division's right flank matters were far from confined to skirmishing. Green continued:

> It was now beginning to be dusk, when an order came for the 68th Light Infantry to descend the hill and take possession of a small village [Moriscos] on the left flank of the enemy. We were to be supported by the Brunswick light infantry who were to form a line of communication between us and the 7th Division.

Little did they suspect that there had been a miscommunication of orders; they should have remained on the hill rather than being sent forward into a very exposed position where the enemy quickly realized their vulnerability!

> We took possession of the village and found that all the people had fled with the exception of an old woman who was nearly frantic. I obtained the liberty to fall out for a few minutes and before I had time to join the column was attacked by a strong body of French infantry.

The 68th's commanding officer, Lieutenant Colonel Johnson, deployed one company to hold the main road into the village from the east and one or more companies in 'small detachments to each of the lanes'. The remainder of the battalion were deployed as supports and a reserve. Companies in support would have been in the village and the reserve probably immediately to the west of the village. Green continued:

> ... a most desperate firing commenced, the enemy advancing up the main street in great force. The colonel ordered two companies to the charge; but finding they were not sufficiently strong, he commanded the whole forward. At this time my right-hand front rank man, a corporal of Captain Gough's company, was killed on the spot, not giving a single struggle.

We charged the enemy to the end of the street, and were so near to them, that the colonel pulled one of the French soldiers into our column. It now became so dark that we could scarcely see each other.

In the ebb and flow of battle around the village the 68th charged three times, driving the French up the main street and out of Moriscos. Meanwhile, the detachments holding the smaller lanes on the periphery to left and right were also in action and casualties mounted. General Graham realized the error and, according to Green:

> ... at length an aide-de-camp arrived from General Graham, with orders for our retreat to the top of the hill; but before we retreated, the colonel made an excellent speech, professing his regard for every man under his command, and at the same time declaring he could keep the town until morning; and if he had not received orders from his superior in command, he would keep possession in spite of the enemy. He added, 'We will not retreat without taking every man that is wounded along with us.' We reached the end of the village in close column, and then called in our detachments, and sent from the column a number of skirmishers, about ten paces in front, who kept up a constant fire on the enemy, who was not more than thirty or forty yards from us. In this position we retreated to the top of the hill: when any man fell, the column halted to ascertain the event. If only wounded, we carried him along with us. We at last arrived at the top of the hill in good order, and there

The rear wall of the church of San Pedro Apóstol in Moriscos still bears the strike of French musket balls.

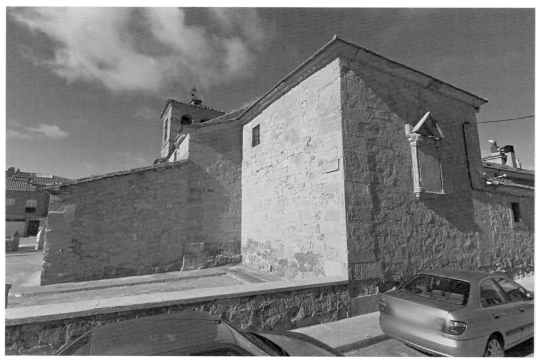

made a stand: the enemy returned into the town, and made a number of fires, and only left a line of sentries to look out for us.

The 68th went into Moriscos some 360 men strong, but suffered 50 killed and wounded. General Graham addressed the battalion and said that any other regiment would have been overwhelmed!

Wellington's Decision

When Marshal Marmont advanced on 20 June with about 25,000 men to the foot of the San Cristóbal ridge, Wellington with approximately 48,000 men offered battle.[13] He came forward to the ridge above Castellanos de Moriscos where the Toro road crosses the ridge and stood near the 1st Division with his senior commanders awaiting developments. Lieutenant Tomkinson was there with the staff of General Sir Stapleton Cotton's cavalry headquarters:

> The general officers of divisions were this evening summoned to Lord Wellington. Whilst standing receiving the orders, several round shot came amongst them, and one close to Lord Wellington, he having a map in his hand. Very little confusion was occasioned – his Lordship moved a few paces and continued his directions. I was with Sir Stapleton, and close to Lord Wellington at the time.

Captain James Stanhope of the 1st Foot Guards overheard a conversation in which Wellington said 'Dammed tempting! I have a mind to attack 'em' but both sides continued skirmishing.[14] Lieutenant Tomkinson, however, raised a question that perplexed many, both at the time and since:

> The position the enemy held close to us was one of considerable risk. We could have attacked them with our whole force in half an hour, and their only chance of getting away was by defending the villages; by sending a large force against one we might have expected success, and so on to the other. Had they both been carried by us; they would then have had to cross the plain before a superior force. The opportunity for an attack was so favourable, we all agreed Lord Wellington had some unknown reasons for not availing himself of their situation. It was said the arrival of a force on the eastern coast of Spain was looked for, and that he delayed, expecting it to operate in his favour in following up any success.

The reason given for not attacking is that most of the senior commanders, particularly Marshal Beresford, were against it. It is also argued that with such an aggressive posture being adopted by Marmont, a defensive battle on the ridge would have been a better option. Wellington reported another factor to Lord Liverpool:

> ... the operations against the forts of Salamanca took up the attention of some of our troops; and although I believe the superiority of numbers in the

Officers of the 16th Light Dragoons still wearing the old-pattern uniform. In most cases 1812 uniform items were not issued until early 1813.

field was on our side, the superiority was not so great as to render an action decisive of the result of the campaign, in which we should sustain great loss.

The general feeling a month later was that a battle on San Cristóbal would have delivered a victory far less complete than that achieved on the field of Salamanca. As the skies on 20 June darkened, Lieutenant Cooke noted that

> Night put an end to the firing. After dark the pickets were placed at the foot of our position, and the whole army slept on their arms in order of battle.
> An hour before daybreak, the troops stood to their arms, fully expecting to be attacked. The dark shades dispersed, and the sun rose, but both armies were tranquil notwithstanding their proximity. The enemy were in full view, without a bush or any obstacle to prevent close quarters.

While Cooke and the Light Division along with most of the army were stationary, there was again action on the allied right flank. Guards officer Captain

The Opening Moves 57

Marshal Marmont, commander of the Army of Portugal.

Stanhope wrote that 'Marmont rode along the front in the day & looked at us & so did Lord Wellington at them.' Andrew Leith Hay commented that this reconnaissance of the flank '... produced a slight affair' in which Marmont avoided capture. Leith Hay records how

> In this instance the Duke of Ragusa advanced so near to the position of his opponents, and removed so far from his own troops, that there appeared a

probability, not only of interrupting his observations, but of intercepting his return. For this purpose, and to discourage these bold attempts at reconnaissance, Lord Wellington directed his aide-de-camp, Captain Burgh, to proceed to the quarters of the 12th Dragoons, and order two squadrons of that regiment to mount, and go forth on this service ... Nothing could be more congenial to the feelings of Colonel Ponsonby than this chase; the men and horses were lightened of every encumbrance ... he placed himself at their head, and at a quick pace sallied forth from the village ... The rapid advance of this body of light cavalry, particularly under the circumstances, excited the curiosity of the enemy; the huts in his encampment poured forth their inmates, who seemed intensely watching the result of this singular encounter, about to take place within cannon-shot of either army. The Marshal and his staff, previously to observing the 12th, were so far advanced that he certainly incurred danger of being intercepted; but with him were some voltigeurs, who, on being approached, covered the plain on his left, and kept up a warm tiraillade on the British dragoons, checking their progress when at a short distance from the French staff, and affording time to secure a retreat, of which the Duke of Ragusa availed himself without the least delay.

The outbreak of firing saw the 51st Light Infantry (7th Division) being ordered up onto the crest of the ridge. Private Wheeler described the resulting events in a letter: 'On the descent from the ridge, the Light Companies of the Guards were engaged with the enemy's skirmishers. We had brought our light guns with us; a few rounds from them and the sight of us caused the enemy to fall back and establish their pickets.'

The guns and howitzers from the siege of the Salamanca forts along with the field batteries were emplaced in freshly-dug fleches while the two armies stood in close proximity to each other. Lieutenant Cooke described the waiting on the ridge:

Our division was now withdrawn from the line and placed as a column of reserve in rear and centre of the army, to protect the [Santa Marta] fords in our rear, and to use as a moveable mass either to resist cavalry or assist where required. The Earl of Wellington was stationary from morning till night, watching the enemy, generally alone and on foot, at the crest of the hill and in the centre of the position. His staff approached him one at a time to receive orders. At night the Earl slept on the ground, wrapped in his cloak.

The troops were much inconvenienced for want of water as the river was at some distance and only a few men could be spared, since it was impossible to know at what moment the enemy might attack ... The Earl of Wellington remained on the hill of Cabrerizos the whole day. The sun shone with great brilliancy; it was burning hot, and one of the soldiers of the 43rd put up a blanket to keep the rays from him. Our bivouac presented a droll appearance as the whole Division had hoisted blankets in a similar manner.

A light infantryman and a camp follower.

Marmont's Indecision

Marmont needed a victory, but was not prepared to attack Wellington without superior numbers or to take on the allies on ground of their choosing. Consequently, he awaited the arrival of his three missing divisions and a 'strong reinforcement' promised from Caffarelli's Army of the North. During the days before the San Cristóbal ridge, French strength grew, with the arrival of two of his divisions, to 36,000 men and 80 guns. Lieutenant Tomkinson, commenting in his diary for the 21st: 'We underrated the enemy at 18,000 infantry; his force is now 30,000, having this day received a reinforcement of 5,000. Two deserters say they are waiting for Bonet's division of 8,000, when they mean to attack.'

Marmont, however, did not attack. General Foy recorded another example of the marshal's indecision:

> At dusk on the 21st there was a grand discussion on the problem as to whether we should or should not give battle to the English. The Marshal

seemed to have a desire to do so, but a feeble and hesitating desire ... I had not the first word: I allowed Maucune, Ferey and La Martinière to express their views before I let them see what I thought. Then Clausel having protested strongly against fighting, I supported his opinion. Because we had left a small garrison in the Salamanca forts, we were not bound to lose 6,000 killed and wounded and risk the honour of the army in order to deliver them. The troops were in good spirits, and that is excellent for the first assault: but here we should have a long tough struggle ... In short, I saw more chances of defeat than victory. I urged that we ought to keep close to the English, 'contain' them, and wait for our reinforcements ... The Marshal was displeased: he fancied that his generals were plotting to wreck his plan: he wanted to redeem the blunder which he saw that he had made in leaving a garrison in Salamanca: he dreads the Emperor and the public opinion of the army. He would have liked a battle, but he had not determination enough to persist in forcing it on.

Without an attack Marmont resorted to an attempt to manoeuvre Wellington from the San Christoval position and on the night of 24/25 June he marched 9 miles to the east to a position from which he could cross the fords at Huerta and threaten the allied line of communication back to Portugal. In response Wellington ordered General Bock's brigade of KGL heavy dragoons to take his brigade across the Rio Tormes to cover Huerta. Captain Stanhope recalled:

> 25th. Before daylight we heard skirmishing across the river and when it became clear we found a large body of the enemy had crossed the river consisting, as we afterwards found out, of 3 divisions of infantry & 3 regiments of cavalry. They began cannonading General Bock who had no artillery but who retreated in the most cool and admirable manner.

Marmont marches east.

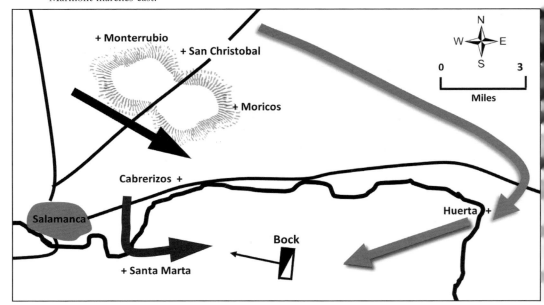

According to Private Wheeler of the 68th Light Infantry, Marmont's move

> occasioned us to cross the river by a ford near the town. This was not a pleasant job, for although the days are excessively hot, the nights are very cold. The river at the ford was up to our waists. We had anticipated the enemy in this movement. For at daylight they found to their mortification the 7th [Division] ready for them.

Wellington had changed his front, deploying the bulk of his army between Moriscos and Cabrerizos but retaining the ability to concentrate his force where required. Stanhope continued:

> General Graham was ordered to cross the ford with the 1st & 7th Divisions. The 5th were in reserve at the [Santa Marta] ford & the left of the line brought to the right ready to act on either side. The enemy occupied Calvarrasa de Arriba but came no further. In the evening they re-crossed the Tormes & so did we. Lord Wellington was convinced they meant to fight and much conversation took place as to the best position. It was determined to throw back our left, fortify a house in the front & put our heavy guns on an island in the Tormes to flank our left.

With the armies in their previous positions, on 26 June Marmont received a message from Caffarelli that Captain Home Popham's Royal Navy squadron had arrived off the Biscay coast and that regular Spanish troops and guerrillas were threatening the north coast ports. He consequently apologized that he could not spare any troops to aid his fellow commander. Marmont, believing that the forts could hold out for another seventy-two hours, was determined to rescue the garrison, but before he could act the forts fell on the 27th.

Once the forts had surrendered and without Caffarelli's reinforcement, the French had little option but to march back to the security of the Rio Duero. The whole period from Wellington's appearance before Salamanca of 16 June to the 27th had, however, left Marmont ignoring his own indecision, brimming with confidence that Wellington would not fight and that he was a defensive general.

The British Cartridge Box

A piece of equipment common to all infantry of the period was the heavy leather cartridge box. It was required to keep the black powder in the paper cartridges dry and to prevent sparks from firing in the closely-packed ranks and setting off an explosion equivalent to a 5.5in howitzer shell.

The British cartridge box was designed to hold sixty cartridges, which in the case of the musket contained more than 13lb of powder. Add to this the weight of the lead balls at 4.5lb and the necessity of the broad cross belt to spread the weight is easily understood.

A number of cartridges – usually twenty-five – for immediate use were placed in holes drilled in a wooden block which sat at the top of the cartridge box. Below this in a tin tray were packs of ten cartridges, which would be opened and the cartridges moved to the block as required, if possible when not in contact with the enemy.

Spare flints and a musket tool plus a 'worm' which could be fitted to the end of the ramrod for extracting complete misfires from the barrel were also contained in the cartridge box.

Existing examples of British cartridge boxes, despite sealed patterns being available to manufacturers, show a significant number of variations in the detail of fittings and in size. Only some of these differences can be accounted for as a result of change of pattern.

A cartridge box, strap, block and tin.

Chapter Four

To the Duero and Back

With the news of the fall of the Salamanca forts on 27 June 1812, Marshal Marmont no longer needed to remain in a risky position in front of Wellington's larger army. His options were to fall back in the direction of Madrid, thus preserving his communications with King Joseph's capital and the Army of the Centre, or to head 50 miles east to the safety of the Rio Duero, where Bonet's division would join him and possibly elements of Caffarelli's Army of the North. He chose the latter course, beginning a two-day forced march before dawn on 28 June. In that time, the Army of Portugal, in three columns, had easily outdistanced the allies heading for Tordesillas and Toro.

Wellington's order of march for the pursuit to the Duero was as follows:

<u>Advance Guard</u>
Alten's Cavalry Brigade, Light Division and Pack's Portuguese

<u>Left Column</u>	<u>Centre Column</u>	<u>Right Column</u>
Le Marchant's Cavalry	1st Division	Bock's Cavalry
3rd Division	5th Division	4th Division
Spanish Infantry	6th Division	
Don Julián's guerrillas	7th Division	
	Headquarters	

The French retreat was followed by the allied cavalry and on the road to Rueda the Light Division was in its normal role of advanced guard. Rifleman Costello recorded a 'smart brush with the enemy', with the main action being confined to Sir Stapleton Cotton's cavalry brigades, which kept the enemy in sight. After three days of withdrawal, the main body of Marmont's army crossed the Duero during 1 to 2 July, leaving a rearguard to cover the destruction of the bridges. Lieutenant Tomkinson wrote in his diary:

> June 30th. We saw the enemy's rear this day on the hills in front of Alaejos ... He moved off before the advanced guard came up.
>
> July 1st. The enemy last night left Castrejón on his route for Valladolid ... The enemy's picquets were a league from us, and Marmont only left Nava del Ray this morning at 7 o'clock.
>
> The [main body of the allied] army marched about three leagues this day and bivouacked on the Trabancos without a tree to shade them or wood to cook with nearer than a league from their camp. The inhabitants frequently use straw to cook with.

64 *Salamanca Campaign, 1812*

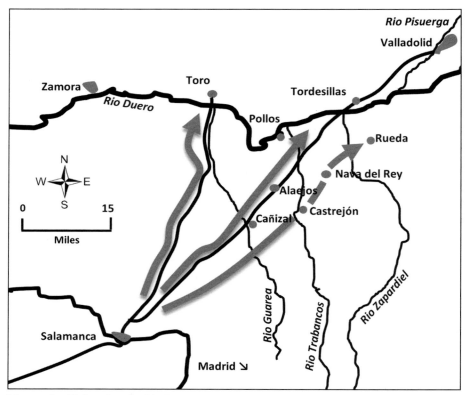

Marmont's withdrawal to the Rio Duero.

July 2nd. Major General Bock's and Le Marchant's brigades [of dragoons] joined the advance this morning, and the whole moved forward at daylight on Tordesillas, situated on the right bank of the Duero. We found the enemy's picquets on the heights about a league from La Nava del Rey, on the right bank of the Zapardiel rivulet, occupying the high ground near Tordesillas. Lord Wellington, in his orders of last night, directed the advanced guard not to cross the rivulet, but to halt there for further orders. Major General [Victor] Alten's brigade gained the heights, and Sir Stapleton supported him with General Anson's brigade, halting the infantry at the bottom. The enemy occupied the plain leading to Tordesillas with their cavalry and had a considerable force of infantry in Rueda.

Lieutenant William Tomkinson's 1796-pattern light cavalry officer's sabre carried by him throughout the Peninsular War.

Sir Stapleton, advancing contrary to Lord W's orders, will not be forgotten by him.

We halted close to their picquets with the two brigades, when Lord W. came up and ordered us to advance. Major General Alten's brigade, with the horse artillery, drove their cavalry over the plain, supported by General Anson's. We left Rueda [7 miles from the Duero] to our right, obliging their infantry to evacuate that place. Our guns did considerable execution, but the cavalry was not allowed to charge. A league from Tordesillas, the ground falls much and suddenly, and on our gaining this point, the guns were opening on their infantry, and had fired a few shots. We thought the opportunity a fair one, when the whole was ordered to halt.

Having marched across the open arid plains in the wake of the cavalry, the Light Division arrived in the wine-growing area around Rueda. Captain Leach of the 95th Rifles recalled coming across bodies of French stragglers found in the wine cellars 'who had been put to death ... and we saw several others in the churchyard, cut and lacerated in a shocking manner. The system of warfare between the Spanish and the French was revolting to the greatest possible degree.'[1]

The infantry divisions were halted between Rueda and Pollos, while Cotton's cavalry brigades were forward with each regiment providing a duty squadron on the river line. The situation in the first week of July with the armies watching their respective banks of the Duero was summed up in Wellington's report to Liverpool, explaining that

> The enemy's position on the Duero is very strong and their army is sufficient to occupy it. On their right they have the strong places of Zamora and Toro which cannot be taken excepting by regular attack [i.e. by siege].
>
> Their left rests upon the Pisuerga, which is not fordable anywhere. They have a fortified post at Simancas, where there is a bridge over that river, and they have fortified, and have a garrison in Valladolid, where there is another bridge. They occupy with their army, and nearly 100 pieces of cannon,[2] the bridge of Tordesillas, and the heights which command the fords of the Duero, from Toro to the Pisuerga.
>
> It is obvious that we could not cross the river without sustaining great loss and could not fight a general action under circumstances of greater disadvantage than those which would attend the attack of the enemy's position on the Duero. In truth, the enemy's numbers are equal if not superior to ours; they have in their position twice the amount of the artillery which we have, and we are superior in cavalry alone, which arm, it is probable could not be used in the attack we should have to make.

Wellington, perennially short of hard cash with which to supplement the commissary's basic rations for his army, could not consider advancing further into Spain. He wrote to Beresford: 'I have never been in such distress as at present, and some serious misfortune must happen, if the government does not attend

Captain Jonathan Leach, wearing the Tarleton helmet worn in the early days of the 95th Rifles.

seriously to the subject and supply us regularly with money.' Marmont expected an attack, but he was under no immediate pressure to resume the campaign and, as long as food was available, he could wait and would only gain strength with the approach of the king.[3]

After a much-delayed march, General Bonet's division numbering almost 8,000 men joined the Army of Portugal on the evening of 7 July, taking up positions on the right flank around Toro, but much to Marmont's fury there was still no reinforcement from Caffarelli. Meanwhile, in order to boost the number of cavalry under his command, Marmont ordered that all horses belonging to officers who did not hold mounted appointments or had extra horses were to be turned over as troop horses. This exceptional and unpopular measure enabled in excess of 700 dismounted dragoons to be put back in the saddle, but as untrained cavalry horses their quality must be questioned.

Of his reinforcement, a week later, Wellington wrote to Liverpool that he expected

> that the 5th, 38th and 82nd regiments will join the army in the course of the next three weeks; and there are not less than 2,000 recruits and convalescents on the road. But at this season of the year it is impossible to rely upon the fitness for service of troops just arrived, or recovered from sickness, after such a march.[4]

General Marie-François Auguste de Caffarelli du Falga, commander of the Army of the North.

The armies now had broad parity, but neither of the competent commanders had the numerical advantage they sought before committing to a general action; the watching, waiting and manoeuvring by both sides would continue. Meanwhile, on the Duero the picquets of the armies were for some ten days watching each other across the river; with bathing parties and bands playing, there was almost a holiday atmosphere. Major William Napier of the 43rd Light Infantry:

> The weather was very fine, the country rich, and the troops received their rations regularly; wine was so plentiful, that it was hard to keep the soldiers sober; the caves of Rueda, either natural or cut in the rock below the surface of the earth, were so immense and so well stocked, that the drunkards of two armies failed to make any very sensible diminution in the quantity. Many men of both sides perished in that labyrinth.

Private Joseph Donaldson of the 94th Scotch Brigade (3rd Division) recorded:

> While here there was an understanding, I believe, between both armies, that they should have use of the river without molestation, our men and the French used to swim in it promiscuously, mixing together at times bringing brandy and wine with them, for the purpose of treating each other; but though friendly with our men, the French soldiers studiously avoided coming near the Portuguese, whom they knew by the dark colour of their skins. This friendly feeling between our soldiers and the French was remarkably displayed during the whole war.

However, this situation would not last, as by 14 July Wellington was reporting that King Joseph had ordered the Army of the Centre to abandon its scattered garrison towns in the Tagus valley and to concentrate at Madrid, along with Drouet's command. This was a significant development that the allied intelligence staff would monitor carefully in order to identify the king's intent, especially as Lord Bentnick's force from Sicily, which Wellington had expected to land on the east coast of Spain as a part of his policy of distraction, had instead landed in Italy. This meant that Joseph was now likely to intervene against Wellington's army, with his 14,000 men swinging the balance decidedly in favour of the French.

Marmont's Offensive

Stung by the loss of the forts and encouraged by King Joseph, now Marmont's force had approximate parity of numbers with the allies, the Army of Portugal prepared to re-cross the Rio Duero. To improve chances of success, the offensive was to open with a *ruse de guerre* designed to catch Wellington off balance. This, however, required his infantry to execute one of their prodigious feats of marching at the beginning of a new phase of the campaign.

Presumably to condition Wellington's intelligence organization to inexplicable troop movements, some of Marmont's divisions were set in motion during

A representation of soldiers of the 94th Scotch Brigade. In 1809 they lost the kilt and in the 1812 dress regulations they adopted grey wool 'trowsers' along with the rest of the infantry.

the days before the offensive. Captain William Warre, ADC to Marshal Beresford, wrote in a letter dated 13 July that

> Yesterday morning we saw a large column of about 4,000 returning towards Tordesillas, from whence they had marched the evening before towards the fords at Herreros and Torrecilla de la Abadesa, but to what end all this marching and countermarching of theirs can be, I cannot guess. If they mean to harass us, they do not succeed, for though we narrowly watch every movement they make, Ld. Wn. is not easily humbugged and lets them wear out their shoes as much they please without disturbing his army.[5]

Wellington was, however, 'humbugged' by Marmont's plan, which was to make a feint march against the allied left, crossing the Duero via the bridge at Toro with two divisions and making an obvious westerly movement with his other formations. Once the allies responded, these divisions would make a forced countermarch back and concentrate at the fords of Pollos and the bridge at Tordesillas, from where they would cross the Duero and turn the allied right flank. If his scheme worked, Marmont's force would be facing only a weakened flank guard.

Wellington's exploring officers were active across the Duero reporting on enemy deployments, including Marmont's sundry deception measures. Headquarters in Rueda also received regular letters from correspondents, with one in particular from Toro revealing that General Foy's division was involved in repairing the bridge near that place. This news contributed to Wellington's conclusion that '... all the intelligence and enemy movements lead to a belief that the enemy intend to cross the Duero at that place.'

To reinforce the picture of a westerly movement, when the offensive began on 16 July, General Picton, covering the fords of Pollos, was quickly reporting that the enemy had withdrawn 'a very large body of cavalry in the morning early and

The opening moves of Marmont's offensive.

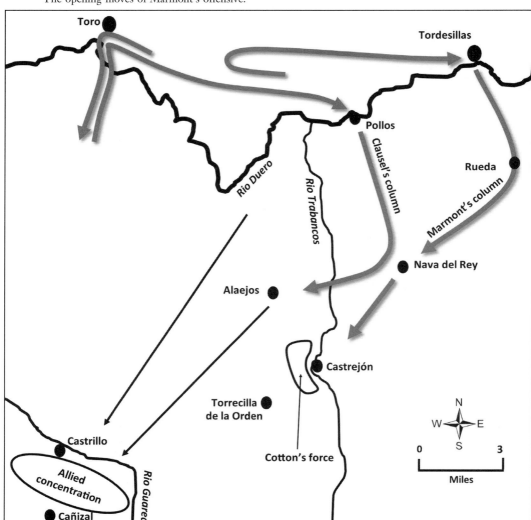

their infantry at about half-past seven and have marched in the direction of Toro'. Wellington wrote to General Clinton, whose 6th Division held the allied left flank near Toro: 'I am anxious to hear from you what movements they have made on their left.' Both Clinton and General D'Urban and his Portuguese cavalry were instructed to keep in close communication with Lieutenant Shanahan, one of the exploring officers. Wellington was in 'no doubt' that he was 'very close to the French columns'.

Wellington, meanwhile, ordered the execution of orders he had already issued for the concentration of the bulk of his army back towards the Rio Guareña at Fuentelapeña, which would cover the Toro to Salamanca road and his lines of communication. Halfway back to Salamanca, they would be in a position to deploy on the high ground behind the Rio Guareña centred on Castrillo. In the event, not entirely convinced by the Toro manoeuvre, he left a substantial covering force or rearguard of two divisions and a cavalry brigade, under the command of General Cotton, to watch Tordesillas. When the allied army marched to its appointed positions early on the 17th, Cotton would be on the Rio Trabancos near Castrejón, some 10 miles from the main concentration. Lieutenant Kincaid of the 1st 95th Rifles recalled the march of the Light Division during the night of 16/17 July:

> After forming on our alarm post, we were moved off in the dark, we knew not wither; but every man following the one before him, with the most implicit confidence, until after marching all night, we found ourselves, on the following morning, at daylight, near the village of Castrejón, where we bivouacked for the day.

Meanwhile, Marmont had counter-marched during the night of the 16th/17th and on the morning of 17 June, just as Wellington's army was moving off to the concentration area, the two leading French infantry divisions and Curto's light cavalry division were crossing the Duero at Tordesillas. They marched on Rueda from which the Light Division had withdrawn that night, and during the day patrols of the cavalry rearguard provided by Anson's brigade noticed a worrying growth in numbers of French troops.

Throughout the morning of the 17th Wellington received conflicting reports regarding French actions on the Toro road. Finally, a personal reconnaissance towards Toro confirmed that the enemy divisions had recrossed to the north of the Duero, but it was not until late in the day, sometime after 1900 hours, that word reached him from Cotton that the enemy had advanced on the Tordesillas road in strength. The French main body was at Nava del Rey, with some divisions having marched in excess of 40 miles, and their cavalry was, unknown to the allies, just 4 miles from the Trabancos. Marmont's very well-executed manoeuvre had forced the allies further back from the Duero, put Cotton's command in considerable peril and the army as a whole in a dangerous situation; one that would require the best from Wellington and his troops to escape.

Curto's division contained two squadrons of the distinctive grey uniformed 3rd Hussars, old opponents of the Light Division.

The Affair at Castrejón

The Light and 4th divisions had spent the 17th west of the Trabancos covered by General George Anson's light cavalry, which fell back in front of the advancing French.[6] Major William Napier of the 43rd Light Infantry described the ground they had found themselves on: 'The country was open and hilly, like the downs of England, with here and there water-gullies, dry hollows, and bold naked heads of land.' The Rio Trabancos was virtually dry, but was a broad tangle of water channels, banks of gravel and parched vegetation. The only easy crossing-place for a formed body of troops was at a bridge at Castrejón, beyond which, on the high ground, were two cavalry outposts and two picquets of thirty men: one provided by the 95th Rifles and the other by the 43rd.

Meanwhile, General Leith's 4th Division had also pulled back behind the Rio Trabancos. Sergeant Douglas of the 3rd Battalion, the Royal Scots recalled that

> We continued to retire until daylight, when we were ordered back to check the advance of the enemy, who were considerably outflanking some of our Division, putting our guns and baggage in danger. We advanced about a league when we came in full view of the enemy and formed line for action with the usual examination of arms; not looking for burnished pieces, but blew down the barrel to see if the touchhole was clear, flints fast and all's well.

The two divisions were some distance apart, but crucially separated by several gullies. Lieutenant Tomkinson, who had by now left General Cotton's staff to join B Troop of the 16th Light Dragoons, wrote:

> The 4th and Light Divisions were encamped close to Castrejón, and General Cole [4th Division], on riding out, fancied the enemy were coming to attack the two divisions *with two squadrons*. He rode back into the town, sent his baggage to the rear, and no doubt would have ordered the troops to turn out had he commanded.

The view from west overlooking the Trabancos and Castrejón to the 'bold naked heads' described by Major William Napier.

General Cotton, however, was not going to withdraw and sent patrols out at dawn, one of which was led by Tomkinson who wrote the following:

> July 18th. Sir Stapleton sent for me before daylight to proceed with a patrol in front of the picquets, with orders to see as many of the enemy's troops as could be overlooked by a patrol, and report immediately... My patrol was of six men, and I was to ascertain particularly if the enemy's infantry had come up to La Nava.
>
> I had scarcely got beyond our picquets when I met a squadron of the enemy's cavalry. More were coming up, and in half an hour the picquets were driven back on Castrejón, and from the number of squadrons shown by the enemy, it was evident they were in force, and advancing. I joined one of the 11th, and with them retired on the brigade. We were a good deal pressed, and once obliged to turn round and charge. Captain Deakin, ADC to Sir Stapleton, with one man of the 11th, was wounded.

Cotton sent the rest of Anson's cavalry forward across the Trabancos, supported by Major Bull's troop of horse artillery. As the brigade advanced over the hills, Napier wrote that these 'troops were soon lost to the sight of the infantry, for the morning fog was thick on the stream, and at first nothing could be descried beyond'. Meanwhile, Lieutenant Kincaid's company of riflemen was providing

The Affair at Castrejón.

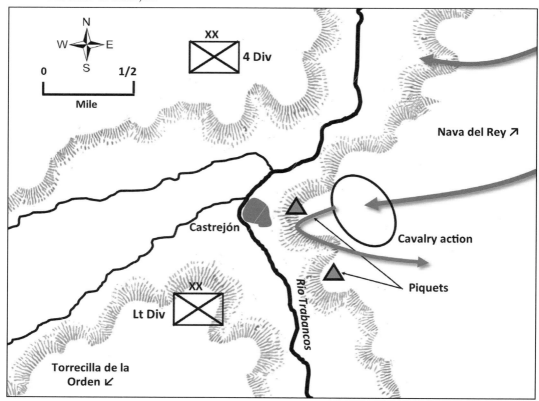

one of the Light Division's picquets just beyond the Trabancos near Castrejón when the action began:

> I was sent on picquet on the evening of the 17th, to watch a portion of the plain before us; and, soon after sunrise on the following morning, a cannonade commenced, behind a hill, to my right; and, though the combatants were not visible, it was evident that they were not dealing in blank-cartridge, as mine happened to be the pitching-post of all the enemy's round shot.

Captain Tomkinson, as he explains, was the target of that French artillery fire:

> The enemy's cavalry all appeared on the plain in front of Castrejón, and on seeing the brigade, halted their guns and ammunition and commenced a cannonade ... It was the sharpest cannonade, for the time, we were, or I, was ever exposed to, and almost impossible to get the men away in complete order. Many shots went over us and struck the 11th Light Dragoons in the rear. On the left, two squadrons, one of the 11th and 12th, were supporting two guns from Major Ross's troop.[7]

The scene was set for a sharp cavalry action with the French engaging with sixteen guns but, as Tomkinson noted, 'Our squadrons were fortunately dispersed over the ground, and at first did not suffer much.' The squadrons covering the pair of guns were promptly attacked. Napier wrote:

> When the French officer saw this squadron, he reined in his horse with difficulty, and his troopers gathered in a confused body round him as if to retreat. They seemed lost men, for the British instantly charged, but with a shout the gallant fellows soused down upon the squadron, and the latter turning, galloped through the guns; then the whole mass, friends and enemies, went like a whirlwind to the bottom ... [of the Trabancos valley].

While Lieutenant Kincaid was attentively watching the progress of the fight,

> there arose, all at once, behind the rising ground to my left, a yell of the most terrific import; and, convinced that it would give instantaneous birth to a hideous body, it made me look, with an eye of lightning, at the ground around me; and, seeing a broad deep ditch within a hundred yards, I lost not a moment in placing it between my picquet and the extraordinary speed.[8]

Meanwhile, Lieutenant Cooke and the remainder of the 43rd who were not deployed on picquets were west of the Trabancos and as the sun rose were alerted by the firing beyond the river:

> Our dragoons became visible retiring before the enemy's horse and light artillery, which at intervals were blazing away. The scene was sublime and beautiful. An officer said to me, 'There will be a row this day; we had better get our breakfast, as God knows when we shall have anything to eat.'[9]

Major Hew Ross, commander of A Troop RHA which habitually served with the Light Division.

Preparations for breakfast were, however, cut short when suddenly squadrons of French dragoons appeared in a valley to the right heading for the main road at full trot. Cooke noted that 'An absurd and ludicrous scene now took place. Into the hampers was thrown the crockery and also the kettle half filled with hot water.'

> To get off seemed impossible, but the company formed column of sections and fixed bayonets, fully determined to cover the old mule [carrying the mess chattels], who went off with a rare clatter and we after him in double-quick

time. The enemy were within 200 yards of us, brandishing their swords and calling out, then they saw some of our cavalry hovering on their right flank and drew up.

Meanwhile, to the left of the Light Division the 4th was in action. Sergeant Douglas takes up the story:

> Our position retarded their progress for some time, until they had examined our strength. We retired again and halted on the side of a gentle declivity with a small rivulet in front and formed line, from line into square, for the purpose of keeping their cavalry in due bounds. Our squares were scarcely formed when Arthur [Lord Wellington] and all his staff came galloping down the hill, his head going like a weather cock while the French 9-pounders whizzed about fiercely. We could see, by the clouds of dust, the march of the enemy, when just in our front a French officer rode to the top of the hill which his Lordship had just descended and fired a pistol. We were pretty well aware of the signal, for in the space of 5 minutes 7 artillery pieces opened fire upon us. 'Twas lucky that Leith had deployed us into line so that the round shot could not do the execution, which it would have done had they caught us in square. The first gunshot told near the colours, which carried away a poor fellow's leg and his boot flew into the air. The adjutant says, 'There's one man down.' After remaining about half an hour under this fire without returning the compliment, the guns ceased, and on came the cavalry. Each regiment now formed into square double-quick ... On came the cavalry, but the menacing appearance of the squares rather cooled their courage.

The 4th Division's battalion squares according to Douglas were deployed 'something like a chequer board, so that the fire of one square would not interfere with another'. The enemy cavalry rode around the squares at a 'humble distance' awaiting any sign of wavering in the ranks of the 4th Division. There was none and the enemy cavalry withdrew. Douglas continued:

> We now deployed, expecting the guns to open and were not disappointed. The object for which we halted being accomplished – viz to let the other divisions of the Army get extricated with the guns and baggage – under this galling fire we went to the right about, retiring in ordinary time; their guns playing on us as long as a shot could reach us.

To the right, with growing numbers of French chasseurs arriving on the plain, the Light Division and Anson's brigade were in difficulty. Wellington had, however, responded to the situation:

> ... in consequence of my knowledge that the enemy had not passed the Duero at Toro, and there was not time to call them [Cotton's force] in between the hour at which I received the intelligence of the whole of the

enemy's army being at La Nava and daylight of the morning of the 18th. I therefore took measures to provide for their retreat and junction.

To extricate Cotton from his isolated position Wellington had ordered three brigades of cavalry – Bock's and Le Marchant's brigades of heavy dragoons and Victor Alten's light dragoons – to march to Castrejón. He also ordered Leith's 5th Division to advance some 3 miles from the Rio Guareña to Torrecilla de la Orden to act as a firm point on the withdrawal route that the 4th and Light

Lieutenant General Sir Stapleton Cotton, later 1st Viscount Combermere, was known as the Lion d'Or due to his practice of wearing his gold-bedecked full dress uniform on all occasions.

divisions could take on their way back to the rest of the army beyond the Rio Guareña.

Wellington, along with Marshal Beresford and their staffs, having ridden hard since well before dawn, had arrived in time to see the two squadrons on the left being attacked and were forced to draw their swords. The staff officers, as Tomkinson explained, did not help!

> The squadrons were supporting one another, and on the advance of some of the enemy's cavalry (inferior to the two squadrons), the one in front went about. Some of Marshal Beresford's staff seeing this, conceived the guns were in danger, rode up to the retiring squadron, calling 'Threes about!' This of course put the other squadron about in the place of fronting the one already retiring. One person gave one word, one another, and the enemy's cavalry came up to the guns.[10]

Lieutenant Kincaid had only just got his picquet of riflemen into cover of a gully

> ... when Lord Wellington, with his staff, and a cloud of French and English dragoons and horse artillery intermixed, came over the hill at full cry, and all hammering at each other's heads in one confused mass, over the very ground I had that instant quitted. It appeared that his Lordship had gone there to reconnoitre, covered by two guns and two squadrons of cavalry, who, by some accident, were surprised, and charged by a superior body of the enemy, and sent tumbling in upon us in the manner described. A picquet of the 43rd had formed on our right.

Lieutenant Simmons added more detail: 'Lord Wellington exposed himself too much, I as well as others did not like to see him within range of musketry; he was slightly hurt by a spent ball, luckily of no consequence.'[11]

Meanwhile, Lieutenant Cooke and the 43rd Light Infantry whose breakfast had been disturbed had re-formed behind one of the steep-sided rivulets that break up the otherwise open and gently rolling plain before advancing:

> The Right [1st] Brigade[12] had moved forward and deployed to the succour of our dragoons first engaged, about half a mile to our right. Two squadrons of our light dragoons then formed on a rising ground 200 yards from us, with two pieces of horse artillery on their right. About an equal number of French heavy cavalry, handsomely dressed with large fur caps, made rapidly towards them while our guns threw round shot at them.[13] Within 100 yards of our squadrons, they drew up to get wind; our dragoons remaining stationary.
>
>   A French officer, the *chef d'escadron*, to beguile a few moments while his squadron obtained a little breathing time, advanced and invited our people to charge. Holding his sword on high and crying *'Vive l'Empereur! En avant, Français!'* he rushed on, followed by his men, and overthrew our light dragoons. Fortunately, the guns had limbered up, and the horse artillery

fought round them with great spirit. The enemy tried to cut the traces, but the drivers held down their heads, and sticking their spurs into the horses' sides, passed the ford under cover of our picquet.

Lieutenant Ferguson, with the 43rd's picquet, on their piece of high ground to the right had hitherto been onlookers of the cavalry engagement:

> The French were led by a dashing officer, who we were delighted to see at last escape. Lord Wellington and Beresford with their orderlies rallied the

An elite company of chasseurs à cheval with an officer in front and a pioneer with the crossed axe badge on his sleeve.

runaways and drove back the enemy. Some of the most advanced of the [French] officers in the number passed close under our musketry. Not a soldier fired. Our men were hurt at the conduct of their British cavalry and were anxious that these few gallant fellows should escape. A brave soldier always admires dashing and bold conduct in his opponent. The French officer was closely pursued and received some several sabre cuts. Notwithstanding he regained his own troops and we heard of his recovery afterwards, although badly wounded.

Kincaid concluded:

> Marshal Beresford and the greater part of the staff remained with their swords drawn, and the Duke himself did not look more than half-pleased, while he silently dispatched some of them with orders. General [Victor] Alten, and his huge German orderly dragoon, with their swords drawn, cursed, the whole time, to a very large amount; but, as it was in German, I had not the full benefit of it![14]

This is just one of the occasions when Wellington was very nearly captured or killed during the course of the Salamanca Campaign.

The cavalry, having recovered their positions on the hills beyond the Trabancos, as recorded by Lieutenant Tomkins held their ground despite enemy pressure: 'The cannonade on the Castrejón plain continued for two hours, during which time we kept our ground with little loss, considering the fire. The enemy's practice was bad.'

The Withdrawal to the Rio Guareña

With clouds of dust marking the arrival of the French infantry and a column branching off to turn the 4th Division's left, General Clinton marched his division off before they became heavily engaged. The Light Division and most of the cavalry were, however, locked in battle and could only withdraw with some difficulty, with Cotton having delayed his withdrawal for longer than was wise. Lieutenant Cooke commented that 'To avoid an action seemed impossible. The enemy's infantry were almost on the run, and we were marching away from them as hard as we could. While the round shot from a flank fire flew over us.' Ensign Hennell, also of the 43rd, recorded that

> We had not formed two minutes before a very warm cannonade opened upon us. A ball came over my head about a foot. A cannon ball makes a tremendous whiz as it passes you. The old soldiers always burst out a-laughing when they see the young ones dip down their heads, which they generally do when a ball passes within a foot or two of them.

Cooke continued: 'The Light Division now commenced its retreat from the vicinity of Castrejón ... We had only retrograded a short way when we obtained a view of the bulk of the French army, pushing forward on a ridge of hills to our

A portrait of an unknown officer of the 43rd Light Infantry.

left.' The enemy infantry's advance would separate the Light and 4th divisions, but Cooke could see that the 4th Division

> were retiring in mass within range of the enemy's fire, critically situated in the valley, while the French cannon rolled on the crest of the hill above and poured in their shot with effect on their right flank.
>
> Our Division was obliquely to the rear, in column of quarter distance, with fixed bayonets ready to form square, surrounded by large bodies of our cavalry.

Major Ross sent Lieutenant Belson's detachment of guns forward, as explained by Sergeant Whitehead:

> The enemy's right flank pushing forward to cut off the Light Division, their cavalry repeatedly charging. The Troop, having changed the gun limbers for

those of the wagon[s], galloped up to them covered by the 12 Lt Dragoons and came into action at 200 yards with common case and put a stop to them. Gunner Beresford is wounded. The Light Division then inclines to the left, the Troop keeps to the road ... this was a smart day's work.[15]

With the enemy cavalry halted, the 4th and Light divisions, with the French infantry approaching from a flank, were on the first leg of their withdrawal, 3 miles to Torrecilla de la Orden, which was by now held by the 5th Division. The 4th Division led with the Light Division bringing up obliquely to the rear, being engaged in 'a bickering fight', as the French attempted to outdistance them and turn their flank, but with most of three cavalry brigades supporting them they were able to keep on the march. Kincaid described the scene:

> The movements which followed presented the most beautiful military spectacle imaginable. The enemy were endeavouring to turn our left; and, in making a counteracting movement, the two armies were marching in parallel lines, close to each other, on a perfect plain, each ready to take advantage of

The withdrawal to the Rio Guareña, 18 July 1812.

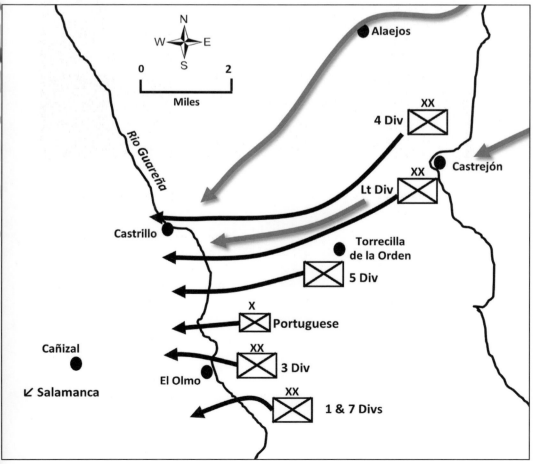

any opening of the other and exchanging round shot as they moved along. Our division brought up the rear of the infantry, marching with the order and precision of a field-day, in open column of companies, and in perfect readiness to receive the enemy in any shape; who, on their part, had a huge cavalry force close at hand, and equally ready to pounce upon us.[16]

Captain Leach described the division's march:

> During this retreat we were exposed to a constant cannonade, and threatened by heavy masses of infantry, ready to close with us if our pace was relaxed for a minute. Nor was the steadiness and gallantry displayed by the cavalry and horse artillery less worthy of admiration. A halt of two or three minutes would have enabled the French infantry to reach us. Thus, we marched for some miles over a country as level as a chessboard, in columns of battalions, ready to engage the French infantry if they should overtake us, and equally so to receive their cavalry, in square or close column, if they attempted to charge. This beautiful series of evolutions of the two armies on this day, and on the three following, were such as a man may never witness again if he lives for ages.

Major Ross's guns, working in sections of two, were in regularly in action throughout the withdrawal and were lucky to escape. On one occasion they

A light 6-pounder cannon and RHA gunner.

remained in action for too long and were caught and overrun while limbering up, but they were rescued by Bock's KGL heavy dragoons who then remained with the division in close support, while Le Marchant's brigade covered the gap between the Light and 4th divisions. Lieutenant Cooke recalled that

> The country was open, and a vast sheet of corn enveloped us for many miles. The men became much distressed owing to the rapidity of the movements and the heat of the day. Owing to our numerical superiority of cavalry, which made a curve down a gentle descent, we were able to regain the road near Castrillo.

In all it was an 8-mile march to the high ground beyond the Rio Guareña and the rest of the allied army. In many respects this was a repeat of the Light Division's epic withdrawal at Fuentes de Oñoro the previous year. Consequently, it required the strongest of nerves and discipline from the division, especially as Major Ross's light 6-pounders were outgunned by the French divisional artillery.

Sergeant Douglas of the Royal Scots with the 4th Division wrote: 'We retired all that day in column of companies, wheeling distance apart,[17] marching over every obstacle that came in our way, fields of wheat, vines, etc which, with the heat of the day, and no water, rendered this as fatiguing a day's march as ever I remember.'

Marmont's dispatch describing the day's events from his perspective reads:

> On the morning of the 18th we found the two divisions at Torrecilla de la Orden. As they did not believe the whole [French] army was assembled they

French infantry on the march.

thought they could gain time without danger. However, when they saw our masses, they hastened to retire to a plateau which dominates the village towards which we marched. Already we had overpowered them. If I had had a cavalry superior or equal in number to that of the enemy these two divisions would have been destroyed. None the less we did not pursue them with less than all possible vigour and during three hours of marching they were overwhelmed by the fire of our artillery, which I fired into their tail and in flanks. They could hardly answer and protected by their numerous cavalry they divided to go up Guareña in order to pass it with more ease.

Crossing the Rio Guareña

The objective of the march was to join the army on the northern part of the high ground beyond the Guareña. The rest of the army was already in position on the ridge as far south as the El Olmo forts. Here Wellington intended to make a stand, but with the French so close on their heels this was one of the most dangerous moments of the withdrawal. For instance, as the 4th Division approached Castrillo the French sent forward horse artillery to a knoll which flanked the allied column. Unlimbering, the French guns opened fire as the column marched on and as a response General Cole sent Sympher's battery to counter the fire and deployed his light companies to gall the enemy gunners. Nonetheless a significant number of the division's 200 casualties of 18 June were suffered during this phase of the retreat.

For the soldiers the retirement from Castrejón had been made far worse by the heat and lack of water on the dusty plain and Captain Leach recorded that 'Many soldiers, particularly of the Portuguese, died on the road, from heat and want of water.' So desperate were men and horses that when the Light Division looked down into the valley where the Rio Guareña was little more than a stream, the division broke ranks and rushed to the lukewarm muddy water to fill their canteens. They were, however, soon sped on their way by the fire of the forty guns of General Clausel's artillery, belonging to the French right column. The 5th Division, however, stopped in the stream to drink their fill rather than drink from their canteens as they went and consequently suffered significant casualties from the artillery fire.

Lieutenant Browne of Wellington's staff voiced the opinion of the army:

> We thought this stream would probably have been the separation of the armies for the day, but by three in the afternoon the enemy had crossed over a force of cavalry & infantry on our left, in that straggling imperceptible manner so peculiar to the French, that made us disregard it, & the more so, as his main movements seemed directed towards the contrary flank ... He manoeuvred mixing infantry with cavalry & at length approached very near our left with two or three battalions & guns.

The French had advanced in two columns and on his own initiative Clausel committed the northern column to an immediate attack off the line of march,

General Bertrand Clausel.

hoping to catch the allied divisions before they were properly formed. Lieutenant Cooke made just that point:

> We had no sooner crossed the river than some squadrons of the enemy's cavalry galloped up a hill immediately overlooking us. The division now moved more leisurely; and everyone was aware that had our cavalry given way the division must have halted to repulse charges, which would have given time for the French infantry to come up; and had that been the case,

the struggle must have been very sanguinary. Our reserves now being at hand, we soon halted on a round hill, and showed front.

Nothing serious, however, developed against the Light Division beyond an exchange of artillery fire. To their left, however, Clausel led his attack on the 4th Division with Brenier's division. Major Vere, the division's assistant quartermaster general, wrote:

> The enemy soon appeared in force on the heights above the river, and several batteries opened successively on the line of the allies. The [4th Division's] line marched with a steady pace, up the slopes of the left bank of the valley, under the fire of the enemy's cannon, with little loss, and took position on the heights.
>
> The enemy's cavalry pushed round the left of the allies; but were met and delayed in their progress by Major General Alten's brigade of light cavalry.[18]

General Carrié's brigade of two French regiments, the 15th and 25th dragoons, were in the act of deploying to threaten the 4th Division when the 14th Light Dragoons and the 1st Hussars KGL charged over the crest line in echelon of squadrons from the left. After a short and confused fight, the French dragoons were routed, falling back behind their infantry to re-form. Carrié, along with 94 men, was taken prisoner, with the total French loss in this short action being 150 all ranks.

> The enemy's cavalry was however ... followed closely by a division of Infantry, which advanced with great boldness and celerity on the left of the position, and up the lower slopes of the heights occupied by the 4th Division. Lord Wellington, who was on the spot, ordered General Cole to attack the French Infantry with his division.

Cole ordered the 27th and 40th regiments to advance in line, leading them upon the enemy's columns which were by now almost halfway up the heights. The 11th and 23rd Portuguese regiments followed in support of the British in two columns at quarter distance. As the line approached, it overlapped the frontage of the columns. Surgeon Botfleur wrote that

> The attack was made by the Division left in front; it fell to the 27th & 40th Regts composing the left Brigade [Anson's] to bear the brunt of the affair. These two regiments, on approaching the enemy, advanced to the charge in the most undaunted manner, notwithstanding the force opposed to them was near three times their number. The French presented a firm front till our people arrived within about twenty paces of them, when they fired a volley, and flew in the utmost confusion. Unfortunately, the assailants were so much exhausted from a long previous march, and the great heat of the weather (which was so excessive that several men and officers actually died on the march), that they were unable to follow them up.[19]

A 27th Enniskillen Regiment officer's crossbelt plate.

Lieutenant Browne offers an alternative explanation for the lack of energy in the infantry's charge:

> The enemy stood & fired a little. They were very firm until within fifty or sixty paces, when our fellows gave them the bayonet with cheers, routed the column & left of the French about 80 dead & 100 prisoners besides wounded. Our men charged at too great a distance, their ranks were in confusion, & they were so breathless & exhausted when they came up with the French, that they could scarcely use the bayonet. It was ascertained from the prisoners that these two battalions of ours had charged six of the enemy, about 3,000 men, & that their force across the stream, & at hand to support consisted of two divisions which had concealed themselves in the inequalities of the ground.

In the two battalions' charge the enemy lost heavily, and an opportunity was afforded to one of Alten's cavalry regiments which had quickly re-formed on the left of the infantry to follow up with 'great effect'. Clausel's losses, mostly near Castrillo, were around 700 men including 250 prisoners, while the British, principally in the 4th and Light divisions, lost 525 men including approximately 50 stragglers.

Marmont, seeing how roughly his right wing had been treated in attacking Wellington in a position of his choosing, did not attack with his other column and the firing subsided. In his report Marshal Marmont stated that his infantry was exhausted, having had little sleep for nearly three days and some of them marching in excess of 50 miles. In that respect his successful opening gambit had ultimately failed. Wellington was in a strong position, covering his line of

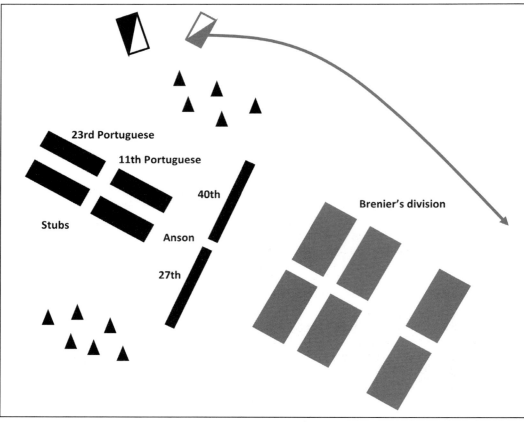

The supposed deployments during the 4th Division's counter-attack. There is no mention in accounts of the 7th Caçadores or of No. 10 Company, 5th 60th Rifles, but they would probably have initially covered Anson's advance but fallen back to protect the brigade's flank as the line and column approached contact.

communications, where he would have concentrated his divisions even if the real attack had been via Toro.

Cooke ends his account, noting the lack of water and a disturbed night:

> We soon halted and faced about. The enemy's guns ceased to play, and a large force of our light dragoons mounted the hill in our rear, with sloped swords.
>
> Night came on and we formed columns in case of accidents. An officer and myself stole down the hill on horseback in search of water for ourselves and animals. Having passed our advanced posts, we heard strange voices. We looked at each other and whispered that to go further would be indiscreet. Re-joining the column, we wrapped ourselves in our cloaks and fell into a profound slumber. We were awakened by a great bustle and the trampling of horses; the Portuguese Caçadores fired some shots. Word passed to stand to our arms, but I was so drowsy I continued in a squatting position, rubbing my eyes, too lazy to move. The confusion was caused by two or three mules breaking their ropes and becoming lively, which was not unusual.

Soldiers' Blanket Tents

Canvas tents for the allied army on campaign in the peninsula were a rarity, even among junior officers; that is until their issue in 1813. In the years up to that date, company mules were reserved for carrying the heavy cast-iron 'Flanders' camp kettles. Consequently, the soldier's white blanket was often used as a part of a tent. Corporal John Douglas of the 1st Royals describes one of the common ways of producing such a tent with the 80in square blanket:

> Our tents were very simple, soon pitched and as easily packed up. They (that is, each tent) consisted of 2 blankets, 2 firelocks and 4 bayonets. At each corner of the blanket a hole was worked similar to a buttonhole, and in the centre another. A firelock stood at each end, to serve as poles. The bayonet of these firelocks passed through the corner holes of both blankets, a ramrod secured the top, and a bayonet at each end fastened in the ground completed our house. These tents certainly were a shade from the scorching rays of the sun, yet the heat inside was intolerable.

A reconstructed blanket tent based on Corporal Douglas' description but also incorporating a convenient sapling.

The advantage of this method was that it did not require the soldiers to carry or disperse to cut large numbers of wooden poles on the plains of Spain. The damage to blankets by repeated use of the bayonet led to whipped holes* and reinforced corners.

As described above, two blankets were required for the tent, a third was used as a ground sheet and the fourth to cover the four soldiers that were using the tent. They would, of course, all usually have had their greatcoats as well.

Other methods using string and rope existed and where materials were available crude huts could be made for shelter.

*The repeated use of bayonets damaged blankets, which led soldiers to reinforce holes by sewing cord around the edges and corners of the blanket.

A French infantry attack.

Chapter Five

The Approach to Battle

'... we have amused ourselves with plenty of marching lately, very little fighting but a good deal of chess-playing with the enemy.'
[Guards officer's letter]

Having laboured on field fortifications overnight, for the allied divisions 19 June 1812 dawned with a confident expectation of battle. Deployed in two lines on the heights above the Rio Guareña they stood and waited, looking for signs of French attack. From the ridge, Lieutenant Cooke spotted Marshal Marmont and his entourage:

> The Duke of Ragusa entered the valley to reconnoitre, surrounded by numerous staff. Two guns of our horse artillery opened, and a ball struck the ground. It knocked up the dust in the very centre of the group, without killing anyone. They took the hint and shifted their ground.

General Cotton, seeing Marmont within range, had ordered the 6-pounders of Major Ross's RHA troop to open fire, an act that the Light Division soon had cause to regret. Cooke concluded that

> Eight of the enemy's guns instantly began a heavy firing on our Brigade. The first shot struck an officer of the horse artillery on the side of his helmet and displaced him from his horse. After a short time, the Brigade went to the right about to get out of range [i.e. about-faced and retired].

The French did not attack and in the full heat of the Iberian summer the allied army remained on the bare ridge into the afternoon. It was not until about 1600 hours that there was any significant movement. At this time Wellington was visiting the Light Division's picquets and he asked Lieutenant Wilkinson of the 43rd 'What are the enemy doing?' Wilkinson replied, 'The French are in motion.' The peer, looking through his telescope, replied 'Yes to the right now.'

Under cover of a French artillery bombardment, probably designed to give their infantry a head-start over the allies, the Army of Portugal marched south in two columns. Marshal Marmont's aim in this manoeuvre was to turn the British right flank and threaten Wellington's line of communication by attempting to place his army on the plateau that extended towards Salamanca. This movement of course required a corresponding response by the allies to prevent them being outflanked. Wellington simply moved his army 7 miles south-west from Castrillo with both sides keeping to the respective sides of the Guareña, but other than a few cannon shot that set the broad tracts of wheat on fire, there was little action.

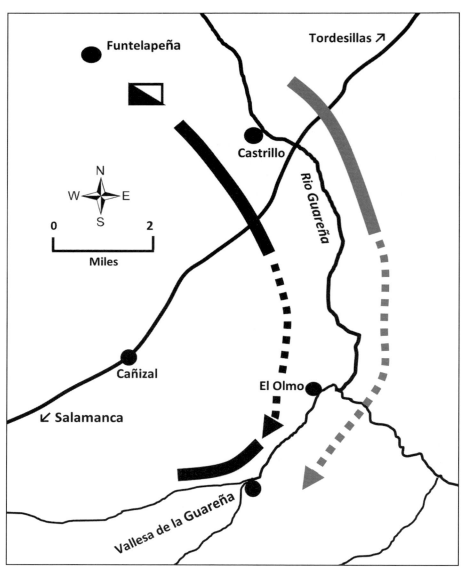

March of the armies on 19 July 1812.

Ensign Hennell of the 43rd Light Infantry wrote in a letter home: 'We moved parallel to them & about 7 o'clock the Light Division formed line directly opposite them, a deep valley between. I had the colours. Our cannon opened before we formed line.' The allies had halted on the heights overlooking Vallesa de la Guareña (Questa Blanca) and the river, with some battalions not reaching their ground until midnight. The French were bivouacked on the opposite side of the stream on the Media Hoja feature. After hours of marching neither side had gained a significant advantage, but Marmont had successfully manoeuvred the allies out of a strong defensive position at Castrillo, which he had not been prepared to risk attacking.

At daybreak on 20 July the opposing armies were deployed again in order of battle. After two hours of indecision Marmont resumed his attempt to turn Wellington's flank marching via Morcuera, Cotorillo and Cantalpino. Private Green of the 68th Light Infantry wrote that he 'expected that in a few minutes we should have been sharply engaged: but instead of this the enemy broke camp, formed column, and marched to a ridge of hills, their bands and drums playing as though they were going to a general field day.'

Lieutenant Browne of Wellington's staff summed up the mood during this period:

> The incertitude in which we were kept by the enemy as to his real direction cannot but be observed. We were also greatly harassed by being in constant readiness, & then racing at a late period to counteract his manoeuvres. Independent of the extreme risk of the system in an open country, this haste to retire before an equal army certainly lowered the spirit of our Troops.

The two armies formed in columns, the French in two and the British in three, and were carefully preserving the distance between the battalions in order to facilitate immediate deployment into battle array.[1] The dust-shrouded march astride the shallow valley of the upper reaches of the Guareña system was again fast as both armies sought to outdistance the other; Wellington and Marmont looked on for errors or disorder on which to pounce. For almost three hours, with the armies between half a mile and a mile apart there was little room for error. While the main allied columns maintained good order, the baggage that followed the army was by the end of the morning strung out over several miles and vulnerable. General Bonet requested permission to attack but, probably as by this time the opposing columns were closing to half a mile apart, Marmont refused.

Lieutenant Martin, riding with Wellington's headquarters, recorded that 'The sight of two well-equipped armies of nearly 50,000 each, marching in two parallel lines within artillery range & frequently cannonading & skirmishing with each other, was the most beautiful and magnificent military spectacle that could possibly be witnessed.' He concluded that 'the movements of the day were of great interest & must have been full of instruction to officers of all ranks.'

By marching fast, Marmont's advanced guard reached Cantalpino first and started to turn from a southerly to a south-westerly direction and for a time it appeared that the allied and French columns would clash. With the armies at close quarters, within a musket shot, Major William Napier recalled that 'the officers, like gallant gentlemen who bore no malice and knew no fear, made their military recognitions, while the horsemen on each side watched with eager eyes

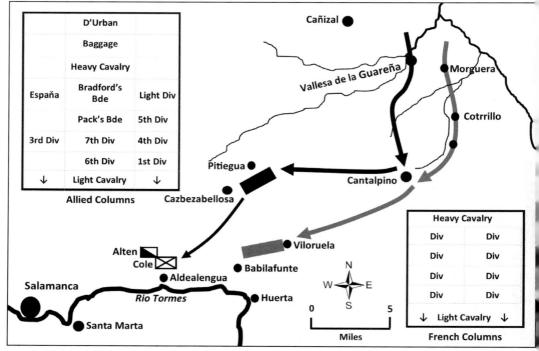

March of the armies on 20 July 1812.

for an opening to charge.' Wellington, however, ordered the head of his columns not to get involved in a fight and to bear away.

Beyond Cantalpino the columns diverged, with the allied army marching to a position between Pitiega and Cabeza Villosa. General Cole's 6th Division and two brigades of cavalry were sent on to the army's right to secure the flank on the Rio Tormes around Aldealengua, while the French took up ground before Wellington's army. Another day's march of some 14 miles had brought a greater change in the situation, with Wellington 'greatly disquieted' that he had again been manoeuvred back towards Salamanca and more importantly that Marmont now had control of the Huerta fords.

With a lack of daylight and knowing that Wellington had occupied another sound defensive position, once again Marmont did not attack but halted his army for the night between Villoruela and Babilafuente.

Browne gave vent to his opinions in his journal:

> ... as to Marmont's movements, I am inclined to think that the credit which he gained with our army for the style & effect of his manoeuvres was principally to be attributed to his having discovered the secret of Ld. Wellington's system of conducting operations, that of declining attack; & therefore while Marmont equally declined to attack in front, he was certain, by flank manoeuvres in a plain country to turn us out of every position we took up, with impunity. No particular preponderance of force had occurred to give him this advantage; but a principle on our side of refusing offensive operations.

Wellington and his staff observing Marmont's manoeuvres.

Intelligence

Wellington wrote in a dispatch to Lord Bathurst that 'The Army of Portugal has been surrounded [by guerrillas] for the last six weeks, and scarcely even a letter reaches its commander', and on 15 July 1812 the duke reported that 'I have an intercepted letter stating that the king would collect 12,000 men of which six regiments are cavalry.' With the guerrillas taking so many messengers, French commanders resorted to typically sending three often concealed copies of messages via different routes or escorted by a very large body of troops. More

98 *Salamanca Campaign, 1812*

often than not, however, they were unable to find such an escort without a compromise in the situation elsewhere. Consequently, Wellington was often better informed than Joseph's marshals and generals, but most of the intercepted messages were in code or partly in code due to the escalating interception of dispatches.

In 1811 Masséna introduced a cipher for use in the Army of Portugal using a combination of 150 numbers, which Major George Scovell of Wellington's staff broke in two days' work during the autumn of that year. In the winter of 1811/12 dispatches with a new encryption started to be intercepted, which was far more complicated and known as the Great Paris Cipher. This code used 1,400 numbers

Major George Scovell as a general in later life.

that represented specific words and, for example, prefixes and suffixes, plus spaces at random in the middle of words.

During the period of manoeuvre, Major Scovell had decoded a substantial part of a message captured on 9 July revealing King Joseph's intent to join Marmont. By the 20th, reports on the progress of the Army of the Centre's march had been added to this important information, from which Wellington was able to calculate that Joseph would join Marmont by 24 July, giving the French a significant advantage in numbers; this could be up to 15,000 without meaningful reinforcement by Caffarelli. Possessing this highly significant intelligence, Wellington knew that he had a finite window of four days for battle with Marmont while still enjoying broad parity, after which he would almost certainly have to fall back to Portugal. His aim, however, remained not to risk battle without a clear advantage. Crucially, Marmont was unaware of when the king would join him and with how many troops.

The Final Approach

As the armies continued marching during the morning of 21 July, Wellington set out his appreciation of what, thanks to Marmont's adroit manoeuvring, was a deteriorating situation to Lord Bathurst, along with his intent:

> I am quite certain that Marshal Marmont's army is to be joined by the King's, which will be 10,000 or 12,000 men, with a large proportion of cavalry, and that troops are still expected from the Army of the North, and some are ordered from that of the South; and it will be seen that I ought to consider it almost impossible to remain in Castille after an action.
>
> I have therefore determined to cross the Tormes, if the enemy should; to cover Salamanca as long as I can; and above all, not to give up our communication with Ciudad Rodrigo; and not to fight an action, unless under very advantageous circumstances, or should it become absolutely necessary.

To cover Salamanca the allies pulled back to their familiar San Cristóbal position. While armed with one of Wellington's captured messages warning a Spanish general that he would not be able to hold his ground, a greatly encouraged Marmont marched for the Huerta fords. The marshal was also able to garrison the fortress that covered the Alba de Tormes bridge from which, unknown to Wellington, the Spanish battalion guarding it had been withdrawn by General d'España the previous day.

With confirmation that the French had manoeuvred to cross the Tormes at Huerta and Encino de Abajo, Wellington followed suit using the bridge at Salamanca and the fords of Santa Marta and Cabrerizos. The 3rd Division, now commanded by Major General Sir Edward Pakenham, Wellington's brother-in-law, due to Picton's Badajoz wound reopening, relieved the 6th Division at Aldealengua. Along with D'Urban's Portuguese cavalry, they were to cover the flank of the army and the road into Salamanca north of the Tormes. Wellington clearly wanted one of his most reliable divisions holding this vital flank in case

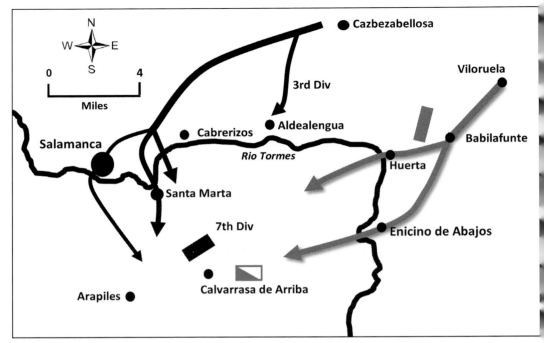

March of the armies on 21 July 1812.

Marmont switched his direction of march as he had done only days earlier on the Duero.

The 6th Division followed by Hope's 7th Division and Pack's Portuguese Brigade were the first of Wellington's formations across to the west of the Tormes and where they fanned out as far as the Salamanca to Alba de Tormes road in rolling country clothed with scrubby oak trees. With interior lines, the allies had a considerably shorter march than the French had via the fords at Huerta and Encino and were quickly in their designated positions while the French were still strung out astride their fords.

Lieutenant William Grattan of the 88th Connaught Rangers was up on the heights of Aldealengua overlooking the river 'throwing up breastworks, and by other means adding to the strength of the position' they occupied. He wrote:

> This division, though encamped on a height of considerable altitude, had received strict orders to intrench [sic] themselves; the earth was thrown up, the works were palisaded, and in time they were so well secured, that they had no fear of an attack or surprise. It is this precaution that marks the great general. Lord Wellington had no idea of being taken aback by any change in Marmont's plans during the night: on the contrary he was convinced that he was serious in his desire to give battle; but to guard against any and every chance was but right.

Meanwhile, thanks to rain further south, the level of the Tormes was rising and the Light Division, which had been providing the rearguard while the army crossed the river, conducted a passage of lines through the 3rd Division and prepared to wade the Santa Marta ford. Major William Napier commanding the 43rd Light Infantry recalled the crossing of the river:

> It was late when the Light Division descended the rough side of the Aldealengua mountain to cross the river, and the night came suddenly down, with more than common darkness, for a storm, that common precursor of a battle in the Peninsula, was at hand. Torrents of rain deepened the ford, the water foamed and dashed with increasing violence, the thunder was frequent and deafening, and the lightning passed in sheets of fire close over the column, or played upon the points of the bayonets ... To a military eye there was nothing more imposing than the close and beautiful order in which the soldiers of that noble Light Division were seen by the fiery gleams to step from the river to the bank and pursue their march amidst this astounding turmoil, defying alike the storm and the enemy.

Lieutenant Simmons of the 95th Rifles seems to have been the only diarist with enough energy following a long day's march to record the events of 21 July:

> Marched with the dawn and continued till 2 p.m. Halted near Moriscos. A little before dark forded the river Tormes above Salamanca. The river was very much swollen from the rain, which made it very deep. Everybody got wet up to near their shoulders in crossing ... The night became excessively dark, the whole army groping their way, up to their knees in mud, to the different bivouacs. The lightning became very vivid; some of the flashes ran whizzing along the men's arms in an extraordinary manner and really checked the march for some time most strangely.

The night was indeed stormy. Lieutenant Tomkinson of the 16th Light Dragoons wrote:

> Dreadful thunder an hour after dark. The greatest number of the horses of the 5th Dragoon Guards ran away over the men sleeping at their heads, by

The Rio Tormes at the Santa Marta ford flows quietly, but rises quickly with rain upstream.

which eighteen in the brigade were wounded, and Colonel and Mrs. Dalbiac, of the 4th Dragoons, were sitting down on the ground in front of the brigade; he had just time to carry her under a gun, which stopped the horses and saved them both. Thirty-one horses were not found the following morning. The loss was said to be accounted for on the 22nd; they returned those lost as horses lost in action on the 22nd.[2]

By each flash of lightning we saw the different columns of infantry marching to their ground for the night very plainly, from the lightning being reflected on their muskets, which at that time of night was beautiful.

Grooms, gunners and cavalrymen spent most of the night at their horses' heads reassuring the mounts and holding on firmly to their reins, while Private Wheeler of the 51st Light Infantry had a lucky escape:

I shall never forget this night. We were in a forest of old oak trees under which we sat for shelter from the storm. I had just left the tree where I had been standing some time to go to one of my comrades for a light. During my

Camp followers of various descriptions marched with the army, sharing its hardships and discomforts.

absence a flash of lightning struck the tree and clave it in two. This was a lucky pipe of tobacco.

By nightfall virtually the whole French army less Sarrut's division, which remained at Babilafuente, had crossed the Tormes at Huerta and another ford 3 miles upstream at Encino de Abajo. Curto's light cavalry, leading Marmont's troops, reached Calvarrasa de Arriba where they sheltered as the storm raged around them, while General Foy's division followed them through the lightning and rain. Less than 1,000 yards east of Calvarrasa de Arriba on the edge of the Teso de la Peña, the Brunswick Oels of Halket's brigade of the 7th Division had established picquets at an old hermitage, the Nuestra Señora de la Peña.

On the eve of battle Marmont had not only been emboldened by a captured dispatch giving word that Wellington was unable to hold his ground, but Lieutenant Browne believed that the felicity with which he had manoeuvred the allies out of a series of positions had gone to the marshal's head, having

> obliged our army, equal in Infantry & superior in cavalry to retire from the defence of the Douro to behind the Tormes almost without a shot; & this by the simplest means. His great care should have been not to rouse the Lion's wrath by treading too close upon him, & had he not assumed too much upon our passiveness we should have turned upon him, until we came to our old haunts upon the Águeda.
>
> His arrogance & an inadvertency of ours were the causes which led to the glorious & happy change in our affairs at Salamanca.

The Musket

By far the most numerous weapon on the peninsular battlefield was the flintlock musket and its close cousin, the cavalry carbine. Today the arguments regarding the superiority of the Tower or 'Brown Bess' musket over the French Charleville* (or vice versa) are endless, complicated by the many different patterns of the two muskets in service at any one time. For example, Napoleon in 1800 commissioned a review of the 1777 Pattern Charleville, resulting in minor modifications to the lock, bayonet and stock to produce the 'corrected' model or *Modèle 1777 corrigé*.

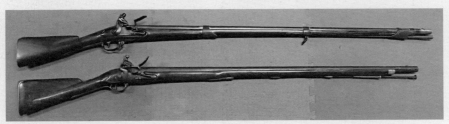

Above the Charleville; below the Brown Bess musket.

*Like the British musket, the Charleville was nicknamed after one of the arsenals at Charleville-Mézières. Its proper designation was the French Infantry Musket.

Both muskets had a smooth bore barrel, which could cope with black powder fouling, and fired a round lead ball. Due to the inherent inaccuracy of the weapon, its primary use was volley-firing en masse, starting at targets within a range of about 100 yards. Skirmishers would typically have to close within 50 yards of the enemy to engage specific targets, though of course they could gall a body of enemy troops at a greater range.

The musket's construction had much to do with its dual role as a close-combat weapon, with the socket bayonet fixed. It had to be robust enough to remain intact during a physical clash of arms and even survive use as a club! Consequently, the military musket was significantly heavier than sporting pieces of the day. Of the two muskets, the Charleville was the lighter.

The following is a basic comparison of the muskets' features:

	Charleville	Brown Bess
Length:	60in	58in
Weight:	10lb	10.5lb
Calibre:	0.69in	0.75in

The Charleville's smaller ball and its tighter fit in the barrel may have provided a better theoretically accurate range, but resulted in slower loading due to normal black powder fouling.

One of the arguments is that the Charleville was easier to maintain in the field due to its use of barrel bands and the level of standardization of parts was greater. Unlike the Brown Bess, Charleville muskets were made in French government arsenals, rather than in the case of the British musket being built in a series of workshops scattered across the UK and the British Empire. Consequently, despite the best efforts of the Ordnance Board, levels of standardization were not high. The technology was, however, simple, with the replacement of the lock being the only challenge to a soldier below the level of artisan or armourer.

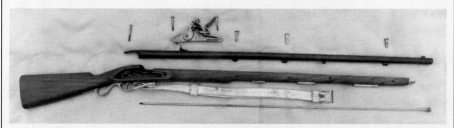

A Brown Bess disassembled for routine cleaning and maintenance.

The key part of any musket is the flintlock or 'lock'. It consisted of some thirty machined, cast and forged components, with the tumbler and sear in particular needing to be accurately machined and placed. Wear of these parts and the main spring breaking were the principal reasons for the failure of the lock. The failure of a musket to fire was usually, however, the limited and variable life of the flint, which would normally need knapping before it became so rounded that it needed changing, typically between fifteen and twenty-five workings of the trigger.

The Approach to Battle 105

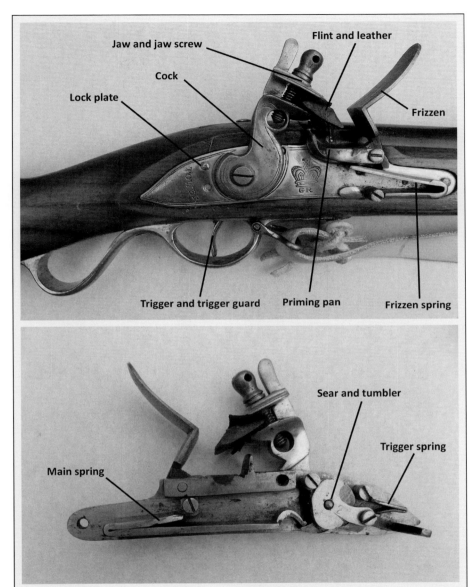

External and internal and views of the Tower lock mounted on an 1805 New Land Pattern version of the Bess as issued to light infantry.

Whatever the narrow technical advantages of one musket over the other were, their effects on the peninsular battlefields had more to do with the situation in which they were being fired and the tactics, training and morale of the soldiers who were using them.

Musket tools, pricker and brush for cleaning the pan and spare flints and lead strips to aid the lock's jaws in securing the flint.

Chapter Six

22 July 1812, Morning

After a thoroughly wet night, the army stood to arms an hour before dawn and day broke clear and bright with a sun that was soon drying men, uniforms and equipment. While the soldiers cleaned rust off their weapons, both Wellington and Marmont, along with their respective staffs were active in the knowledge that this was a crucial day in the campaign. Full of confidence, following the previous days of manoeuvre, the commander of the Army of Portugal firmly believed that Wellington was a defensive general who would not fight. If he could not be brought to battle, a resumption of manoeuvre would at the very least see the allied army forced to retire to the borders of Portugal. That he would be back in Salamanca that night Marmont was in little doubt; according to Lieutenant Kincaid he reputedly sent a message through to his habitual lodging in the city to have his 'usual dinner ready for 6 p.m.'.[1] The marshal wrote in his after-action report to the Minister for War that in crossing the Tormes:

> My object was... to continue the movement on my left, in order to force the enemy in the surroundings of Salamanca to fight on more advantageous ground [for me]. I intended to take a good defensive position, where the enemy could do nothing against me, and he would finally come close enough for me to be able to take advantage of the first mistakes he makes, and attack him with vigour.[2]

Captain Parquin, an officer in Marmont's escort of 200 chasseurs,[3] read out the marshal's order of the day to his troops on the morning of 22 July, which 'produced on everybody an excellent impression':

> In it the Marshal reminded his troops that the English Army, which for the last two years never faced us except when backed by armed breastworks, had suddenly changed its tactics; that it had at last decided to come up to the scratch and fight us at close quarters and that the Emperor, although now five hundred leagues away from the Army of Portugal, was intently observing the brave men that composed it. The marshal added that he had united his army to march against the English and do them battle to the cry of 'Long live the Emperor'.[4]

For Wellington the situation described in his dispatch of the previous day was changed only in as much that with the imminent arrival of French reinforcements, particularly cavalry, he could not hope to cover Salamanca beyond the

22nd unless 'advantageous circumstances' presented themselves. He wrote after the battle that

> There was no time to be lost therefore; and I determined that, if circumstances should not permit me to attack him on the 22nd, I would move towards Ciudad Rodrigo without further loss of time, as the difference of the numbers of cavalry might have made a march of manoeuvre, such as we have had for the last four or five days, very difficult, and its result doubtful.

So adroitly had Marmont hitherto manoeuvred that 'advantageous circumstances' were not expected, and the army's baggage had the previous evening been ordered to march at dawn on the high road back to Ciudad Rodrigo.

By 0800 hours, the two commanders with their entourages were clearly visible to each other across the valley. Marmont reported that

> On the morning of the 22nd, I went to the heights of Calvarrasa de Arriba to reconnoitre the enemy. I found a division [Foy's] there which had just arrived; others [Ferey's division] were on their way there. Some skirmishing began to occupy observation posts, of which we remained the masters.

What Marmont could see were elements of a single division, General Hope's 7th Division, but what he could not see were the further five allied divisions and the two Portuguese brigades concealed in the woods behind a distinct ridge line.

Adjacent to the hermitage of Nuestra Señora de la Peña is the rocky eminence of Teso la Peña which was probably used by Marshal Marmont during his reconnaissance.

Consequently, Marmont drew the erroneous conclusion that this was a rearguard. Through his telescope Wellington, however, could see further French divisions, albeit imperfectly at this stage, marching through the woods from the fords.

The sound of skirmishing that Marmont reported approaching from the east was Victor Alten's light cavalry,[5] which was engaged in a running exchange of shots between Foy's light troops as they marched towards Calvarrasa de Arriba. At about 0800 hours Alten was wounded by a musket ball in his leg and Colonel Arentschildt of the 1st Hussars KGL took over command of the brigade. As Foy's men reached Nuestra Señora de la Peña, the 7th Division's picquets in the area provided by the Brunswick Oels were initially reinforced by the 68th Light Infantry and Lieutenant Colonel Bryan O'Toole's 2nd Caçadores, which had both been ordered forward to aid the Brunswickers who had been forced back from the Hermitage.[6] Private Green of the 68th recorded:

> Early on the morning of the 22nd July, we heard the firing of the advanced guard, and in less than ten minutes our regiment, being light infantry, was ordered forward: having reached the front, we saw the French picquets advancing on ours, and both were sharply engaged. In a moment the left wing was ordered to the front: no sooner did our advanced picquets perceive that they were supported by such a number of light troops than they advanced on the French picquets, and drove them in confusion to the summit of a high hill; but the enemy receiving strong reinforcements bore down on my brave comrades, who contested every inch with them. At this

The Hermitage stands on the edge of a rocky ridge overlooking the valley and wooded ridge that concealed Wellington's army.

period a general came to the front, to see how things were going on: in a fit of passion he enquired, 'Who commands here?' The answer was 'General Hope'. He said 'Where is he? The whole of the advance picquet will be taken prisoner.' General Hope came up at this time but did not appear at all afraid that the men would be taken. He sent one of his Aides-de-Camp with directions to a squadron of light dragoons to support the picquet immediately: they came forward and had only just taken their stand when one of them, a youth of about twenty-one years of age, was killed.

While the 68th and 2nd Caçadores were skirmishing, the rest of the 7th Division were in the cover of the oak trees. Private Wheeler of the 51st Light Infantry recalled that

> The 68th Regiment was soon after ordered to the front, we soon lost sight of them amongst the trees. They were soon engaged and from the great number of wounded brought to the rear in wagons it was clear they had dropped in for a hot breakfast ... There was much skirmishing and heavy cannonading at intervals 'til after midday, but from the thickness of the forest we could not see what was going on.

Green of the 68th, still skirmishing in the valley between the ridges, continued:

> The enemy now retired to the top of the hill [the Peña plateau] and brought six pieces of cannon to play on us. About this time the watering parties of the 7th Division came to the valley for a supply of water: the French guns began to play on these unarmed and defenceless men; but not one of them was hurt, although shot and shell fell thickly amongst them. After this the enemy continued firing on us for some hours. In this skirmish Major Miller and several privates were wounded, and one of the latter had to undergo amputation.

As the fighting settled down on Wellington's left flank, the light cavalry were redeployed to the west. The situation remained unchanged, with the French holding Nuestra Señora de la Peña and elements of the 7th Division, including some KGL light troops, established in a skirmish line in the valley below, until about midday.

The day of 22 July is often simplistically characterized as a wait until Marmont saw the dust of the allied baggage on the road to Ciudad Rodrigo. As the morning progressed, however, both commanders were watching their opposite number's manoeuvring and making adjustments to their deployments accordingly. Marmont recalled:

> I spent the morning making arrangements, initially for a good defensive, and then to attack, if the circumstances made me hope for benefits. After the arrangements I had made, everything seemed to presage the best odds. I thought it necessary to occupy a plateau to our left which completed our

A representation of an officer of the 68th Light Infantry.

defence, and which at the same time was to be very useful in the event that we should act in offensive, to which I was almost determined.

The plateau referred to by Marmont is the 'Greater' of the two features known as Los Arapiles.

Los Arapiles

In taking up his ground during the night General Lowry Cole had apparently not realized the significance of the Arapiles features, nor had the 4th Division been ordered to occupy and hold them or to have troops positioned close at hand in cover behind them. Captain Leith Hay, his uncle's ADC adds more detail including that overnight

> General Cole immediately saw the necessity for occupying the lowest Arapile [with a picquet] and ordered a detachment to take possession of it.[7]
> It was then nearly daylight, when Lord Wellington rode up to the General. By the indistinctness of objects, as seen by the early morning light,

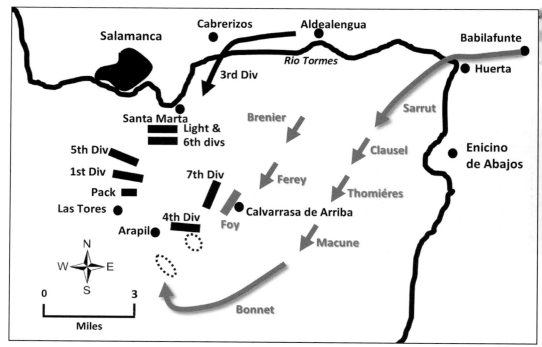

The situation during the first half of the morning.

> the greatest Arapile appeared to be much more distant than it really was – but by the time full daylight allowed its true distance to be seen, Lord Wellington ordered it also to be occupied; but before the order could be executed, it was in possession of the enemy.

As Marmont intimated, possession of the Arapiles would both aid the turning of the allied flank and hinder the retirement of the 7th Division which the marshal assumed was Wellington's rearguard. Consequently, at around 0800 hours, with the French seeing no redcoats, three battalions of the 120th Infantry Regiment of Bonet's division were dispatched to seize the Arapiles without attracting attention. Lieutenant Browne described their methodology:

> Whilst it was a doubt, from the closeness of the enemy's manoeuvres whether Marmont would attack or not he had by degrees, inclined two or three battalions thro' standing corn & undulations of the ground, close to an isolated hill on our right, & got near it so suddenly, that he was in possession before we could occupy it, & we had only just time to secure a second hill [the Lesser Arapile].

The 120th's advance to the Greater Arapile was spotted too late for the 7th Caçadores to prevent its seizure, with the French soldiers breaking ranks in a final rush to seize the crest. Major John Scott Lillie recalled a bizarre situation:

> I received orders through the Duke of Richmond to occupy the Greater Arapile[8] … on arriving close to it I found it was too steep to ascend on horseback, and consequently rode round, while my men made the best of

Marmont's view from the Teso la Peña south-west to Los Arapiles.

their way directly to the top. I was not aware of any enemy being in the immediate vicinity, as some Spaniards had been there a short time previous; thus, when I came suddenly on some troops advancing from the opposite direction, I took them for Spaniards, and questioning them in Spanish, they replied that they were Spanish: they were partly covered by the high corn and the uneven ground, and I rode up in the same direction with them until we met our men at the top of the hill, when all doubts on the subject were removed by their opening fire on us at a few paces distance. We contested the point so long as anything like an equality of numbers permitted us; but as their numbers rapidly increased, and we found that we were encountering the head of a brigade, we were overpowered and closely pursued in the direction of the other Arapile, for which the enemy made a push, and which they would have succeeded in taking had not the fusilier brigade and the Duke himself been sufficiently near to arrive there first.

Marmont reported that the 120th had 'chased the English detachment which occupied the heights and overthrew it. Until then we had only had success, and everything indicated that success would be complete.'

With the 7th Caçadores pushed off the Greater Arapile and falling back, the situation was saved by the deployment of the 4th Division's artillery onto the Teso de San Miguel and the 27th Enniskillens of General William Anson's infantry brigade onto the Lesser Arapile:[9]

Hauptmann Sympher's battery of the 4th Division was immediately hurried off to defeat the enemy's object, but the French being nearer to the hill, gained its summit before he could offer any resistance. Sympher, however, made an excellent disposition of his guns, placing them above the village of Arapiles and, in such positions as to command the passage between the heights and part of the approach to that which had just been seized by the enemy. Meantime, the smaller hill was secured by a battery of horse artillery, and soon a cannonade opened from these neighbouring points.[10]

A bemedalled Major John Scott Lillie wearing the brown country cloth uniform of the 7th Caçadores.

Sympher, it seems, had four guns on the Teso de San Miguel and a pair on the Lesser Arapile. They were later joined by some of the 6-pounders of Macdonald's E Troop RHA. While Sympher's guns were deployed by General Cole, Captain Dyneley received his orders for his troop via one of Wellington's ADCs:

> On the day of the battle after a very few minutes' fighting, an order from his Lordship came desiring me to get my guns upon a height to receive an attack the enemy were about to make. The order I received had certainly a very awkward signification: 'His Lordship desires you will get your guns up that height and wishes you to defend it as long as you have a man left to your

General Sir Lowry Cole, Commander 4th Division.

guns. In the event of you being obliged to retire, you will spike your guns and leave them and the General officer commanding has most positive orders that he supports you to the last; in fact,' his Lordship says, 'he must have the hill kept.'

From these orders I made sure of an 'ex' or 'dis'-tinguish. I got my guns up with the assistance of a company of the 40th Regiment, unloaded my limbers and sent them to my gunners' horses to the rear, as I thought, if we have to run for it, my men should get away as fast as the infantry.[11]

Captain Parquin was with a dismounted section of Marmont's escort on the Greater Arapile:

> Toward eleven o'clock of this beautiful summer day, the Duke of Ragusa, with field-glass in his hand, was intently surveying the English position. His butler had just spread upon the grass the silver tableware containing the marshal's cold breakfast, and His Excellency, with his aides-de-camp and chief of staff, were about sitting down to a comfortable meal, when some shells discharged from howitzers on the opposite mountain terminated very abruptly the luncheon that had not quite begun. The English commander had masked the battery of these pieces by interposing an infantry battalion, which he at once removed out of the way when the firing began. Falling into our mountain position entirely unexpected, the projectiles forced us to hurry down to the plain to recover our horses. I had already mounted when I heard the Duke of Ragusa's voice loudly calling out: 'Nicolas, Nicolas, my horse!' Nicolas was His Excellency's chief groom, but he did not happen to be at hand when the marshal reached the plain. I at once dismounted and offered my horse to the duke, who accepted it on account of the critical circumstances. He had already put a foot in the stirrup when the groom rushed forward, leading by the bridle his master's charger. The commander returned me my horse and started on a gallop to reach the line of battle, having first, however, given me the order to take over to General Foy and direct him to bring his division forward. I at once fulfilled the mission confided to me.

To complete his deployment Wellington instructed the 40th Somersets to remain in support of the Inniskillings and ordered the light companies of the 1st Division's Guards and Fusilier brigades, plus companies of the 5th 60th Rifles and Brunswick Oels to occupy the village itself.

The 6th and Light divisions that had been bivouacked near the Santa Marta Ford were also ordered forward, the 6th to the area of Las Torres and the Light to the woods behind the main body of the 7th Division. An officer of the Light Division wrote:

> Our division advanced and took up the ground the 7th Division had occupied in the morning. The wood extended a short way to our front. The division was formed in open column, concealed from the enemy, who were

A view of the allied positions on Teso de San Miguel from the area between Los Arapiles.

stationed in a small force a mile to the front, with two pieces of artillery. From our situation we [and the 1st Division] formed a corps of reserve.[12]

With the allied deployment around Arapiles complete, Bonet did not commit his remaining nine battalions to the capture of the lesser feature and the village but kept them assembled behind the Greater Arapile, ready to support the 120th Regiment. These columns were reported by officers of General Leith's 5th Division who had been sent forward to some high ground near Arapiles from which they could see the French deployment. Leith Hay reported that

> Large bodies of the enemy's troops were perceived marching to their left, forming in rear of the Arapiles, and on the skirts of a wood extending towards Alba de Tormes. These columns were considered by General Leith to be within the range of the artillery of his division, which he ordered in advance to a height in front of his position, from whence was obtained a better view of the formation taking place under cover of the Arapiles. Having reached this eminence, Captain Lawson opened his fire with such effect that the nearest of the enemy's troops made rapid, and not very orderly, change of position, proceeding to a distance greatly out of reach of the point where the British artillery were annoying them. To counteract the galling effects of this attack, the enemy brought forward some guns, which he placed so as to bear diagonally on the height occupied by Captain Lawson; from these, immediately opened a destructive fire, killing and wounding several men and horses, and damaging one of the carriages. Captain Tomkinson's troop of the 16th Light Dragoons had been sent forward to protect the British cannon: it was formed under shelter of the height, and not exposed to the cannonade that was now kept up with great spirit. I was sent down to direct the artillery to retire, and to bring the light dragoons back across the ravine, which was now swept by a shower of balls and howitzer shells. The 16th separated, and galloped back without sustaining serious loss; but I was more apprehensive for the artillery, its carriages of course presenting larger objects, and not moving with the same rapidity: they, however, did not suffer so much as might have been expected.[13]

The French also established part of a battery on the Greater Arapile despite its very steep and rocky sides. To achieve this, they had to dismount the gun barrels and employ infantry to carry them up to the flat top of the feature. In a similar manner the gun carriages, tools and ammunition were hauled up the slope.

Wellington's reaction to the loss of the Greater Arapile during mid-morning was to succumb to temptation and order the recapture of the feature by Campbell's 1st Division supported by elements of the 4th. According to Lieutenant Browne, a staff officer in the allied headquarters, it had become increasingly apparent that

> The enemy's possession of it, hemmed us in so unpleasantly that it was resolved to retake this hill, & attack the enemy, if not very generally, at least

to liberate ourselves from an encroachment that threatened the safety of our retreat. The attack of this hill [by the 1st Division] was on the point of moving off, when it was perceived that the enemy had brought up a very heavy column to support his acquisition, & Ld. Wellington balanced, I believe from the hope that the French Marshal having this hill, would attack us, & indeed all his dispositions now looked very like it. The intention of repossessing ourselves of the hill was therefore given up or deferred.

The heavy columns mentioned by Browne, in addition to Bonet's nine battalions at the base of the Greater Arapile, were those of Clausel's division, which Marmont had ordered forward to support Bonet and to be ready to take the offensive when the moment presented itself. The 1st Division might have succeeded against Bonet with a slight superiority of numbers but with another division coming up in support, Wellington, in the opinion of most, wisely cancelled the attack. On the other hand, the hesitant movement must have confirmed Marmont's views on Wellington as a defensive general.

An account by Corporal Douglas of the 3rd Battalion, Royal Scots, offers another possible factor in Wellington's decision:

> In our present position, his Lordship wished to find out where the enemy's guns were planted and pitched upon the following stratagem. He ordered our regiment, being the first at hand, down the hill, to move towards the enemy that their guns might open upon us; and thus, by devoting a few to

The 1806 Pattern cap plate of the 1st Royal Scots or Royal Regiment. A thistle replaces the GR cipher and the title 'The Royal' is inserted beneath the lion. Its replacement, the 1812 Pattern, did not start arriving in the peninsula until the annual kit issue during the winter of 1812/13.

destruction, be the means of saving a great many. We fixed bayonets, loaded and down the hill we went, marching on towards the French lines. Our position, you may be assured, was none of the most enviable. The ground being thick studded with short brushwood, which rendered it very difficult to keep proper order, we were covered by some squadrons of the Greens but when we came on a level with their guns, such a murderous fire was opened as surpasses description. Here we stood a knocking down without the most distant hope of returning the compliment. In my opinion there is no situation in which men can be placed so trying as to keep them exposed to a heavy fire and not be allowed the privilege of self-defence. In about half an hour we were ordered to retire, at which time the heath was in flames around us from the bursting of the shells. Thus, having ascertained where their guns were planted, we joined the Division again.

Watching and Waiting

At the same time Marmont, still convinced that Wellington's main force was heading west, despite being able to see more allied troops from the Greater Arapile, he ordered Thomières' division along with much of the reserve artillery and some light cavalry to start to extend the French flank to the left. This deployment took most of the morning but Marmont's intent was not immediately apparent to Wellington.

An air photo showing the Los Arapiles features and the village in the centre.

The marshal was equally unaware of quite how much more difficult his deployment had made Wellington's potential withdrawal to Ciudad Rodrigo. Lieutenant Browne wrote: 'The hill on our right, which I have said the enemy carried by surprise was very important to the compactness of our position & rendered fresh dispositions necessary.' These additional moves saw d'España's Spanish troops and Bradford's Portuguese Brigade being redeployed into a position behind the 4th Division. A further move was prompted by information that Marmont's final division, Sarrut's, was crossing the Tormes. Consequently, with the danger of attack north of the river removed, Wellington was able to order the 3rd Division to also cross by the ford of Cabrerizos and march west across the rear of the battlefield to the Teso de los Zorreras near Aldeatajeda.[14] This and other moves extended his right flank, not only to cover Thomières' move westward but also to strengthen his right in preparation for a withdrawal which seemed increasingly likely. Aldeatejada was a rearguard position for a withdrawal to Ciudad Rodrigo, intended to be used by Wellington and anticipated by Marmont.

As time slipped by with the prospect of attack by Marmont lessening, Wellington indeed outlined a plan to Colonel Murray for another withdrawal. Murray duly prepared detailed orders covering sequencing and routes and disseminated them to the divisions. Inevitably, the word spread across the army

Wellington's redeployments made during the morning.

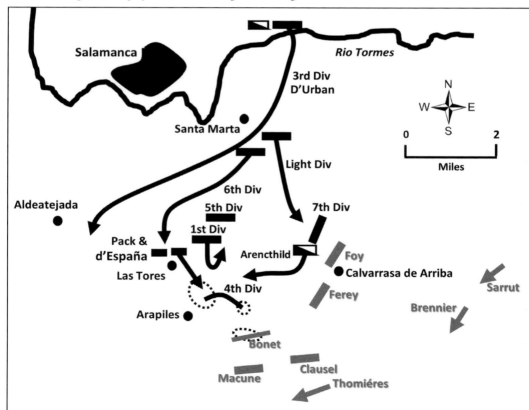

22 July 1812, Morning 121

that they were not going to fight but were to resume the march back to Portugal. Spirits fell.

As the hot sun had now dried the ground and dust was being raised by foot, hoof and wheel, Marmont took the 3rd Division's dust cloud and further to the north-west that of the allied baggage as a sure sign that Wellington's expected withdrawal was already under way. This confirmed in his mind that he was only facing the rearguard around Los Arapiles and that the rest of the allied army was on its way back via the new rearguard position at Aldeatejada. Unknown to the marshal, five divisions were concealed in positions behind the ridge.

Lieutenant Browne described an anxious morning marked by exchanges of artillery fire and some skirmishing:

> By the time this change [in deployment] was completed the enemy had made great progress. We cannonaded his columns near the steep hill with effect & they retired, taking up ground as in position. This was about twelve o'clock & he [Thomières] was gaining upon our right flank very fast. Ld. Wellington then found that the enemy would be able to inconvenience his retreat exceedingly if he delayed any longer, & that he must attack or retire. Marshal Beresford's opinion was asked & he was against an attack, considering the strength of the enemy's position, that the river was almost upon our rear, &

Marmont's perception of the situation at midday.

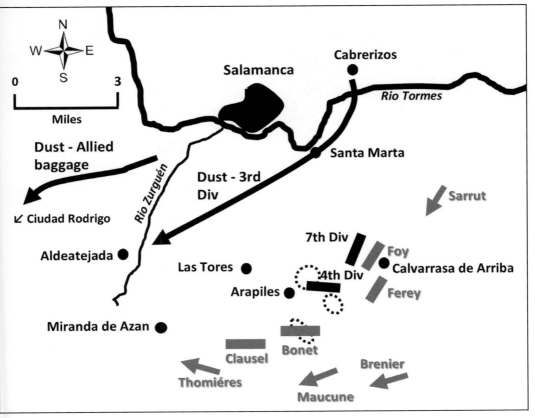

British infantry marching across the Salamanca battlefield during the 200th anniversary commemoration. Note the dust thrown up by relatively few feet.

also upon the principle which had hitherto made Ld. Wellington decline acting on the offensive. Some time elapsed, during which there was some cavalry skirmishing for the hills further on our right which the enemy obtained. Every instant our situation became more & more critical, & the feelings of those officers of the army, who from their situation had been enabled to observe all the movements of the enemy & the consequences which they threatened were anything but confident or comfortable.

Browne concluded that 'Ld. Wellington appeared only to be delaying retiring in hope that he might be attacked, & when the enemy were gaining ground to the right he said "We must be off as fast as we can or fight him".' In addition to the abandoned attack by the 1st Division, attacks were discussed throughout the morning by Wellington and his staff, with the likes of Colonel Gordon supporting offensive action and Marshal Beresford counselling against taking the risk involved in an attack. Meanwhile, across the valley, as recorded in General Foy's diary, Marmont again hesitated, unsure of the situation:[15]

> The Marshal had no definite plan: he thought that the English army was already gone off, or at least that it was going off, to take position on the heights of Aldeatejada on the left bank of the Rio Zurguén. He was tempted to make an attack on the one visible English division, with which a skirmishing fire had already begun. He was fearing that this division might get out of his reach!

For most of the morning, the two commanders were both at the critical point observing. Marmont and his flamboyant entourage, having earlier been up on the Greater Arapile, were reported as 'galloping along the front repeatedly'. A mile to the north Wellington and his staff were on the Teso de San Miguel for several hours, but with the bulk of the French divisions stationary on the ridge opposite, the peer retired to the village of Arapiles for lunch.

As recorded by Major William Napier:

> ... at three o'clock, a report reached him that the French left was in motion and pointing towards the Ciudad Rodrigo road; then starting up he repaired to the high ground, and observed their movements for some time, with a stern contentment, for their left wing was entirely separated from the centre. The fault was flagrant, and he fixed it with the stroke of a thunderbolt.

What Wellington saw was a westward extension of the rest of the Army of Portugal for which Marmont had issued his orders sometime after 1300 hours, and nearly two hours later the movement of French divisions out of the woods and along the ridge could plainly be seen from the Lesser Arapile. The marshal had seen the 4th Division strengthening the area around Arapiles and was concerned that Wellington would occupy the tactically important broad Monte de Azan plateau, which extends for a mile and a half to the south-west of Arapiles village, terminating at the Pico de Miranda. Marmont recorded in his dispatch:

> Accordingly I ordered the 5th Division [Maucune] to move out and form up on the right end of the [Monte de Azan] plateau, where his fire would link on perfectly with that from the [Greater] Arapile: the 7th Division [Thomières] was to place itself in second line as a support, the 2nd Division [Clausel] to act as a reserve to the 7th. The 6th Division [Brenier] was to occupy the high ground in front of the wood, where a large number of my guns were still stationed. I ordered General Bonet at the same time to occupy with the 122nd Regiment a knoll [Pt 883, Teso del Judío] intermediate between the plateau and the hill of the [Greater] Arapile, which blocks the exit from the village of the same name. Finally, I directed General Boyer to leave only one regiment of his dragoons to watch Foy's right, and to come round with the other three to the front of the wood, beside the 2nd Division. The object of this was that, supposing the enemy should attack the plateau, Boyer could

A French general of division.

charge in on their right flank, while my light cavalry could charge in on their left flank.[16]

These were not orders to attack but, though he does not admit it, they extended his flank to the left in order to manoeuvre Wellington back to Spain. Marmont wrote in his memoirs that he did not now expect a general action: 'I hoped that our respective positions would bring on not a battle but an advantageous rearguard action, in which, using my full force late in the day, with a part only of the British army left in front of me, I should probably score a point.' In execution of the orders, however, his army became strung out and extended over a 6-mile frontage in a manner that had arguably not been intended by Marmont. His divisional commanders conditioned by days of hard marching to outflank the allies simply continued the army's practice since the crossing of the Duero six days earlier.

Unchecked by his army commander, Curto's division of chasseurs and Thomières' division continued their march west towards Pico de Miranda rather than halting within supporting distance of Maucune. Not only that, Marmont's centre had become denuded with only Bonet's division around Los Arapiles, which was in itself distanced from Foy and Ferey's divisions, which had remained in the area of Calvarrasa de Arriba facing Wellington's left flank. Thus Marmont, with his orders being poorly executed by his divisional commander, had allowed his army to become split into four parts, which were crucially unable to provide immediate support for each other.

Expecting defensive battle but seeing the opportunity to attack, as the French divisions moved out of mutual supporting distance, Wellington calculated the relative times and distances for him to take the offensive and for the French to march to support each other. In doing this he was able to confirm in his mind that this was the 'advantageous circumstances' he had waited for over the previous six days. Having made his decision to act, there are several claims as to what he said and to whom. In a conversation in 1838 with Charles Grenville, Wellington gave his own account of how an ADC gave him news that finally there was movement opposite:

> The Duke was anxiously waiting for some advantageous occasion to attack Marmont, and at last it arrived; he saw it happen and took his resolution on the spot. He was dining in a farmyard with his officers, where (when he had done dinner) everybody else came and dined as they could. The whole French army was in sight, moving, and the enemy firing [with artillery] upon the farmyard in which he was dining. 'I got up,' he said, 'and was looking over a wall round the farmyard, just such a wall as that' (pointing to a low stone wall bounding the covert), 'and I saw the movement of the French left through my glass. "By God," said I, "that will do, I'll attack them directly".'[17]

Having determined on action, as Napier concluded, 'A few orders issued from his lips like the incantations of a wizard.'

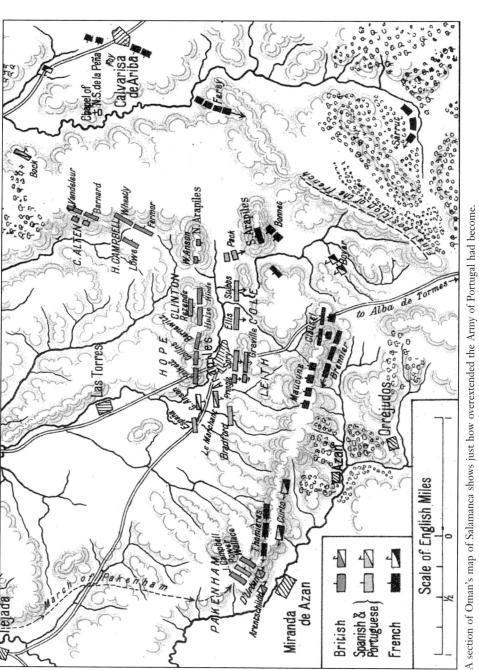

A section of Oman's map of Salamanca shows just how overextended the Army of Portugal had become.

22 July 1812, Morning   127

Hamilton Smith's representation of British staff officers in 1812.

The Plan for Battle

ADCs were soon spurring their horses into a gallop to disseminate Wellington's orders for the attack on an overextended French army. On the left, the 7th Division was to be replaced by the Light Division, supported by the 1st Division. Together these two divisions were to threaten and thus fix the divisions of Foy and Ferey on that flank. Meanwhile, in the centre, the 5th Division was to deploy to the right of the 4th and joined that division in forming in two lines. Beyond the

5th, Bradford's Portuguese with Le Marchant's heavy cavalry were to take post to the right. Forming a second line of divisions behind the Teso de San Miguel and the village was the 6th Division, which was joined by the 7th, who were in turn flanked to the right by George Anson's light cavalry. Covering the gap to the right, out towards the 3rd Division were Bradford's Portuguese and d'España's Spaniards. Finally, Pack's Portuguese Brigade was to capture the Greater Arapile.

Having given orders to his centre, Wellington, accompanied by his orderly dragoon and a handful of staff officers, galloped west to the 3rd Division who were in cover north of the Teso de las Zorreras near Aldeatejada. Here he gave General Pakenham his orders from the crest of the Teso. Lieutenant Grattan of the 88th was with a group of officers and witnessed Wellington's arrival and described the scene:

> As Lord Wellington rode up to Pakenham every eye was turned towards him. He looked paler than usual, but notwithstanding the sudden change he had just made in the disposition of his army, he was quite unruffled in his manner, and as calm as if the battle about to be fought was nothing more than an ordinary assemblage of the troops for a field day. His words were few and his orders brief.

Wellington's deployment and plan of attack, afternoon of 22 July 1812.

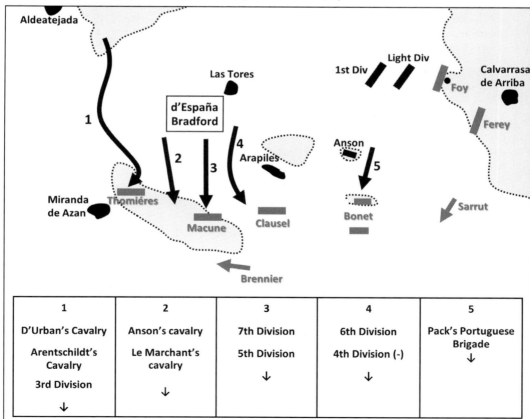

Captain Lightfoot of the 45th Regiment was at the head of the division's column and heard what was said:

> His Lordship's orders to General Pakenham in our hearing were 'Pakenham, you will carry that height [the Pico de Miranda] where the enemy's left is posted by storm, and when you have gained it, go at them hard and fast with the bayonet.' 'Yes, my Lord,' said Pakenham, 'That I will by God' and galloping off, placed himself at our head.

The division was at the time preparing its lunch and 'our camp kettles were in a moment overturned and mounted on the mules. Many men looked blank at having to go without a meal.'[18] Quickly under arms and deployed in columns, the 3rd Division set off to the attack.

Marching in quick time of 108 paces per minute, it would have taken the head of the division some thirty minutes to cover the distance from the Teso de las Zorreras to Monte de Azan. The division was flanked by two squadrons of the 14th Light Dragoons and covered by Brigadier General D'Urban's Portuguese cavalry which had crossed the Tormes with the 3rd Division and now formed the extreme right of the allied army.

Deployment

Our two diarists from the 7th Division, Wheeler of the 51st and Green of the 68th describe the division's march from the army's left to the centre. They were unaware of what was happening on either the extreme left or right. Wheeler first:

> In the afternoon we broke into open column of divisions right in front and marched up the rear of our army. This was not a very agreeable job as the enemy were cannonading the whole length of the line, and our route lay within range of their guns. The fire at length became so furious that it was expedient to form grand division, thus leaving an interval of double the space for their shot to pass through.

The guns that were playing on the 7th Division were Maucune's own battery, plus four batteries of Marmont's reserve artillery, which were moved forward to Maucune's left. General Brenier's division marched on beyond Maucune's and halted behind the guns. The five batteries outmatched those of the allies at this stage in the battle and as the 7th Division appeared from behind the Teso de San Miguel they came under fire. Wheeler continued:

> Our support being required on the right of the line we now moved on in double quick time. This raised such a dust that together with the heat of the day we were almost suffocated. The want of water now began to be severely felt, those who had some in their canteens were as bad off as those that had none, for what with the heat of the sun and the shaking it got it was completely spoiled. Those who drank of it immediately threw it up.
>
> As we proceeded the fire increased. We were wet with sweat as if we had been in the Tormes, and so great was the quantity of dust that settled on our

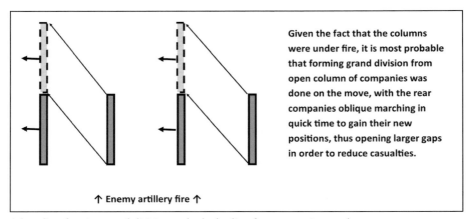

A battalion forming grand division; only the leading four companies are shown.

faces and clothes that we scarce knew each other. In fact, we more resembled an army of sweeps or dustmen than any one thing I can conceive. Almost fagged to death we arrived at our position on the right of our line; in our front was a hill on which was posted the enemy's left [sic]. They welcomed us opening about 16 guns and several howitzers. We found some water near us but it was so bad we could not drink it, however it served to rinse our mouths and wash the dust off our faces, this refreshed us much.

While the rest of the division marched to its new position, the 2nd Caçadores and the 68th Light Infantry waited to be relieved of responsibility for skirmishing beneath Nuestra Señora de la Peña by the Light Division. Private Green wrote:

About three o'clock the 95th Rifle Corps arriving, took our places, and we immediately marched off to join the division. About this time the cannonading commenced: the French had nearly one hundred [sic, 70] pieces of cannon firing on our army, which was forming for the attack: we had about sixty [sic, 48] pieces; and the thunder of these one hundred and sixty guns was terrible, and beggars description.

The exchange of artillery fire continued, while Maucune's tirailleurs advanced on Arapiles village, which was held by the Guards' and Fusiliers' light companies. The French penetrated into the outskirts of the village on two occasions, but were ejected by counter-attack. The tirailleurs' success was, however, not to be supported, as both Generals Maucune and Bonet were instructed not to send battalions to join the attack. At this stage, Marmont from his position back up on the Greater Arapile claimed that he could see that Maucune was in danger of becoming too closely engaged and Thomières was being drawn too far west. To stop his left becoming overextended he was about to leave the Arapile when a shell fired by a howitzer of Dyneley's RHA battery on the Lesser Arapile burst among the French staff, badly lacerating Marmont's right arm and cracking two ribs.[19] Meanwhile, Thomières marched on further west on the Monte de Azan ridge. Green continued:

> Having joined the division and taken our place on the left of the first brigade; we halted a few minutes, and then advanced to the spot where our artillery were stationed. We now came into an open plain and were completely exposed to the fire of the enemy's artillery. Along this plain a division of the army was stationed: I think it was the 4th Division: the men laid down in order to escape the shot and shells, the army not yet being ready to advance. As our regiment was, marching along the rear of this division, I saw a shell fall on one of the men, which killed him on the spot; a part of the shell tore his knapsack to pieces, and I saw it flying in the air after the shell had burst.

The 5th Division did not have as far to march to its position south-west of Arapiles, where a ridge gave them protection from aimed artillery fire but not from shot that bounced over it, nor from shells. Corporal Douglas recorded that the

> 3rd Brigade on coming down did not please Sir James [Leith]. He marched them back under the whole fire in ordinary time and back again to make them do it in a soldier-like manner. The Brigade, on coming to its ground, the centre sub-division of the 15th Portuguese was struck with a shot (I mean cannon shot) which did fearful execution. It scarcely left a man standing.

The battle was well under way, but with Marmont wounded there was only a short hiatus in command while General Bonet was summoned from his nearby division to take command of the army.

On the Column

A body of troops moving in line has to maintain its dressing in order to preserve its integrity while on the move. With the average two deep British battalion line being some 200 yards long and the French three deep line at 130 yards, moving in line was inevitably slow, at their respective ordinary step of seventy five and seventy six paces a minute.

Moving in a column of smaller bodies, be they divisions (two companies), single companies, platoons or sections, with a much reduced frontage was faster, with a quick step of 108 and 100 being used in practice.

The French intent when advancing in column was to deploy into line to exchange volleys, beat the *Pas de Charge* ['Old Trowsers'] and deliver an attack at 140 paces per minute. During the Revolutionary Wars against many of the European armies it was found that the enemy having been galled by the tirailleurs, often gave way as the undeployed French columns bore down on them. In the Peninsular, however, from the earliest battles they discovered that this tactic rarely worked against the British two deep line, but many persisted in trying to use the columns' momentum to bludgeon their way through. On other occasions, such as at Buçaco Ridge in 1810, they believed that the heavy screen of skirmishers deployed by the Light Division was the main battle line and thought that they had broken through, only to be confronted by a British line as they reached the crest. On other occasions, French officers found that it was too late to deploy when advancing on a British line sited on a reverse slope position, a musket shot from the crest. In that case they had little choice but to press on.

When caught in column the French frontage was invariably overlapped on both sides by the British two deep line, which could bring many more muskets to bear against a single or double company column. Using the average British battalion strength at Salamanca (less a number for the reforming light companies), this was 450 muskets versus sixty five if the French were on a full strength single company frontage and 130 if doubled.

The French at times, where there was sufficient open ground, employed *ordre mixte* to benefit from the weight of the column and the firepower of the line.

Column deployed in *ordre mixte*.

The other types of battlefield column are shown in the flowing diagrams:

Column by Division. A battalion advancing in column would usually be in column by division i.e., two companies (*peletons*) wide. These columns for a six company battalion could be 'open', that is to say the gap between companies equated to the length of the frontage, half or quarter distance. This was more akin to multiple lines than our conception a solid column.

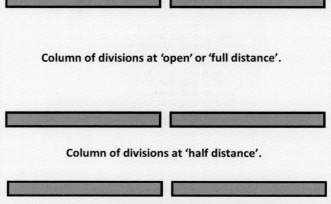

Column of divisions at 'open' or 'full distance'.

Column of divisions at 'half distance'.

Column of divisions showing two of the different distances between divisions. Note: These diagrams include the light company which would often be deployed skirmishing, necessitating rearrangement of the battalion's deployment.

Column by Company. On the constricted ground of much of the Peninsular, the British often encountered columns a single company wide. Initially French battalions advanced open formation designed to minimise casualties from artillery fire but as it approached the Allied position it would normally start to close the distance between companies.

Column of companies at quarter distance. In this diagrams the light company is deployed for skirmishing.

Serrée en Masse. The preceding columns were for battlefield manoeuvre. *Serrée en masse* was used for maximum weight and momentum as the column approached to the attack. The intervals between successive companies was closed up to 18 inches. The battalion was now in almost a solid mass designed to batter their way through the enemy's line.

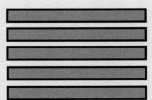

Column deployed in *Serrée en masse*.

Cavalry combat: a French 3rd Hussar versus a British light dragoon.

Chapter Seven

The Right Wing

With his divisions and brigades in place, at about 1600 hours Wellington's attack on the French left and centre was under way. Off to the west General Pakenham's 3rd Division flanked by D'Urban's Portuguese cavalry marched south astride the Cañada de Miranda track to attack the Pico de Miranda, the western extremity of the Monte de Azan plateau. They were deployed in four columns, with Wallace's brigade leading the infantry fronting three of the columns and D'Urban's cavalry forming the right column.

Lieutenant William Grattan of the 88th Connaught Rangers wrote a rather colourful account of the march and action of Wallace's brigade, but as he makes a number of interesting points he will be quoted selectively:[1]

> When all was in readiness Pakenham departed at the head of ten battalions [*sic*][2] and two brigades of guns, to force the left of the enemy. Three battalions, the 45th, 74th, and 88th, under Colonel Alexander Wallace of the 88th, composed the first line; the 9th and 21st Portuguese of the line, under the Portuguese colonel, De Champlemond, formed the second line; while two battalions of the 5th,[3] the 77th and the 83rd British, under the command of Colonel Campbell, were in reserve.

General D'Urban's column, which consisted of six Portuguese squadrons, had been ordered to cover the Division's right flank, followed by Arentschildt's brigade, which had been ordered over to this flank to provide sufficient cavalry to counter General Curto's chasseurs that were following Thomières west. On the division's left flank, Lieutenant Colonel Williams and his three companies of the 5th 60th Rifles along with the 12th Caçadores provided patrols and formed bodies of light infantrymen. Le Marchant's three regiments of heavy cavalry were deployed in reserve in a hollow to the left rear of the advance.

Based on Grattan's account of the deployment above, such notes as there are on Thomières' movements *and* the detail of the tactical methods of the day, I present a probable method of attack, though given the conflicting accounts it is far from possible to be certain exactly how Pakenham manoeuvred.

Captain Campbell on Wallace's staff wrote:

> To me, as Brigade-Major of the right brigade, Sir Edward Pakenham, in his quick decided manner, pointed out the direction we were to take, and desired me to tell Colonel Wallace, 88th regiment, the officer in the temporary command of the brigade, to move on with as much rapidity as possible, but without blowing the men too much. We soon descended into a kind of

The Cañada de Miranda track down the centre of the valley was the 3rd Division's axis of advance to the Pico de Azan. The hillsides in 1812 were clothed with scattered oaks. The track is a part of the southern camino, Via de la Plata, from Andalucía to Santiago de Compostela.

Probable deployment of the 3rd Division's columns for the advance, afternoon of 22 July 1812.

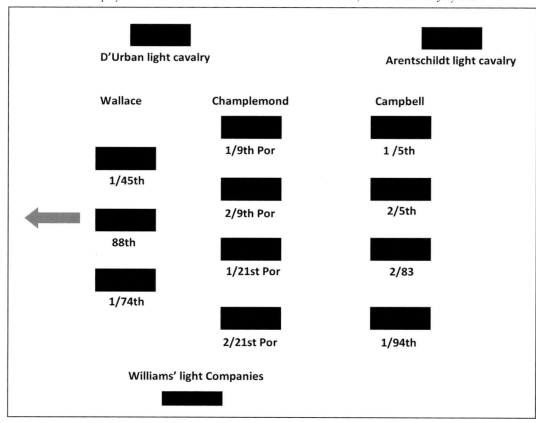

valley, or rather hollow, and having brought up our left shoulders a little, we pushed on at a quick pace, but in excellent order.[4]

An advance of more than 2 miles across open terrain to Monte de Azan at the southern end of the valley could have been costly if a single French battery had been in a position on the high ground at the head of the valley to engage the columns. General Thomières was, however, unaware of the approach of the 3rd Division, despite being supported by virtually the whole of General Curto's division of light cavalry.[5] In normal circumstances light cavalry would provide patrols deployed to the front and rear, but certainly none were on the crest of the ridge to the right of Thomières' division from where they would have been bound to see Pakenham's division. Consequently, by not taking this simple precaution the 3rd Division and D'Urban's cavalry were able to reach the foot of Monte de Azan unobserved. The only plausible explanation is that Thomières and Curto also believed that the allies were withdrawing and were still fixated on the practice of previous days of attempting to reach a position from which they could turn Wellington's flank.

Thomières did, however, have an advance guard battalion deployed ahead of the bulk of his division. D'Urban explains how he located the 3rd Battalion of the 101st Regiment of the *Ligne*, also marching without having deployed patrols:

> The enemy was marching by his left along the wooded heights, which form the southern boundary of the valley of the Arapiles, and the western extremity of which closes in a lower fall, which descends upon the little stream of the Azan,[6] near the village of Miranda. As the head of our column approached this lower fall, or hill, skirting it near its base, and having it on our left, we became aware that we were close to the enemy, though we could not see them owing to the trees, the dust, and the peculiar configuration of the ground. Anxious, therefore, to ascertain their exact whereabouts I had ridden out a little in front, having with me, I think, only my brigade-major Flangini and Da Camara, when upon clearing the verge of a small clump of trees, a short way up the slope, I came suddenly upon the head of a French column of infantry, having about a company in front, and marching very fast by its left. It was at once obvious that, as the columns of the 3rd Division were marching on our left, the French must be already beyond their right, and consequently I ought to attack at once.[7]

Unaware that they had been seen, the French battalion marched on, while D'Urban quickly returned to his brigade and ordered three weak squadrons totalling some 200 horsemen of the 1st Portuguese Dragoons to attack. He led them forward hoping to surprise the enemy battalion and charge them before they could react and form a square. Colonel Henry Watson commanding the 1st described their approach: 'The cavalry was pushed forward in contiguous columns, and were protected from the enemy by a small rising ground, which as soon as I had passed, I was ordered to wheel up, and charge the front in line' (see map, p. 141).

Major General Benjamin D'Urban.

Bursting over the horizon within several hundred yards of the enemy, the disconcerted French infantry column had just enough time to form an incomplete square[8] and when the dragoons pressed home their attack two of the squadrons received a volley of musket fire. The right-hand squadron, however, overlapped the head of the column and was able to fall on the infantry's unprotected flank. Colonel Watson recorded:

> In this charge we completely succeeded, and the enemy appeared panic-stricken, and made no attempt to prevent our cutting and thrusting at them

in all directions until the moment I was about to withdraw; then a soldier, at not more than six or eight paces, levelled his musket at me, and shot me through the shoulder, which knocked me off my horse, where I continued to lie till the whole of our infantry passed over.

With the dragoons sabring the disordered infantrymen, the French battalion broke and fled back along the ridge, pursued by the Portuguese cavalry. The 11th Portuguese Dragoons deployed to support the 1st Dragoons along with two squadrons of the 14th Light Dragoons of Arentschildt's brigade that were just arriving.

Meanwhile, Pakenham's columns were climbing up onto the high ground with Colonel Williams' riflemen now leading, deployed as a skirmish line. Not only did Thomières have the fleeing battalion and enemy cavalry approaching from his front, but he was now confronted by the heads of three battalion columns appearing on the crest line less than 1,000 yards to the east of the rest of the 101st. Colonel Wallace's major of brigade Captain Campbell remembered:

> Having moved a considerable distance in this order (field officers and adjutants prolonging the line of march), the head of the column, by bringing up the right shoulder, began gradually to ascend the hill, on the top of which we expected to find the enemy still extending to their left. At length, having fairly outflanked the French left, the whole formed line, and with Sir Edward Pakenham in front, hat in hand, the brigades advanced in beautiful style, covered by our sharpshooters, the right of the first line admirably supported by the left brigade.

Grattan recorded that 'Wallace's three battalions advanced in open column until within two hundred and fifty yards of the ridge held by the French infantry', where just beyond the effective range of massed musket fire, the columns were ordered to form line while on the march:

> Pakenham, who was naturally of a boiling spirit and hasty temper, was on this day perfectly cool. He told Wallace to form line from open column without halting, and thus the different companies, by throwing forward their right shoulders, were in line without the slow manoeuvre of a deployment. Astonished at the rapidity of the movement, the French riflemen [sic] commenced an irregular and hurried fire, and even at this early stage of the battle a looker-on could, from the difference in the demeanour of the troops of the two nations, form a tolerably correct opinion of what would be the result.

Deploying in this way saved considerable time at a point when not giving the French time to recover from the surprise was crucial. At this juncture, the 12th Caçadores were also deployed to reinforce the 5th 60th Rifles in the skirmish line.

Thomières had little time to react, hurriedly deploying his own tirailleurs into a skirmish screen and bringing the 8-pounders of his divisional artillery battery

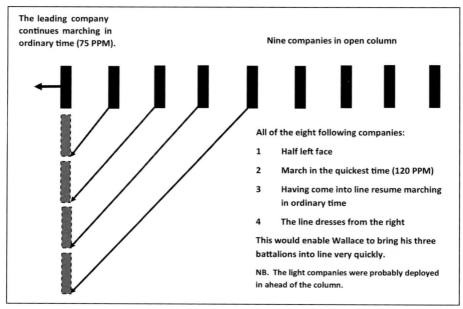

One of the methods of a battalion deploying into line from column.

into action. This resulted in a duel with Captain Douglas's battery of the 3rd Division, which had taken position on a hillock to the division's left rear. Captain Bull's RHA guns fired common shell and shrapnel over the heads of Wallace's brigade, which was now on the final slope up to the crest of the ridge.

Private Joseph Donaldson of the 94th recorded that Pakenham had 'completely succeeded' in catching Thomières strung out; 'for having formed across the enemy's flank, we advanced under a heavy fire from their artillery, overthrowing everything before us.' Grattan continued:

> All were impatient to engage, and the calm but stern advance of Wallace's brigade was received with beating of drums and loud cheers from the French, whose light troops, hoping to take advantage of the time which the deploying from column into line would take, ran down the face of the hill in a state of great excitement.[9]

As the two bodies of skirmish closed on each other they opened fire but, as Captain Campbell recorded, the line coming up behind them did not await the outcome:

> The enemy's skirmishers and ours now set to work, yet we did not wait for their indecisive long shots; but advancing still rapidly and steadily, our right soon came into contact with their left, which had opened a very heavy and destructive fire upon us, and which would have lasted long enough had the brigade been halted to return it, but it was instantly charged and overthrown.

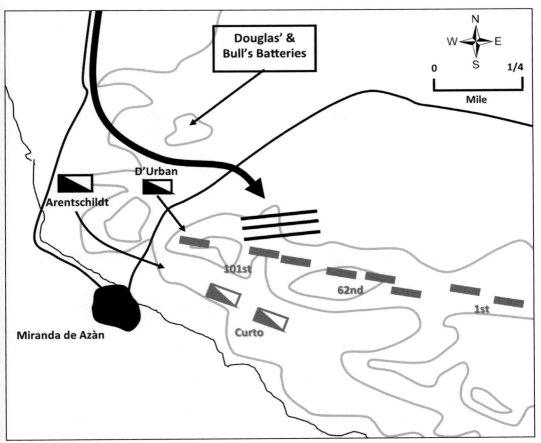

Attack of the 3rd Division on Thomières' division, which was marching north-west along the Monte de Azan ridge.

It was now evidence to us all that Sir Edward Pakenham knew how to handle Picton's division.[10]

The French were clearly shaken by the sudden turn of events, but Napoleon's veterans would not collapse without a fight. Grattan continued:

> Regardless of the fire of the tirailleurs, and the showers of grape and canister, Pakenham, at the head of Wallace's brigade, continued to press onward; his centre suffered, but still advanced; his left and right being less oppressed by the weight of the fire, continued to advance at a more rapid pace, and as his wings inclined forward and outstripped the centre, the brigade assumed the form of a crescent. The manoeuvre was a bold, as well as a novel one, and the appearance of the brigade imposing and unique, because it so happened that all the British officers were in front of their men – a rare occurrence.[11] The French officers were also in front; but their relative duties were widely different: the latter, encouraging their men into the heat of the battle; the former keeping their devoted soldiers back! – what a splendid national contrast! Amongst the mounted officers were Sir Edward Pakenham and his

staff, Wallace of the 88th, commanding the brigade, and his gallant aide-de-camp, Mackie.

In spite of the fire of Thomières' tirailleurs, they continued at the head of the [enemy's] right brigade, while the soldiers, with their firelocks on the rest,[12] followed close upon the heels of their officers, like troops accustomed to conquer. They speedily got footing upon the brow of the hill, but before they had time to take breath, the entire French division, with drums beating and uttering loud shouts, ran forward to meet them [in a counter-attack], and belching forth a torrent of bullets from five thousand muskets,[13] brought down almost the entire of Wallace's first rank, and more than half of his officers.[14] The brigade staggered back from the force of the shock, but before

Major General Sir Edward Pakenham.

the smoke had altogether cleared away, Wallace, looking full in the faces of his soldiers, pointed to the French column, and leading the shattered brigade up the hill, without a moment's hesitation, brought them face to face before the French had time to witness the terrible effect of their murderous fire.

The French, two battalions of the 101st Regiment and three of the 62nd, were now clearly not properly formed in either line or column and their 'discharge of musketry, though heavy 'was unlike the former, – it was irregular and ill-directed, the men acted without concert or method, and many fired in the air':

> The French officers did all that was possible, by voice, gesture, and example, to rouse their men to a proper sense of their situation, but in vain. One, the colonel of the leading regiment, seizing a firelock, and beckoning to his men to follow, ran forward a few paces and shot Major Murphy dead in front of the 88th. However, his career soon closed: a bullet, the first that had been fired from our ranks, pierced his head; he flung up his arms, fell forward, and expired.

The 88th's two ensigns carrying the colours thought that they were the target of the French colonel. Lieutenant Thomas Moriarty with the Regimental Colour said 'That fellow is aiming at me!' 'I hope so,' said his fellow, Lieutenant John D'Arcy, carrying the King's Colour, 'for I thought he had me covered!' As Major Murphy fell, a French musket ball sliced through D'Arcy's epaulette and smashed the Colour pole into two pieces.

Wallace's hitherto silent men who had continued to advance into the waning French fire, sensing the moment had come to charge home, cheered and, according to Grattan, 'The effect was electric':

> Thomières' troops were seized with a panic, and as Wallace closed upon them, his men could distinctly remark their bearing. Their moustachioed faces, one and all, presented the same ghastly hue ... as they stood to receive the shock they were about to be assailed with, they reeled to and fro.

As the brigade charged, the fleeing tirailleurs carried away the disordered ranks of the 101st, which in turn fell back in chaos on the 62nd Regiment who joined the flight too late, a brigade of Curto's chasseur regiments, some seven squadrons strong, appeared to support Thomières' division. Several squadrons charged the two flanking British battalions: the 1st Battalion 45th Line and the 1st 5th Fusiliers. As General D'Urban had only a short time before, the French had been able to get within charging distance unseen by using the slopes of the feature as cover. The 1/45th Foot, rather than forming square, only had time to wheel back three companies to produce a defensive flank. Private Brown wrote:

> During the action, as our brigade was marching up to attack a strongly posted column of infantry, a furious charge was made by a body of cavalry upon our Regiment, and, not having time to form square, we suffered severely. Several times the enemy rode through us, cutting down with their

A French foot artillery battery in action.

sabres all that opposed them. Our ranks were broken and thrown into the utmost confusion. Repeatedly our men attempted to reform, but all in vain – they were as often cut down and trampled upon by their antagonists. At length, however, the enemy were driven off by some squadrons of our cavalry who came up in time to save us from being totally destroyed. Numerous and severe were the wounds received on this occasion. Several had their arms dashed from their shoulders, and I saw more than one with their heads completely cloven. Among the rest I received a wound, but comparatively slight, although well aimed. Coming in contact with one of the enemy he brandished his sword over me, and standing in his stirrup-irons, prepared to strike; but, pricking his horse with my bayonet, it reared and pranced, when the sword fell, the point striking my forehead. He was, however, immediately brought down, falling with a groan to rise no more.

Off to a flank of the 3rd Division, as recalled by Private Donaldson: 'The fifth regiment, in attacking a body of infantry posted on a small height, were furiously charged by the enemy's cavalry, and thrown into some confusion.'

Being on the right flank of the division it is presumed that the 1st 5th was sent to deal with a part of the 101st that had rallied and was resisting the allied cavalry, but it seems that the enemy pressed home their attack less vigorously on them as they fell back into clumps. Sergeant Morley of the 5th Fusiliers wrote that

> There was a pause – a hesitation. Here I blush – but I should blush more if I were guilty of a falsehood. We retired – slowly, in good order, not far, not

100 paces. General Pakenham approached, and very good-naturedly said 're-form', and after a moment 'advance – there they are, my lads – let them feel the temper of your bayonets.' We advanced – rather slowly at first, a regiment of dragoons which had retired with us again accompanying ... and took our retribution for our repulse.

The cavalry mentioned by Brown and Morley were probably the 11th Portuguese Dragoons, but in addition to the two squadrons of the 14th Light Dragoons, three of the 1st Hussars KGL, also of Arentschildt's brigade, had arrived to lend support to the 3rd Division. The leading brigade of chasseurs was thrown back and they joined Thomières' division in fleeing towards the French centre.[15] General Curto's second brigade was deterred from intervening by the presence of Arentschildt's men covering the right flank.

Captain Campbell recorded that the infantry:

> were again ready for another dash at the enemy, who were trying to reform on a gentle height, a short distance in front of us. But how truly inspiring the scene had now become, and how 'beautifully the practice' of Major Douglas's artillery was telling among the French! Another charge was intended; the French would not, however, stand, and retired in tolerable order, but most severely galled by our sharpshooters, who were close at their heels.

The pursuit was led by the light companies and the 88th Connaught Rangers, but once the Portuguese dragoons had re-formed, they took over harrying the

If attacked by cavalry and unable to form a square, soldiers would form defensive clumps or 'Rally Orb' as demonstrated by the 95th Rifles living historians.

French. Grattan observed that 'The confusion of the enemy was so great, that they were mixed pell-mell together without any regard to order or regularity.' Tomkinson related a story illustrative of the pursuit:

> A soldier of the 3rd Division said he was after a French chap with his bayonet, who tried all he could to get out of his way; at a last resource he threw away his musket and attempted to leap up one of the low oak trees on the field when he ran his bayonet into him as he was getting up.

Private Donaldson was following in General Campbell's brigade and this time recorded the unusual experience of Douglas's 8-pounders firing through their ranks as they marched east along the ridge following Wallace's pursuit:

> In this manner driving in their left, we came in front of where our artillery were playing on the enemy; but no time was lost, for by marching past in open column, they continued to fire without interruption, sending their shot through the intervals between each company, without doing us any injury, although it created rather unpleasant sensations to hear it whistling past us.

As Donaldson noted, the pursuit was not unopposed or without cost:

> The enemy's shot and shell were now making dreadful havoc. A Portuguese cadet who was attached to our regiment received a shell in the centre of his

Capture of the 'Jingling Johnnie' by the 88th Connaught Rangers, which has in the past been confused with the capture of an Eagle.

body, which, bursting at the same instant, literally blew him to pieces. Another poor fellow receiving a grape shot across his belly, his bowels protruded, and he was obliged to apply both his hands to the wound to keep them in; I shall never forget the expression of agony depicted in his countenance. These were remarkable cases, but the men were now falling thick on every side.

Eventually the soldiers of the 62nd and 101st regiments started to re-form behind the three battalions of the 1st Regiment which had not been substantially attacked by the 3rd Division and were able to fall back towards Maucune's division in relatively good order. After a mile of pursuit, however, resistance grew and Grattan noted:

> Led on by the ardour of conquest, we had followed the column until we at length found ourselves in an open plain, intersected with cork-trees, opposed

Centre company soldiers of the 1st Royals wearing the 1806 Pattern regimental caps.

by a multitude who, reinforced, again rallied and turned upon us with fury. Pakenham and Wallace rode along the line from wing to wing, almost from rank to rank, and fulfilled the functions of adjutants, in assisting the officers to reorganise the tellings-off of their men for square. Meanwhile the first battalion of the 5th drove back some squadrons of Boyer's dragoons; the other six regiments were fast approaching the point held by Wallace, but the attitude of the French cavalry in our front and upon our right flank caused some uneasiness.

At this point, having outmarched his supports, closing in on Maucune and with Brenier's division to be seen approaching through the woods to the south, Wallace brought the pursuit to a halt. During the forty minutes of action, Thomières had been killed, his divisional artillery overrun, and the Eagle of the 22nd Regiment eventually fell into the hands of the 12th Caçadores, having been found among a pile of dead Frenchmen by a Portuguese soldier. It was handed to Lieutenant Pratt, who passed it on to his commanding officer Major Crookshank.[16] Of the two leading French regiments the 101st had lost 1,031 men out of 1,449 in action and the 62nd *Ligne* 868 men out of 1,123, many of which were taken prisoner. Generals Pakenham, D'Urban and Colonel Arentschildt had suffered some 500 casualties in overthrowing Thomières.

The remnants of Thomières' division would be pursued back to the wooded ridge, not only by D'Urban and Arentschildt's cavalry but by Bradford's Portuguese Infantry and as we will see by the 5th Division and General George Anson's light cavalry as well.

The Eagle of the 22nd *Ligne* recovered at Salamanca by a soldier of the 12th Caçadores but often attributed to Lieutenant Pratt.

Attack of the 5th Division

According to Captain Leith Hay, ADC to his uncle General Leith, while the 3rd Division's attack was developing, the 5th Division

> remained for a considerable time without movement, or being assailed ... About three o'clock, a force of not less than twenty pieces of artillery were assembled by the enemy on the heights directly opposite to the 5th Division. The ground upon which the division stood was flat, and the troops without any means of shelter. It became consequently advisable to make the regiments recline on the field, and, by so doing, avoid in some measure the effects of what was evidently to become a very heavy cannonade. For at least an hour did these brave soldiers immovably support the efforts made to annihilate them by the showers of shot and howitzer shells that were either passing over or ricocheting through the ranks. General Leith, on horseback, passed repeatedly along the front of his division, speaking to, and animating the men, who earnestly expressed an anxious desire for permission to attack the enemy.[17]

Having set Pakenham in motion, 'Lord Wellington arrived from the right and communicated to General Leith his intention of immediately attacking the enemy':

> General Leith was directed to form his division in two lines, the first of which was composed of the Royals,[18] 9th and 38th regiments, with part of the 4th regiment from General Pringle's brigade, necessarily brought forward for the purpose of equalizing the lines, of which the second was formed by the remainder of General Pringle's and the whole of General Spry's Portuguese infantry. When General Bradford's brigade came up, the division was to *appui* [deploy to support] itself on to his left, march directly up the heights, and attack the enemy's columns. Lord Wellington on this, as on all occasions, gave his orders in a clear, concise, and spirited manner; there was no appearance of contemplating a doubtful result; all he directed was as to time and formation, and his instructions concluded with commands that the enemy should be overthrown, and driven from the field.

Corporal Douglas was waiting with the Royals, lying down behind the crest line:

> General Leith rode up about two o'clock. The cannonading at this time was terrible. Addressing the regiment, he says, 'Royals', on which we all sprang up. 'Lie down men,' said he, though he sat on horseback, exposed to the fire as calm as possible. 'This shall be a glorious day for Old England, if these *bragadocian*[19] rascals dare but stand their ground, we will display the point of the British bayonet, and where it is properly displayed no power is able to withstand it. All I request of you is to be steady and to obey your officers. Stand up men!' Then taking off his cocked hat and winding it around his head he gives the word 'March!' A few paces brought us to the crest of

the hill when we became exposed to the fire of all the guns they could bring to bear on us. I think the advance of the British at Salamanca never was exceeded in any field. Captain Stewart of our company, stepping out of the ranks to the front, lays hold of Captain Glover and cries, 'Glover, did you ever see such a line?' I am pretty confident that in the Regiments which composed our lines there was not a man six inches out of his place.

As the division would be advancing from behind the ridge west of Arapiles, across half a mile of open ground under fire from French artillery, as ordered by Wellington, the division advanced in line in order to reduce casualties. Ahead of them were about 1,000 skirmishers made up of two companies of the Brunswick

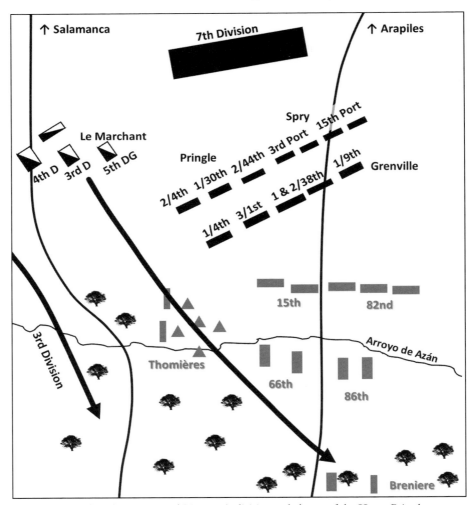

Deployment of the 5th Division and Maucune's division and charge of the Heavy Brigade.

Oels, the 8th Caçadores and the light companies of Grenville's brigade. Leith Hay recorded that

> the ground between the advancing force and that to be assailed was also crowded with light troops in extended order, carrying on a very incessant *tiraillade*. The general desired me to ride forward, make the light infantry press up the heights to clear his line of march, and if practicable make a rush at the enemy's cannon. In the execution of this service, I had to traverse the whole extent of surface directly in front of the 5th Division: the light troops soon drove back those opposed; the cannon were removed to the rear; every obstruction to the regular advance of the line had vanished.[20] In front of the centre of that beautiful line rode General Leith, directing its movements, and regulating its advance.

Leith Hay stressed the importance of controlling the march so as to arrive 'in perfect order close to the enemy, and at all points making a simultaneous attack'. To achieve this, with himself in the centre, in front of the 1st 38th, Leith sent two of his ADCs to the left and right 'to restrain any effort at getting more rapidly forward than was consistent with' retaining cohesion.

With the enemy skirmishers driven in, the 5th Division's leading line closed in on the enemy who, seeing Le Marchant's heavy cavalry approaching between the 3rd and 5th divisions were at least partly in square. It would seem that Grenville's brigade overlapped the French and struck Maucune's line at an oblique angle, with the centre of the brigade being most heavily engaged.

Through the dust and smoke General Leith and his staff saw the enemy, the five battalions of the 15th and 82nd *ligne* that made up Maucune's first defensive line. Behind them, beyond the Arroyo de Azan, almost certainly still in column, were the four battalions of the 66th and 86th *ligne*. Leith Hay continued:

> He was drawn up in contiguous squares, the front rank kneeling, and prepared to fire when the drum beat for its commencement. All was still and quiet in these squares – not a musket was discharged until the whole opened. Nearly at the same moment General Leith ordered the line to fire, and charge: the roll of musketry was succeeded by that proud cheer that has become habitual to British soldiers on similar occasions ... In an instant every individual present was enveloped in smoke and obscurity. No struggle for ascendency took place: the French squares were penetrated, broken, and discomfited; the victorious division pressed forward, not against troops opposed, but a mass of disorganized men, flying in all directions.

The number of muskets firing in Grenville's line greatly outnumbered those the French could bring to bear, even with the front rank of the square kneeling. Corporal Douglas of the 3rd Royals confirms Leith Hay's account:

> The enemy seemed to have formed parts of squares, and parts of lines, and before they could recover from their panic, our murderous fire opened,

Lieutenant General Sir James Leith.

which swept all before it. Their first line we fairly ran over, and saw our men jumping over huge grenadiers, who lay down exhausted through heat and fatigue, unhurt, in the hope of escaping. Of course, we left them uninjured, but they did not behave honourably, for as soon as they found us at a little distance, they resumed the posture of the enemy and commenced to fire on our rear; but nearly the whole of them paid the price of their treachery with their lives.

Sergeant Hale of the 9th Norfolks wrote that

as our regiment formed part of the first line, we did not forget to let them hear and feel the effects of our small arms, and according to English custom,

The dry course of the Arroyo de Azan, astride which Maucune's division was deployed.

as soon as we could make it convenient, we showed them the point of the bayonet, and gave them a grand charge, by which we obliged them to leave three pieces of cannon in our possession in a short time.

With General Maucune's forward regiments beaten, the 5th Division resumed its advance. Douglas continued his account:

> The first line of the enemy being broken and falling back in confusion, the 2nd lined the side of a deep trench cut by the torrents of water which roll down from the hills near the village of Arapiles, and so deep and broad that it took a good spring to leap over it.[21] Here the 2nd line kept up a heavy fire of musketry, which checked our centre for a few minutes, while our poor fellows fell fast. To remain long in this way was too much to be borne. The cheer was raised for the charge, a general bound was made at the chasm, and over we went like so many beagles, while the enemy gave way in confusion. The cavalry now came in for their share and cut them down in great number.

Hale commented that 'the enemy's line continued retreating for some considerable distance, and we continued firing advancing, till it was thought necessary for us to halt.'

With Thomières defeated and Maucune's first line dispersed, into this scene plunged General Le Marchant's heavy cavalry to complete the defeat of a quarter of the Army of Portugal. The pursuit of the French by infantry and cavalry continued across the plain to the wooded ridge. The historian of the 9th Norfolk Regiment wrote:

> ... the Ninth sloped arms and pressed forward without firing a shot; they were near Major General Le Marchant's brigade of heavy cavalry when it executed its brilliant charge on the French infantry ... Pressing rapidly forward along with the dragoons, and sharing with them in their successes against the French infantry ... the Ninth were at length a quarter of a mile in front of the other regiments of their brigade, when one of Lord Wellington's

aides-de-camp rode up, and said 'The 9th is the only regiment formed, advance.' This was instantly obeyed.[22]

At this point General Leith, along with his ADC nephew, was wounded and in his absence at the head of his division, Lieutenant Colonel Grenville, who was in command of the brigade, ordered the 9th Foot to withdraw and join the other battalions of their brigade. The 9th's historian complained 'thus yielding a post so strong that the 6th Division lost many men in retaking it!' More of this later.

Charge of the Heavy Brigade

Le Marchant's brigade, with one squadron detached, consisted of eight squadrons from the 5th Dragoon Guards and the 3rd and 4th dragoons. This was a total of up to 1,000 big men mounted on big horses who would ride boot-to-boot delivering shock action. They had hitherto been waiting dismounted, holding their horses, in a hollow to avoid French artillery fire.

Wellington, on his way from the 3rd Division stopped at General Sir Stapleton Cotton's cavalry before returning to oversee Leith's attack. He gave Cotton perfectly timed orders, telling him that 'The success of the movement to be made by 3rd Division would greatly depend on the assistance received from the cavalry; and that he must therefore be prepared to take advantage of the first favourable opportunity to charge the enemy's infantry.'

The allied attacks on the ground of the centre right.

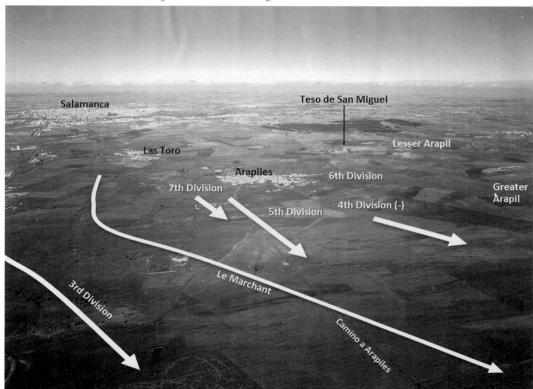

Adding the memorable phrase 'You must then charge at all hazards', Le Marchant's biographer continued: 'After some brief remarks on the chances of the day, Lord Wellington rode towards the centre, having desired the dragoons to remain in the same position until the time for action was come.'

In the wait while Pakenham's attack developed, the usual issues of avoiding enemy fire, finding routes around unexpected obstacles and preserving surprise for as long as possible during the move forward from their position in the rear were addressed. While orders were being given, Lieutenant Colonel Dalbiac led a reconnaissance of the route forward from Las Torres, leaving picquets to mark the way, which used folds in the ground as partial cover from fire and view.

With Le Marchant at its head, the brigade advanced for the first mile at a walk or at most a trot, as the canter that has been claimed by some would have resulted in the horses being blown before reaching the battle area and joining any serious action.[23] As they approached the gap between the 3rd and 5th divisions, the first problem was the passage of lines through the flank of Wallace's brigade, which was now halted. Grattan recalled that

> The smoke was so thick that nothing to our left was distinguishable; some men of the 5th Division got intermingled with ours; the dry grass was set on fire by the numerous cartridge-papers that strewed the field of battle; the air was scorching; and the smoke, rolling onward in huge volumes, nearly suffocated us. A loud cheering was heard in our rear; the brigade half turned round, supposing themselves about to be attacked by the French cavalry. Wallace called out to his men to mind the tellings-off for square.[24] A few seconds passed, the tramping of horses was heard, the smoke cleared away, and the heavy brigade of Le Marchant was seen coming forward in line at a canter. 'Open right and left' was an order quickly obeyed; the line opened, the cavalry passed through the intervals, and, forming rapidly in our front, prepared for their work. The French column, which a moment before held so imposing an attitude, became startled at this unexpected sight. A victorious and highly-excited infantry pressing close upon them, a splendid brigade of three regiments of cavalry ready to burst through their ill-arranged and beaten column, while no appearance of succour was at hand to protect them, was enough to appal the boldest intrepidity.

The left-hand companies of the 74th had wheeled back in order to create gaps through which the six leading cavalry squadrons could pass.

The timing was perfect. Seeing cavalry moving in his direction, some of Maucune's battalions were ordered into square, as already discussed, only to be confronted by the 5th Division's attack. With Maucune's first line defeated, the second line was unprepared and failed to present an organized front, being caught not in square but in column. Douglas of the Royals wrote 'The French seemed taken by surprise as ... [British cavalry] advanced with us on our right ... the enemy seemed to be rather in confusion ... They seemed to have formed part of squares and parts of lines.'

156 Salamanca Campaign, 1812

Major General John Gaspard Le Marchant.

A cavalry officer who took part in the charge, writing at a time when it was fashionable to decry the performance, particularly the heavies, explained that the brigade

> moving rapidly forward ... came first into contact with the 66th (French) regiment, consisting of three battalions, and formed in a sort of column of half-battalions, thus presenting six successive lines, one behind the other. Strange to say, though drawn up in that formidable manner, their fire was so

ill-directed, that it is believed scarcely a single dragoon fell from its effects; and no check taking place, the cavalry bore vigorously forward at a gallop, penetrating their columns, nearly the whole of which were killed, wounded, or taken.[25]

It would seem that the brigade attacked with six squadrons, two each of the three regiments, in echelon from the 5th Dragoon Guards on the left. Two squadrons were in reserve. Lieutenant Grattan was watching:

> The plain was filled with the vast multitude; retreat was impossible; and the troopers came still pouring in to join their comrades, already prepared for the attack. Hastily, yet with much regularity, all things considered, they attempted to get into square; but Le Marchant's brigade was forward before the evolution was half completed. The column hesitated, wavered, tottered, and then stood still! The motion of the countless bayonets as they clashed together might be likened to a forest about to be assailed by a tempest, whose first warnings announce the ravage it is about to inflict.

The destruction of the 66th Line was terrible, losing almost 50 per cent of its 1,100 strength killed, wounded or taken prisoner. The 86th on the right of Maucune's second line escaped relatively lightly with 200 casualties. The cavalry continued to advance:

> ... leaving the broken infantry to be made prisoners by the 3rd Division as they cleared the ground before them, to assist in which one squadron of the

Charge of the 5th Dragoon Guards. They had not yet received the new 1812 helmet or uniform.

4th Dragoons was for the moment detached. They presently came upon another column, however, of about 600 men, who brought down some men and horses by their fire, but attempted no stand of any consequence, and, falling into confusion, were left as before to be captured by the advancing infantry ... The conflict was severe, and the troopers fell thick and fast; but their long heavy swords cut through bone as well as flesh. The groans of the dying, the cries of the wounded, the roar of the cannon, and the piteous moans of the mangled horses, as they ran away affrighted from the terrible scene, or lay with shattered limbs, unable to move, in the midst of the burning grass, was enough to unman men not placed as we were; but upon us it had a different effect, and our cheers were heard far from the spot where this fearful scene was acting.

At some point before the Heavy Brigade outdistanced the infantry, the 2nd Battalion, 44th Foot was at hand when two squadrons of the 5th Dragoon Guards rode down a body of the 62nd Line of Thomières' division. The regimental historian recorded:

The French officer who carried the eagle had just wrenched it from the pole, and when Lieutenant Pearce first saw it, he was endeavouring to conceal it under the grey greatcoat, which he wore over his uniform; Private (afterwards Sergeant) Finley aided in the capture, and the French officer making resistance, was assisted by one of his men, who attacking Lieutenant Pearce with his fixed bayonet, was shot dead by Private Bill Murray, of the 44th light company. Privates Blackburn and Devine, of the same company, had also a hand in this affair, and Lieutenant Pearce divided twenty dollars – all the money he had with him – amongst the four, for their gallant exertions.

The cavalry now advanced well ahead of most of the battalions of the two infantry divisions, who with the squadron of dragoons were rounding up the prisoners and

The Eagle of the 62nd Line captured by the 44th East Essex Regiment.

A halberd and pennant carried by the escort to the Eagle of the 62nd Line.

re-forming lines to hold their gains. The 7th Division, no longer under fire, remained in support. Meanwhile, as the cavalry pursued the enemy south:

> The nature of the ground, which was an open wood of evergreen oaks, and which grew more obstructed as they advanced, had caused the men of the three regiments of cavalry to become a good deal mixed in each other's ranks; and the front being at the same time constantly changing as the right was brought forward, the whole had now crowded into a solid line, without any intervals.

Captain Bragge of the 3rd Dragoons in a letter home wrote: 'Our brigade literally rode over the regiments in their front and dashed through the wood at a gallop, the infantry cheering us in all directions. We quickly came up with the French columns ... it was impossible to see for dust and smoke.'

Meanwhile, in the true manner of a Napoleonic cavalry commander, Le Marchant led the fighting from the front. His biographer noted that

> The General himself had some narrow escapes. He fought like a private soldier, and as many as six men fell by his hand. It was only after a fierce struggle that the French yielded, and the General had the satisfaction of seeing them fly before him in dismay and confusion.

An officer of heavy dragoons dressed and equipped for campaign.

Their single mass of cavalrymen:

> without any confusion, pressed rapidly forward upon another French brigade,[26] which, taking advantage of the trees, had formed a *colonne serrée*,[27] and stood awaiting their charge. These men reserved their fire with much coolness till the cavalry came within twenty yards, when they poured it in upon the concentrated mass of men and horses with a deadly and tremendous effect. The gallant General Le Marchant, with Captain White, of his staff, were killed; Colonel Elley[28] was wounded; and it is thought that nearly one-third of the dragoons came to the ground; but as the remainder retained sufficient command of their horses to dash forward, they succeeded in breaking the French ranks, and dispersing them in utter confusion over the field. At this moment Colonel Lord Edward Somerset, discovering five guns upon the left, separated from the brigade with one squadron, charged, and took them all.

It was the 5th Dragoon Guards that bore the brunt of the 22nd Line's volley and as the heavies' formations broke up in pursuit, General Le Marchant was killed as explained by Oman:

> Le Marchant endeavoured to keep a few men in hand, in order to guard against any attempt of the French to rally, but he had only about half a squadron of the 4th Dragoons[29] with him, when he came upon some companies which were beginning to re-form in the edge of the great wood. He led his party against them, and drove them back among the trees, where they dispersed. But at the moment of contact he was shot dead, by a ball which entered his groin and broke his spine. Thus fell an officer of whom great things had been expected by all who knew him, in the moment when he had just obtained and used to the full his first chance of leading his brigade in a general action.

The three regiments of the heavy brigade had by this time become intermingled: 'The officers rode where they could find places: but a good front, without intervals, was still maintained, and there was no confusion.'[30] The column that the dragoons had come up against was one of the battalions of the 22nd Line, the leading regiment of General Brenier's division, which having marched hard was just emerging from the forest to help Maucune's dissolving battalions.

This must have been the stage at which Wellington turned to General Cotton and said 'By God Cotton! I have never seen anything more beautiful in my life!' Out of sight, beyond the plateau, and unaware of the cumulative success of the attack, General D'Urban's Portuguese Horse were still in the fighting. The general wrote:

> We were so far in their rear that masses of their routed infantry (to our astonishment as we did not know the cause) in the wildness of their panic and confusion and throwing away their arms, actually ran against our

An engraving of Le Marchant wearing a Tarleton helmet of the light dragoons.

horses, where many of them fell down exhausted and incapable of further movement.

Following behind D'Urban's heavies and heading to the right were Anson's Light Brigade[31] of three regiments of light cavalry. Colonel Money wrote:

> The rapid move of the cavalry which now began to gallop, and the 3rd Division pressing them, they ran into the wood, which separated them from the army; we charged them under a heavy fire of musketry and artillery from another height; near two thousand threw down their arms in different parts of the wood, and we continued our charge through the wood until our

brigade came into an open plain of ploughed fields, where the dust was so great we could see nothing, and halted; when it cleared away, we found ourselves within three hundred yards of a large body of French infantry and artillery, formed on the declivity of a hill. A tremendous battle was heard on the other side, which prevented the enemy from perceiving us. At last, they opened a fire of musketry and grapeshot, and we retired in good order and without any loss.

The heavies were not, however, entirely unopposed, as evidenced by Lieutenant Norcliffe's post-battle letter home:

We were pursuing the French Infantry, which were broken and running in all directions. I was cutting them down as well as I could, when in the hurry and confusion I lost my regiment and got with some soldiers of the 5th Dragoon Guards; on looking behind me, I could only see a few of the 5th, and we were in the centre of the enemy's infantry, amongst whom were a few chasseurs and dragoons. Nothing now remained but to go on, as we were in as much danger as by going any other way.

I rode up to a French officer, who was, like the rest, taking to his heels, and cut him just behind the neck; I saw the blood flow, and he lost his balance, and fell from his horse. I perceived my sword was giving way in the handle, so I said to the officer who lay on the ground: '*Donnez-moi votre épée*' – I really believed he was more frightened than hurt; I sheathed my sword and went on with his. I had not gone 10 yards further before my horse was wounded in the ear by a gunshot; he turned sharp round, and at the same instant I was shot in the head. I turned giddy and fell off. I can recollect a French dragoon taking away my horse. I was senseless a few seconds, and when I recovered, I saw the French dragoons stripping me of everything; they began by turning my pockets inside out, to look for money which they stole; my sword and sash, hat, boots, and spurs off my feet, dragging me along the ground in the most barbarous manner ... At last I was left by the cavalry, and the French infantry came all round me, and I expected the same treatment. Judge of my surprise, when I experienced quite the contrary: '*Courage, mon ami.*' I asked for water, being very faint from loss of blood ... Presently an officer came up with five; each took a leg and an arm, and the fifth supported my head, which was bleeding profusely, and I will say I never saw men more careful; if ever I groaned, owing to the pain of being carried, they said to each other: '*Gardez-vous, gardez-vous, camarade.*' They carried me into the very centre of the French column.

One, Colonel of Grenadiers, poured some brandy into a cup and wanted me to drink it; I just wet my lips. He then ordered five grenadiers to fall out and carry me further into the wood. I made a sign that I had rather be carried by the men who brought me there, fearful of falling into fresh hands. Our infantry was at the time advancing again to the attack; the five men who carried me were desired by all the French officers to take particular care that no-one ill-used me, and that if I could not get away, I was to be laid under a tree. The five men seeing our infantry advance, laid me down very carefully under an olive tree, and each of them shook hands with me before they left me, and said: '*Je vous souhaite bien, Monsieur*', and they also desired that I would remember they belonged to the 65th Regiment.

The cavalry pursuit ended in the wood, but for the French it was now a matter of the four unbroken regiments of Thomières, Maucune and now Brenier's divisions extricating themselves. In this they were aided by General Curto's

A mounted officer of the 3rd Dragoons.

The 1st Hussars of the King's German Legion fought under their commander Colonel Arentschildt.

chasseurs, which had been rallied and reinforced by their second brigade. Consequently, the allies had opposition.

Further back and to the west, Colonel Arentschildt and D'Urban's brigades were rounding up prisoners when they were attacked by Curto's troopers. In one recorded incident, two squadrons of the 3rd French Hussars charged the 1st KGL Hussars and were only beaten off 'after severe combat' during which Arentschildt rallied his hussars, along with some Portuguese and troopers of the 14th Light Dragoons.

Meanwhile, the 3rd and 5th divisions were re-forming a line, having advanced and pursued the enemy for somewhat over a mile; meanwhile, to their left the course of the battle was not so straightforward.

The French Soldier

Unlike their British counterparts, the majority of French soldiers were conscripts. Introduced during the Republic, men between the ages of 20 and 25 were eligible for military service, with each department assembling the men once a year to draw numbers to keep its associate regiment(s) up to strength. Those with the lowest numbers were automatically selected for service and those in the middle were put on a reserve list. By 1812 the qualifying age had been lowered and in times of manpower crisis, ballots would be held more frequently and, particularly after the disasters of 1812, even younger age groups would be eligible for ballot as well. The almost continuous wars from the revolution onwards had made serving in the army increasingly unpopular and there was wholesale avoidance, necessitating sweeps of the country to round up *refractaires*.

As in all armies, the majority of underdeveloped and underfed youths found the demands of marching long distances with heavy loads extremely taxing. Of those soldiers who became worn down or sick, few were lucky to reach a hospital and stragglers who fell out from the ranks were particularly vulnerable to murder in the peninsula.

The French conscripts invariably fought alongside veteran officers, NCOs and men who provided a knowledgeable steadying example on campaign and in battle. This cadre of veterans was, however, regularly raided to supply a burgeoning Imperial Guard with manpower, which had a detrimental effect on the quality of *ligne* battalions. Once acclimatized to war in the peninsula, French soldiers earned the respect of their enemy. Private Mills of the Coldstream Guards wrote:

> Their movements compared with ours are as mail coaches to dung carts. In all weathers and at all times they are accustomed to march when our men would fall sick by hundreds ... Another peculiar excellence of the French soldier is their steadiness in manoeuvring under fire.'

Even with magazines and some supply convoys, French soldiers had to live off the land and after years of experience, veterans leading foraging parties could find even the most carefully concealed cache of food and drink. However, near starvation was not uncommon.

A pair of centre company fusiliers. The man on the right wears the simplified 1812 infantry uniform coat and the new shako plate.

Even though pay for all armies was perennially scarce, for the French, being in a hostile country, taking food and looting was the normal state of affairs as this paragraph from a soldier's letter indicates:

> Do not send money until I say otherwise because as soon as we take a city we eat all its food. Then, we use either bayonets or cannons to take another one. We care about nothing. It is true that we sometimes receive food, but we are the masters everywhere. We fight bad soldiers. The priests lead the armies. The greatest evil comes from the monasteries and the churches. They *foutre* [f**k] with their muskets from the windows. They have cannons in the bell towers. We cannot fight them in the field as we would. They are only capable of hiding. Despite this misery, I hope that God will save me.

As intimated above, the guerrillas, an almost ever-present hidden enemy, were a source of frustration for French soldiers and contributed significantly to the unpopularity of the war in their minds.

A French grenadier company advancing with arms supported.

Chapter Eight

The Centre

In the centre of the battlefield General Lowry Cole's 4th Division was not as fortunate as the 5th, which was fighting to their right. Thanks to having Anson's brigade detached, and until relieved committed to holding the Lesser Arapile, Lowry faced a challenge in opposing both Bonet's and Clausel's divisions. They were, however, supported by General Hope's 6th Division, which had been moved across from its overnight position near the Santa Marta ford and, unlike the other division supporting the centre, General Hope's 7th and Clinton's 6th would be heavily committed to battle during the afternoon.

The French 120th Regiment still held the Greater Arapile and the 122nd also remained in its outlying position on the Teso del Judío, originally linking Bonet and Maucune.[1] Both regiments were supported by the remaining six battalions of Bonet's division, which were tucked away south of the Greater Arapile; largely out of sight but well-positioned to intervene against attacks to either east or west of the feature. By this time General Clausel had arrived and deployed his division on the ridge to the right of Maucune. General Ferey was also marching his division towards the centre, from its morning position near Calvarrasa de Arriba. General Foy and his men remained around the Nuestra Señora de la Peña, where they continued skirmishing with the 95th Rifles. The final French division, Sarrut's, having marched through the woods from Alba de Tormes was approaching the rear of Clausel's division (see map on following page).

The fighting in the centre began sometime after that on Wellington's right and centre right, with one source stating it was 1745 hours. The 4th Division was delayed in its move forward, having to thread their way through Arapiles, which had been set on fire by French shell fire, in file before forming up on the south side of the village. Colonel Charles Vere, the division's assistant quartermaster general, wrote that the lines were formed 'upon their Sergeants regularly sent out and then the line advanced in great order and regularity, under a heavy fire from the enemy's guns'.[2] The three battalions of the Fusilier Brigade were formed on the right and the four battalions of Stubbs' Portuguese Brigade on the left. The lines were covered by a thick screen of skirmishers, the whole of the 7th Caçadores on the left and on the right, commanded by Captain von Wachholtz, the three light companies of the Fusilier Brigade and one of the Brunswick Oels.

Colonel Vere recorded that as the division advanced on General Clause's position, they came under heavy artillery fire:

> General Cole ordered the skirmishers to fall into the line as it came up to them. But as an attack, which Brigadier General Pack was to make upon the

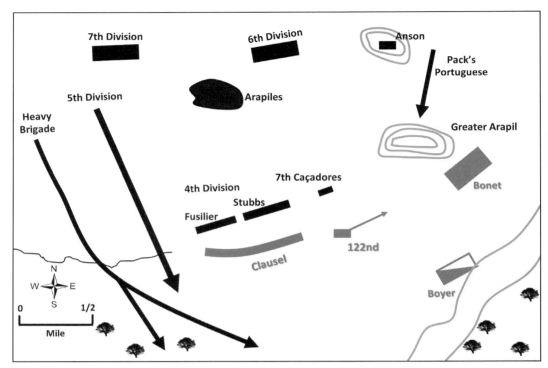

The advance of the 4th Division.

highest Arapile, had not taken place at that time; and the left of the Portuguese [Stubbs'] Brigade of the 4th Division, by its forward movement became exposed to interruption by the troops of the enemy from behind the Arapile; the [7th] Caçadores attached to the division, were directed to keep on the left flank of the line, as it moved forward, and to direct their attention towards any movement of the enemy on that side.

The further the 4th Division advanced, the greater became the hazard posed by the French guns on the Greater Arapile and Bonet's six uncommitted battalions. The march south, however, continued but with mounting casualties. Stubbs' Portuguese were first into action on the left, driving the 122nd Regiment off its isolated crest. The 7th Fusiliers' historian wrote of the division's first attack on Clausel's division:

> As the British columns advanced, they deployed into line, marching over heavy ploughed ground, through the storm of grape that smote them with deadly effect. This forward movement was splendidly maintained, sweeping all before it. The Fusiliers were in the front line; they stormed and carried a height upon which the French had thrown 30 guns into battery, and of these they captured eighteen.[3]

Colonel Vere noted that 'The enemy was forced by the 4th Division [some 200 yards] down the reverse of his position; but he collected, and rallied on the high ground beyond and parallel to it and re-opened his fire.'

Pack's Attack on the Greater Arapile

Meanwhile, Wellington had ordered General Pack, commander of the Portuguese Brigade to seize the fortress-like Greater Arapile as Bonet's division was advantageously positioned on the flank of the 4th Division's advance. Through their telescopes, the central section of the Greater Arapile appeared for most of its length less steep than the rocky extremities of the feature and presented a glacis-like avenue of attack. The 4th Caçadores were ordered forward to provide covering fire for the assault by the 100-strong storming party which was deployed in front of the four battalions of the 1st and 16th line. As Pack's brigade advanced from the cover of the Lesser Arapile's northern extremity it was immediately fired on by the French artillery that had hitherto been duelling with the British and KGL artillery on the Lesser Arapile.

Pack's major of brigade Captain George Charles Synge wrote the most detailed of any account of the battle, revealing the nature of the fighting and is therefore quoted at length:

> In a moment all the commanding officers were under way. As the General and I were riding to Major Fearon's storming party, he remarked that both on the right and left of the point of direction which the storming party were

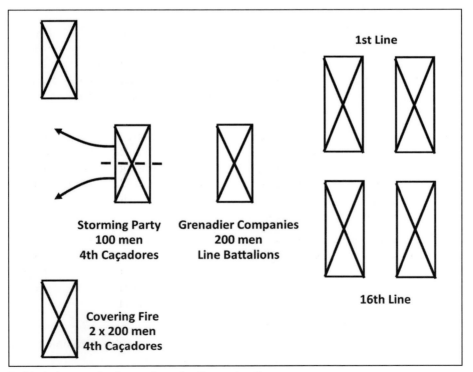

Pack's deployment for the attack on the Greater Arapile.

taking there appeared better openings to get to the top, and he added, 'I wish I had divided Fearon's party into two and sent half towards each of the openings, but it is too late now.' I said, 'Not if you choose to let me gallop at once and give him the order and allow me to take command of one.' He hesitated for a second, but on my repeating the offer and urging the necessity of my being off or it would be too late, he consented. I was soon up with Major Fearon. He took fifty to the left, and I the same number (not that we stopped to count) to the right. Immediately after this change, my direction led through a patch of standing rye, where several of my little party fell, at first I supposed killed, for the enemy opened their guns as soon as they saw what we were about; but one man near my horse fell in such a manner that it struck me it was sham, and as he lay on his face I gave him rather a sharp

Major General Denis Pack, commander of an independent Portuguese brigade.

prod with my sword – there was no time for any other appeal to his 'honour' – on which he turned up perfectly unhurt! What became of him afterwards I know not; I had other matters to think of … While I was appealing to feelings of all sorts and had just got through the last of the rye, Pack overtook me, and said in a whisper, 'Synge! I think those fellows won't carry it for you.' I said 'Oh! Yes, they will, we are over the worst of it.' I meant the ground. The roar of the enemy's guns was tremendous as we approached the top, and somewhat unusual in its sound, for they tried to depress the muzzles of their guns as much as possible, and though they could not do so much harm, so steep was it, it sounded as if it all but touched the top of our heads. I have never heard the like before. Those following in support fared worse.

The last part of the ascent was so steep that it was almost impossible for a horse to climb it; even the men did so with difficulty – but I had a horse that would do what scarcely any horse would attempt. It was not until I was close upon the summit that I knew what we had to contend with, for I found the ground, which had at a little distance the appearance of a gentle slope, formed a natural wall of I suppose between three and four feet high, at the top of which it spread out into a level table-land, on which the enemy were drawn up in line about ten yards from me. We looked at each other for a moment. I saw immediately that what we had undertaken was impracticable, as the men could not mount the scarped ground without first laying their arms upon the top, and even then, in such small numbers that it would be absurd – but I also saw that we were so easily covered by 'the wall', and

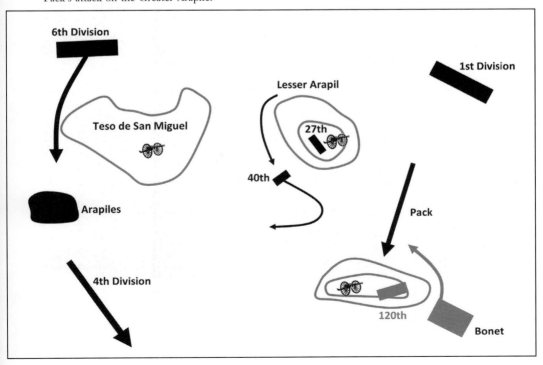

Pack's attack on the Greater Arapile.

the enemy so exposed from head to foot, that if we fired they could not remain an instant. At this critical moment, the head of Sir Noel Hill's column [1st Portuguese Line], which had followed me in support, was close up, and Hill himself called to me to ask what to do and what was before us (he could not see). I said, 'Be quick, and let your leading company close up to this bank and fire away while the others deploy as fast as they can and fire as they get up – the enemy are exposed and we are protected by this parapet.' To my horror Hill replied, 'You forget we are not loaded!' 'Well,' said I, 'we have no other chance. Load away as fast as you can.' He gave the word of command, and the men were in the act – I was addressing some few words of encouragement as well as the breathless state of anxiety I was in permitted (my poor old Ronald with great difficulty keeping his position on the steep), and two or three of the storming party were trying to scramble up the scarp, when the whole line opposed to us fired, knocked me over and literally cut to pieces the few that had climbed 'the wall'. My thigh was broken, and in falling, having no hold of the saddle, I could not in any manner save myself. Ronald made a couple of springs down the hill while I was falling, and this, together with the mangled bodies of those who fell back off the scarp on the head of Hill's column, which in the confusion of loading was unable to see what was happening above, caused a sensation of panic which was complete.

The French line followed up their volley by charging up the edge of the scarp, down which they leapt when they saw our confusion. Sir Neil Campbell's Grenadiers [16th Portuguese Line], the left column and all, went! – the disaster was complete. I had fallen to the ground on the near side of my horse, it being the left thigh that was broken, and was in great agony owing to a sort of instinctive effort to use the broken limb in which the marrow also seemed to be breaking. A gallant little fellow, an ensign, who was adjutant of Hill's Regiment, ran up to me and put his arms under mine to try to raise me, and if his strength had equalled his courage and goodwill,

The eastern face of the Greater Arapile attacked by Pack's brigade.

The rocky lip that brought the Portuguese attack to a halt.

he would have carried me off, but he was of the smallest stature. I told him that my thigh was broken, and that it was of no use. The bayonets of the charging army were all but touching him before I could persuade him to save himself, and I actually pushed him away. A lot of the French ran over where I was, and amongst them an officer, cheering them on. As he passed over me, seeing me twirling about in frightful agony owing to the position in which I had fallen, he called out at the appalling spectacle my state exhibited. '*Oh! Mon Dieu!*' and then asked, '*Est-ce-que vous etes Anglais?*'[4] I said, 'Yes,' and he pointed to a man by his side as he ran by and told him to save me. The man, who I suppose was a non-commissioned officer, did stop for a second or two, which perhaps saved my life. Some of the enemy then began to plunder those who had fallen, wounded, dying or dead, and several began at me. I was in Hussar uniform, and worse all my riches about me, with some smart things about my neck, which there was a scramble for. Most foreign soldiers, at least such as I have known, conceal their money in the waistband of the dress or inside the leg of the boot. To see if I had any such store some began cutting my clothes off, as you might have seen a sheep in the act of being shorn, and one began to pull off my boots. This was horrid, for my overalls were fastened down by curb-chain piping, and the attempt to get the boot off the broken limb was intolerable. I was soon left to go out of the world nearly as naked as I had first entered it.

Just then my attention was called from my own state to a fine young fellow of the 1st Grenadiers, who was defending himself with his musket against four or five men who surrounded him, and who were all trying to bayonet him. I called to them to spare him as he was now their prisoner. Someone, who I believe was in authority, thought I wanted something for myself, and seemed disposed to ascertain what I stood in need of, but when he learnt I was appealing for the young Portuguese sergeant, he turned away. 'Oh! As for these *canaille!*' was all I heard, and how it ended I do not know, for I myself became an object of the same sort of extinguishers. Suddenly they were called off to re-form on their original position on the top of the Arapiles, and I and the bodies of my comrades were left to our fate.[5]

Clausel's Counter-Attack

'Clausel made a surprising effort, beyond all men's expectations, to restore the battle.' [Major William Napier, 43rd Light Infantry]

With Clausel's first line battalions having re-formed behind the second, Vere noted that

> At this moment, it became evident that the danger to which the left of the line of the two brigades of the 4th Division was exposed, in their forward movement, had not been lightly estimated. General Pack had attempted to gain the height opposite to him (the highest Arapile) and failed – and the left battalion [7th Caçadores] of the Portuguese Brigade of the 4th Division, had been arrested in its forward movement to the plain, by a movement of the enemy from behind the Arapile upon it; and it was now engaged with the enemy, about halfway from the heights from which the enemy had been driven and the remainder of the line ... This detached battalion struggled gallantly against very superior forces, but it was overwhelmed and broken; and it suffered much from the French cavalry.

With Bonet attacking the 4th Division's left flank, Clausel's second line joined the counter-attack on the 4th Division along with Boyer's eight squadrons of dragoons. Attacked by a combination of infantry and cavalry, the 7th Caçadores were inevitably, as Vere recorded, broken but as they ran being sabred by the dragoons, panic spread along the line from Stubbs' brigade to the Fusiliers. Here, according to Napier, 'the French came up resolutely without firing a shot.' Lieutenant Cameron of the 7th Fusiliers wrote:

> We were at this moment ordered by Colonel Beatty[6] to retire and form square, a most hazardous movement when the enemy's Infantry were advancing, and within thirty yards of us. The order was only partially heard and obeyed on the right, while on the left we kept up a hot fire on the enemy, who were advancing uphill, and within a few yards of us. The companies on our right having retired in succession we found ourselves alone, but the ground the enemy were ascending was so steep that we got off without loss and joined the rest. Luckily while we were forming square to receive the cavalry, the 6th Division came up and received the charge intended for us.

With Thomières and Brenier's divisions to his right defeated by Pakenham and Leith and being harried off the field by the British cavalry, Clausel's decision to launch a counter-attack was bold and opportunistic. He could have with all honour withdrawn to the woods, but as Oman and others have observed, Clausel's counter-attack is an example of how dangerous Napoleon's generals could be in adversity.

Vere continued his account:

> During these reverses, and under favour of them, the enemy had moved a large body of his force against the left of the line of the 4th Division that had gained the enemy's position; and nearly at the same time, as that of the overthrow of the Portuguese Battalion in the plain; drove the line of the division from the position and recovered it.

Major Scott Lillie of the 7th Caçadores described the situation:

> I happened to be at the time with some companies of the Caçadores and the 40th Regiment ... This was one of the few occasions on which I saw the

Clausel's counter-attack.

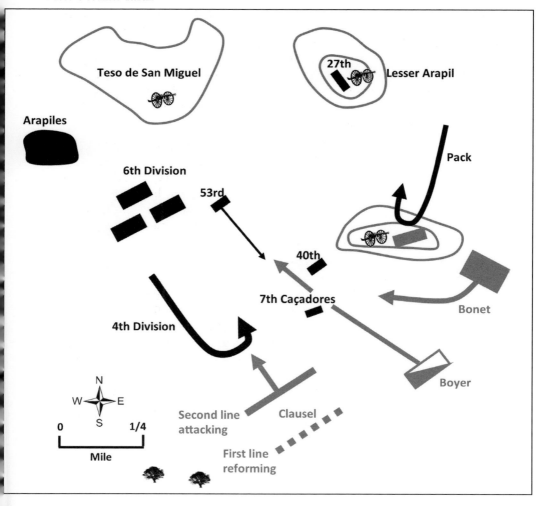

The blue coated uniform of a Portuguese line infantryman. Much of it and his equipment was supplied by Britain.

A Caçadore soldier in this example from a musket-armed company. He wears a uniform similar in style to that of the British riflemen.

bayonet used; the 40th under the late Colonel Archdall, having come into close contact with Bonet's French brigade in consequence of this movement, which was directed by General William Anson in person; he was moving on with the 40th, leaving the [Greater Arapile] on his left and in his rear, on which a corps moved from behind the hill in rear of the 40th for the purpose of attacking it, the regiment being at the time engaged in front. I happened to be between the 40th and the enemy and rode after the former to tell Colonel Archdall of his situation, on which he wheeled round and charged the enemy's column with the bayonet and this terminated the contest at that point.[7]

Bonet's battalions and Boyer's dragoons fell on the Portuguese and the 40th Foot to the left of the Fusilier Brigade; some managed to form square before the cavalry brushed past them and they were then confronted by Bonet's troops as described by Scott Lillie. Despite 'terminating the contest' with Boyer's infantry, losses to the 40th were significant, losing 128 officers and men killed and wounded.[8] According to Vere the Portuguese 'suffered much from the French Cavalry, which continued to advance, till met and checked by the 53rd regiment'. This regiment belonged to the 6th Division, which was advancing some distance behind the 4th Division and with both of Cole's brigades in line there were no reserves to support the 7th Caçadores. Consequently, the 53rd of General Hulse's brigade had been sent forward to be their supports. Their commanding officer, Lieutenant Colonel Bingham,[9] writing two days after the battle, described that having just arrived, the Portuguese:

> gave way, and our left was uncovered just as the French gained a temporary advantage on our right. In this situation, unsupported, we were attacked by the enemy's Heavy Dragoons; we retired in good order, in line, and twice stopped their advance by halting and firing. At last, a circular rocky hill, about two hundred yards in the rear, offered an advantage; I determined to profit by it; the Dragoons being too near, and the ranks too much thinned to attempt a square, we made a dash for the hill. The dragoons came thundering on the rear and reached the hill just as our people faced about. The fire checked them, and it was soon obvious they would make no impression. At this moment I saw a part of the Regiment which had not reached the rock, running down the hill in great confusion, without however being pursued by the Dragoons. Giving the charge of the hill to Mansell, I dashed through the dragoons, who made way for me, and succeeded in rallying the men round the regimental colour that I had with me. The several attacks of the dragoons on the mass failed, although at one time they seized the end of the king's colour, and there was a struggle who should have it; when a sergeant of grenadiers wrested it from the Dragoon who held it, or rather tore the silk from the pole, which I rather think remained with the enemy; at the same time our people gained ground on the right, and the dragoons retired in confusion. They would not have been with us so long had not our men been almost left without ammunition.[10]

An impression of French dragoons.

Major Frederick Newman of the 11th Foot recorded that they were also approached by Boyer's dragoons:

> The brigade now advanced in line, and when we rose the hill a body of French cavalry was coming up at a hard canter, either to cover their retreating infantry, or to put a finishing hand to the 4th Division; we at once halted and gave them a volley which sent these cavaliers to the right-about in much quicker time than they came, leaving several horses and men on the ground.

The 11th and 61st contributed to Boyer's defeat, but it was the 53rd that lost most heavily and the reorganized remnant only rejoined the action later. The 6th Division was, however, criticized by the 4th for being slow to arrive in their support, but the same delaying factor of getting round Arapiles applied to the 6th Division as it had to the 4th in their advance. Hulse's brigade, for instance, passed to the east and west of the village in column of companies.

It was probably during this period that General Cole was also wounded and General Anson took command of the 4th Division. Fortunately, Marshal Beresford was present in the centre and ordered Spry's Portuguese Brigade forward,

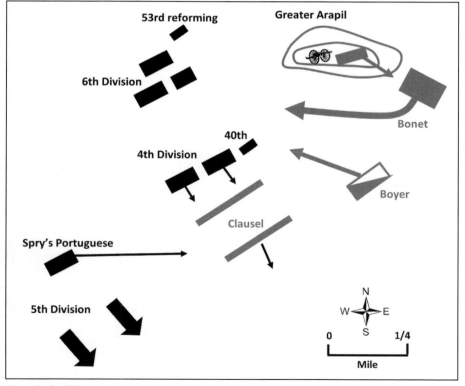

Clausel rebuffed.

being the 5th Division's uncommitted reserve. Lieutenant Browne of Wellington's staff recalled that

> The Portuguese Brigade of the 5th Division from being on the left took these Battalions of the enemy completely in flank; but there was so much hallooing that instead of charging they began firing which was as dangerous to the British as to the French. Marshal Beresford & his staff put a stop to this firing, & he was making a disposition to charge the enemy in flank, which these Regiments, the 3rd & 15th Portuguese were not very willing to try – a few companies made a sort of shabby charge which these French troops would scarcely have regarded but that the 4th Division again attacked & the 5th took them in rear.

In encouraging his troops, Beresford was severely wounded. Captain Warre, one of Beresford's ADCs recalled that

> It was near sunset, and in endeavouring to make a Portuguese brigade charge the enemy (who were driving the 4th Division back with five battalions) in flank, that our excellent marshal was wounded, while exerting himself, as he always does with the greatest zeal and gallantry, and by his noble example, to cover the 4th Division by this flank charge.

The sight of Spry's brigade and elements of the 3rd and 5th divisions marching towards the flank of Clausel's division was enough to halt the French battalions on the left, where the regiments halted and threw back a defensive flank. Colonel Burgoyne wrote of the Fusilier Brigade's recovery:

> No sooner had they arrived at the bottom, than they came to their senses, and were furious with themselves for having allowed the enemy to gain the advantage. In about five minutes, they were formed in perfect order at a short distance below, and they then re-ascended the hill most gallantly, and drove the French down the other side as quickly as they themselves had been driven before.

With Clausel's division thrown back, further left, the rest of the 6th Division was coming into action, but despite advancing at the double south of Arapiles, they were too late to provide immediate assistance. The French infantry were so mingled with Stubbs' men that the 61st South Gloucester Regiment had to be prevented from firing for fear of hitting friends as well as the enemy. Major Newman of the 11th Foot recalled:

> At the time our brigade advanced in contiguous columns ascending a rising ground, you may recollect that just before we reached the top the 4th Division came over it in a state of disorder, the enemy [122nd Line] closed upon them, the French officers in advance, and actually making use of their swords against our retreating men: our brigade was immediately halted and began to deploy. By the time three companies had formed, the portion of the

Colonel John Burgoyne of the Royal Engineers.

4th Division opposite to the 11th passed round the right flank; these companies at once opened their fire and swept away nearly the whole of those officers; this checked them, and after some firing, they turned about and fled.[11]

Meanwhile, beneath the Greater Arapile Bonet's battalions including the 122nd renewed their attack on to the high ground of the Teso del Judío where Hulse's brigade (11th and 61st) stood and attacked 'impetuously'. One theory for this was that both battalions had only recently received their annual clothing issue, the 61st the day before. Therefore, they did not present the normal washed-out pink hue of British uniforms in the days before colourfast dyes. Consequently, the French reputedly thought they were militia or newly-arrived and therefore unseasoned troops. The French battalions were, however, greeted by a steady line, a volley, three cheers and a charge with, as Cannon described, 'so much resolution that the torrent of battle was arrested, and, after a desperate effort, the French were overpowered, and the hill was re-captured.'

Having driven the enemy from the crest, Hulse's battalions were ordered to halt and to 're-form the line'. Bonet's battalions similarly re-formed and the 11th and the 61st were ordered to attack. As the lines approached each other they both fired volleys, but the British battalions, 'unstoppable', continued to advance until they were given the order 'Charge bayonets'. At this point the French wavered and, knowing what the 'Hurrah' meant, they broke and ran. The 61st's historian wrote that 'In this second charge the two corps drove the enemy in their front across the plain more than halfway from the Arapile to the heights of Alba de Tormes [*sic*, Peñas Águeda ridge].'[12]

Captain Harry Ross-Lewin of the 32nd Foot (Hinde's brigade) later commented that 'As we advanced, we marched over a brigade lying on the ground.' Lieutenant Smith of the 11th wrote that

> The advance of the brigade was so rapid, that very many of a body of riflemen [tirailleurs], more numerous than the British, covering the retreat

A miniature portrait of an officer of the 11th North Devonshire Regiment.

of the main body of the defeated enemy, had not time to get out of our way, threw themselves on the ground as dead, and were run over. It was known that many of them fired at the back of the advancing line. One, it is certain, drove his bayonet through the back of a grenadier of the 11th, and before he could withdraw it, he was cut down by Brigade Major Cotton who was following the regiment on foot, his horse having been killed, and in that position both lay dead.

With the pursuit of Bonet having reached the foot of the ridge crowned by the French rearguard, the 6th Division's advance came to a halt under fire. Major Newman, who had taken over command of the 11th when Lieutenant Colonel Cuyler was wounded, wrote:

> During this time their artillery played incessantly on us with shot and shell by which I lost about forty men; and the loss increased so fast by their getting

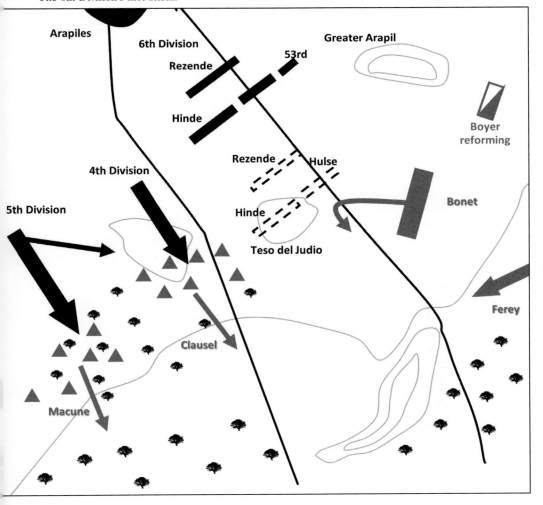

The 6th Division's first attack.

the range that I told Hulse something should be done, either in retiring or by the line lying down. The latter he agreed to, and we hardly had a casualty after.[13]

The crisis in the centre had seen the 4th Division, weakened by the storm of Badajoz just three months earlier, checked and the French thrown back, having been attacked in turn by one of Wellington's reserve divisions, the 6th, and Spry's Portuguese. Napier summarized: '... the allies righting itself as a gallant ship after a sudden gust, again bore onwards in blood and gloom through ... one vast cloud of smoke and dust that rolled along the basin, and within it was the battle with all its sights and sounds of terror.'

An officer of the 11th Foot's Grenadier comapny dressed and accoutered for campaign.

Chapter Nine

End of the Battle

While Clausel and Bonet launched their counter-attack, Ferey's fresh division and Sarrut's command, which had struggled to contain the 3rd and 5th divisions, plus the unbroken parts of Maucune's division, formed on the wooded ridge a mile to the rear of the action. The remnants of Boyer's dragoons and Curto's chasseurs re-formed and covered the flanks. These positions stood astride the routes from the centre of the battlefield to Alba de Tormes and the fords of Huerta and Encinas. Foy, also a key component of the rearguard, remained on the French right sparring with the Light Division's riflemen.

The centrepiece of Clausel's rearguard, astride the road to Alba de Tormes a few hundred yards in advance of the woods, was Ferey's fresh division, but the remainder was largely made up of infantry that had not hitherto been very heavily engaged. Of these regiments the 15th *Ligne* had been involved in Maucune's route but was largely intact, while Sarrut's men had marched some 10 miles to join the battle and had fought the 3rd and 5th divisions. Other regiments thickened up the line, but the cavalry after its earlier fighting was probably not fit for offensive action. The role of the rearguard was to allow the broken French regiments to march hard through the woods, the 7 miles to the Alba de Tormes bridge and safety.

During this period General Clausel had taken command of the Army of Portugal when General Bonet had also been wounded, but it was not long before he too was forced to quit the field with a wound. Fortunately for the now leaderless French, this was not until Clausel's clear and concise orders to establish a rearguard had been effected.

At this stage Wellington ordered the 1st Division to attack with the intention of turning the flank of the new French position and possibly cutting off the direct line of retreat to Alba de Tormes. For unexplained reasons the message either did not reach General Campbell or he failed to act on it as intended. He advanced towards the Greater Arapile apparently at a 'leisurely pace', possibly reluctant to proceed further until he was sure that the French 120th *Ligne* had abandoned it. Consequently the division for the time being simply acted as a link between the Light Division and the main body of the army in the centre.

The rest of Wellington's plan was for the 6th Division to attack the Peña de Águeda ridge supported by the Fusilier Brigade on its left and parts of the 3rd and 5th divisions to the right, while further to the left the Light Division was to attack the heights around Nuestra Señora de la Peña. The 7th Division and General d'España's Spanish plus, *de facto*, the 1st Division were his reserve. The allied

188   *Salamanca Campaign, 1812*

Simpkin's portrayal of the uniform of the 32nd before the issue of the 1812 Pattern uniform.

cavalry were at this point re-forming following their epic charges and only able to play a limited part.

Regrouping for the attack, however, took time. As already recorded, the 6th Division, which had pursued the French to the foot of the ridge, where 'They were then ordered by General Hulse to sit down, being within range of a dozen pieces of artillery and a brigade of infantry. In this situation they remained for nearly three-quarters of an hour.' While the other brigades deployed on their flanks, the fire endured by the division was not only from tirailleurs but from French guns which were probably distributed in sections of two along the defensive front.[1]

According to Cannon in his history of the 11th Foot during this time:

> A round shot (probably fired at the colours), took the heads off the two serjeants,[2] posted between the colours, and of a black man who beat the cymbals in the band, and who was in rear of them, without injuring either of the officers carrying the colours; one of them (Ensign Scott) was afterwards killed. So fast did the men fall, that it appeared as if not one would be left; it was remarked with what steadiness the men closed [ranks], without orders, to the centre as vacancies continually took place, the supernumeraries were soon disposed of.

Consequently it is claimed that General Clinton could not wait for the flanking brigades to be fully formed and, in the gathering darkness, ordered his men to their feet and the advance to begin, apparently ignoring Pakenham's warnings not to do so until his troops had turned the enemy's left flank. Colonel Vere of Headquarters 4th Division wrote:

> The brigade of the 6th division, under General Hulse, was ordered by Lord Wellington to attack the right of the enemy in his new position, and the Fusilier Brigade of the 4th division, commanded by Lieutenant Colonel Wilson of the 48th Regiment, was moved forward to the attack, on the left of General Hulse's Brigade.

Major General Sir Henry Clinton.

Ahead of the 6th Division, Ferey had deployed his nine battalions on the uneven crest of the ridge in a single three-deep line that was almost a mile long, with those at either extremity formed in square.

General Clinton inserted Brigadier General Conde de Rezende's Portuguese between Hinde's on the right and Hulse's on the left. As there was a relatively short distance to advance, Brigadier Hinde elected to group his three light companies on his right flank which was largely open.

Grattan of the Connaught Rangers watched the 6th Division's attack:

> It was nearly dark; and the great glare of light caused by the thunder of the artillery, the continued blaze of the musketry, and the burning grass, gave to the face of the hill a novel and terrific appearance: it was one vast sheet of flame, and Clinton's men looked as if they were attacking a burning mountain, the crater of which was defended by a barrier of shining steel.

Contributing significantly to the 'sheet of flame' were the allied guns firing obliquely from the left. The explosion of shells, burning wadding and cartridge paper from cannon, musket and rifle set the tinder-dry grass on fire and as the conflagration spread, blazing pines and oaks were added to the dramatic fiery backdrop.

Attack of Hinde's Brigade

Captain Ross-Lewin of the 32nd recalled that

> It was half-past seven when the 6th Division, under General Clinton, was ordered to advance a second time and attack the enemy's line in front ... The ground over which we had to pass was a remarkably clear slope, like the glacis of a fortification – most favourable for the defensive fire of the enemy, and disadvantageous to the assailants, but the division advanced towards the position with perfect steadiness and confidence. A craggy ridge, on which the French infantry was drawn up, rose so abruptly that they could fire four or five deep, but we had approached within two hundred yards of them before the fire of musketry began, which was by far the heaviest that I have ever witnessed, and was accompanied by constant discharges of grape. An uninterrupted blaze was then maintained, so that the crest of the hill seemed to be one long streak of flame. Our men came down to the charging position, and commenced firing from that level, at the same time keeping their touch to the right, so that the gaps opened by the enemy's fire were instantly filled up. At the very first volley that we received, about eighty men of the right wing of my regiment fell to the rear in one group; the commanding officer immediately rode up to know the cause and found that they were all wounded.

As Ross-Lewin recounted, the result of the advance was that along the whole of the 6th Division's line a protracted and costly fire-fight began. General Clinton has been much criticized for this and has been contrasted with Pakenham's eschewing volley fire and going straight in with the bayonet. There were, however, significant differences in the situation: Pakenham had to capitalize on surprise and numbers against Thomières' division, which was strung out. The 6th Division was, however, far from fresh and already much reduced in strength, as well as facing a well-formed French division in its first action of the day. In addition, winning the fire-fight before attacking was a key part of the British approach to battle during the period. When that indefinable moment which commanders could almost feel came, it was time to advance and charge in with the bayonet. In Clinton's defence, it should be remembered that he needed to order the attack without waiting for the flanking formations to be properly formed.

When that moment came, the 2nd, 32nd and 36th foot attacked the left of Ferey's position held by the 70th *Ligne*. Captain Ross-Lewin recalled that

> as we moved on, one of the enemy's howitzers was captured by the light company of the 32nd regiment. It had been discharged once, but before the gunners could load it again, it was taken by a rush. The success of the attack was complete; for as soon as the sixth division got near enough, they dashed forward with the bayonet.

Ross-Lewin's brother Thomas, a lieutenant in his company, wrote a letter home from the battlefield which adds more information: 'We charged up a steep hill and carried it, and then advanced to another, which our Brigade also carried, driving the French columns before us and taking five pieces of cannon. Our Light Company had the honour of taking two guns.'

The attack on the Peña de Águeda ridge.

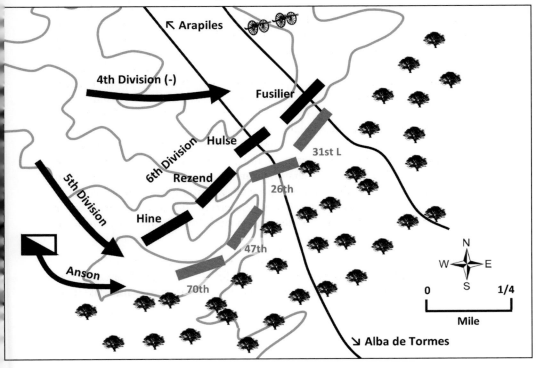

With French artillery distributed along the ridge, most battalions lay claim to capturing one or more pieces of cannon. The 70th *Ligne* fell back from the ridge to the edge of the wood, while Hinde's battalions re-formed.

Attack of Hulse's Brigade

With the 53rd still moving up to their rear, General Hulse only had two battalions with him which he ordered forward into the attack. The 61st's Digest reports that

> The Major General finding that the brigade was losing many men from the fire of the enemy called the COs of the Regiments to him to intimate his intention of attacking the hill in front ... [and told] them to make the same known to their respective corps. The communication was received by the two corps with an instantaneous shout of 'Yes, we will!' and three cheers.

Of the advance against defenders on the ridge, probably the 26th *Ligne*, Major Newman commanding the 11th wrote:

> The next advance of the 6th Division was to the attack of the French position. As soon as the French saw this, a cloud of their skirmishers came down to the foot of the hills forming their position, and as we neared them opened their fire, supported with terrible effect by their artillery with grape; however, the brigade kept moving on, and in spite of every obstacle carried the position. Not a shot was fired by the 11th until we reached the top, when we gave them a farewell discharge. By this time the loss of the 61st and 11th was most severe.[3]

Grattan again paints a vivid picture of the action:

> But nothing could stop the intrepid valour of the 6th Division, as they advanced with a desperate resolution to carry the hill. The troops posted on the face of it to arrest their advance were trampled down and destroyed at the first charge, and each reserve sent forward to extricate them met with the same fate.

Meanwhile, having gained the ridge and speeding the 26th *Ligne* off with that final volley, Newman could see that the Portuguese brigade to the right of the 11th was in difficulties. They were attacking the steepest and highest portion of the Peña de Águeda ridge, which enabled the French, probably the 47th *Ligne*, to hold their positions and eventually counter-attack in column. The 61st's Digest resumes the account: 'On the arrival of the brigade at the summit of the hill, the enemy again formed their troops into column [to attack the Portuguese] and faced a proportion of their files outward to receive the attack of the 11th and 61st who threatened their flank.' Major Newman continued:

> I saw this and proposed to Hulse to wheel up the 11th to their right and attack them in flank, but for the present he declined, thinking we were

too much reduced. After a while poor Bradford, the [Division's] assistant adjutant general, came up, and instantly went to the rear and brought up to our support a brigade of the 4th Division [Stubbs' Portuguese], which had been reformed; the 61st and 11th then changed their front to the right, and attacked this hill and carried it.[4]

At the time of Salamanca a drummer of the 11th Foot would have still worn a reversed colours regimental coat. In other words, the normal regimental green facing colour formed the body of the jacket, with the collars and cuffs being of madder red.

194 *Salamanca Campaign, 1812*

An officer's 11th Foot gilt button. Similar buttons have been recovered from the Salamanca battlefield. Such finds have enabled identification of the scene of Hulse's action on the Peña de Águeda ridge.

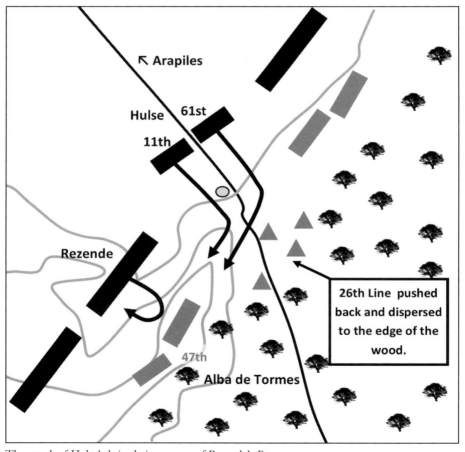

The attack of Hulse's brigade in support of Rezende's Portuguese.

End of the Battle 195

The 61st's Digest concludes: 'The two Regiments formed to the right, on the right file of the 11th and then opened their fire upon the column ... and soon compelled it to retire.' This cleared the majority of the Peña de Águeda ridge of French troops.

At some point during the fighting on the Peña de Águeda ridge the 11th captured a large green standard or colour on a pole with a point. It was assumed that it was of an Irish unit in French service, but none were involved in the action. With the Eagles being a regimental distinction carried by the 1st Battalion of a regiment,[5] coloured fanions were carried by other battalions for identification,

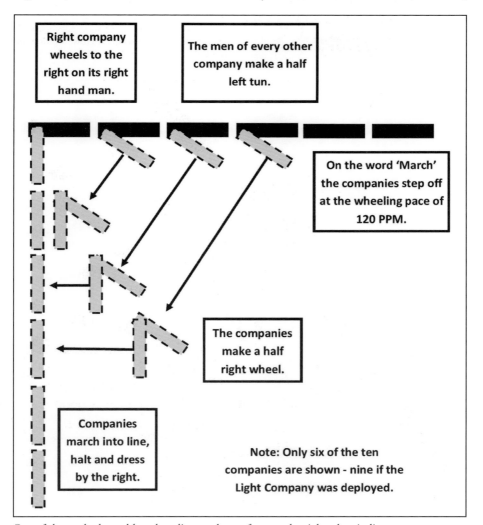

One of the methods used by a battalion to change front to the right when in line.

rallying, etc. Officially fanions were of plain colours to avoid them becoming trophies, but it is known that unofficial adornments were often added.[6] Although regulated in April 1812, it is likely that non-standard fanions were still present in French regiments in the peninsula 500 leagues from the emperor's eye! The battalion fanion captured by the 11th, one of two taken at Salamanca, was that of a junior battalion in one of Ferey's regiments, probably of either the 26th or 47th *Ligne*.

Along with their earlier action, the 11th had suffered grievous losses of no fewer than 340 men out of 516 and the 61st 366 from 546.[7]

The regimental adjutant was responsible for the battalions' fanions.

The Fusilier Brigade

The casualties in the Fusilier Brigade had thus far not been confined to the rank and file, with Lieutenant Colonel Ellis being wounded and command of the brigade falling upon Lieutenant Colonel Wilson. There was the same heavy French fire on the left of the British attack with the Fusilier Brigade facing two battalions of the 31st *Légère* Regiment. Captain Lemonnier-Delafosse recalled in his memoirs that 'The cruel fire cost us many lives. Then, slowly, having gained almost an hour's respite for the army, we retired, still protected by the squares.'[8] Of the attack, Colonel Vere recorded that

> The attack was spirited, and well executed. The Fusilier Brigade moved up the heights under a heavy fire, without returning a shot; and drove the enemy in its front, from his ground. The Brigade then brought up its left, for the purpose of assisting General Hulse, by a flank and raking movement. But the formation was no sooner effected, than the enemy [26th *Ligne* at the edge of the wood] gave way before the General [Hulse], and the defeat was completed. As the day had closed, the troops halted and picquets were pushed into the wood.

The Last Stand

Driven off the crest, back several hundred yards to the edge of the wood, the remnants of Ferey's division bravely made their last stand. So heavy had the casualties been in Hinde's and Hulse's brigades that the task of attacking was given to Stubbs' Portuguese. Raked by artillery fire from the right, according to Captain Lemonnier-Delafosse, the rearguard

> ... no longer with any artillery to help, saw the enemy marching up against us in two lines, the first of which was composed of Portuguese.[9] Our position was critical, but we waited for the shock: the two lines moved up toward us; their order was so regular that in the Portuguese regiment in front of us we could see the company intervals and note the officers behind keeping the men in accurate line, by blows with the flat of their swords or their canes. We fired first, the moment that they got within range: and the volleys which we delivered from our two first ranks were so heavy and so continuous that, though they tried to return fire for fire, the whole melted away. The second line was coming up behind – this was English, we should have tried to receive it in the same way, still holding our ground though under a flank fire of artillery, when suddenly the left of our line ceased firing and fell back into the wood in complete disorder.

This was caused by the arrival of leading elements of the 5th Division and Anson's light cavalry that outflanked the 70th *Ligne*, which panicked and fled into the woods. Lemonnier-Delafosse continued:

> The 70th *Ligne* had found its flank turned by cavalry; it broke; the rout spread down the front to the 26th and 47th; only our two battalions of the

Salamanca Campaign, 1812

31st *Légère* held firm, under the fire of the enemy, which continued so long as we showed outside the edge of the forest. We only withdrew as the day ended, retiring some 250 yards from our original position, and keeping our voltigeur companies still in a skirmishing line in front.

The 3rd Division, further to the right, was by the end of their earlier attack tired, much dispersed and in sore need of reorganization, which consequently delayed their participation in the attack on the ridge. Once they moved forward, they only did so at the speed to be expected of exhausted troops. As a result, Sarrut's

General Claude Ferey was mortally wounded leading his division's rearguard action.

Sketches of a carabinier and officer of the 31st *Légère*.

division and other 'steady' regiments and battalions that had been positioned as a westward extension of the rearguard were able to melt away into the forest.

The Advance of the Light Division

Wellington's divisions of the centre and right were ordered to pursue the French into the woods, but a combination of exhaustion and darkness prevented any great results being achieved. On the allied left, however, there were 2 miles of far more open country before reaching the woods and on this flank waited General von Alten's Light Division. For most of the day the officers and men of the division only had a distant view of the billowing clouds of smoke and dust, along with the sound of the thundering guns. Between 1800 and 1900 hours, however, William Prince of Orange, serving as an extra ADC to Wellington, rode up and ordered the Light Division 'to move on the left of the attack'. Facing them was General Foy's veteran division which had served in Marshal Ney's renowned VI Corps for many years.

William Prince of Orange served as an aide-de-camp to Wellington during the campaign.

The division initially advanced in battalion columns with, according to Lieutenant Browne, 'Ld. Wellington himself conducting the three divisions of our left, viz. the Light, First and Seventh.' As the Light Division crossed the valley, the columns deployed into line preceded by a thick screen of skirmishers, which drove in the French tirailleurs. 'The shades of evening were beginning to fall when the enemy made their last effort, amid flashes of cannon and small arms'. Ensign Hennell, who was carrying the regimental colour of the 43rd, recalled that

> Lord Wellington was within fifty yards of the front when the advance [skirmishers] commenced firing. As he passed the 43rd, he called out, 'Come, fix

your bayonets, my brave fellows', which they instantly obeyed, and were upon the point of charging, when the enemy, having fired a volley or two, which passed mostly over their heads, disappeared.

As Foy retired, the Light Division followed them past the chapel and on towards the village of Calvarrasa de Arriba and as Napier wrote, Foy threw

> out a cloud of skirmishers, [and] retired slowly by wings, turning and firing heavily from every rise of ground upon the light division, which marched steadily forward without returning a shot save by its skirmishers, and for two miles this march continued under musketry, which was occasionally thickened by a cannonade.

Lieutenant Cooke provides more information on the 43rd Light Infantry's part in the battle, which was certainly not uncontested:

> The enemy's light infantry increased and retired very deliberately; the ascent was gentle. The 1st Brigade deployed, supported by the 2nd. The 1st Division was marching in reserve. Our skirmishers were obliged to give ground to the obstinacy of the enemy, and nearly ceased firing. The line marched over them, dead and alive.
>
> Appearances indicated a severe fight, for we were near the enemy's reserves. The Earl of Wellington was within 50 yards of the front when the adverse lines commenced firing. He ordered us to halt within 200 yards of the enemy. They gave us two volleys with cheers, while our cavalry galloped forward to threaten their right flank. I heard that a musket ball perforated the

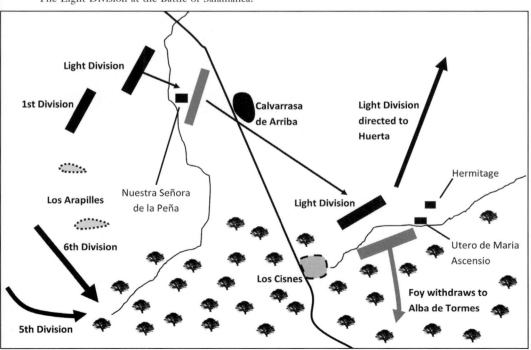

The Light Division at the Battle of Salamanca.

Earl's cloak, folded in front of his saddle. As we were about to charge, the enemy disappeared, not being in sufficient force to withstand the attack. This advance was beautifully executed. Night coming on, the firing died away.

Major William Napier was a witness to Wellington being hit by a spent musket ball:

> ... the Duke rode up alone behind my regiment, and I joined him; he was giving me some orders when a ball passed through his left holster and struck his thigh; he put his hand to the place, and his countenance changed for an instant, but only for an instant; and to my eager inquiry if he was hurt, he replied sharply, 'No!' and went on with his orders. Whether his flesh was torn or only bruised, I know not.

As the pursuit developed, only the division's artillery and skirmishers were seriously engaged and only the latter came into close contact with the enemy, as they followed Foy's battalions through the scrub. Sergeant Whitehead wrote in his account that at

> About 6 o'clock we limbered up to the right and galloped off some distance when an order was given to change left in front by right flank; this done we formed line for action at 500 yards, firing 7 or 8 rounds a gun. Limbered up to front advancing at the gallop ... continued this until 12 o'clock.

Cooke continued his account:

> Our line continued its movement. A French cavalry picquet fired on us at ten, but the *ruse de guerre* would not do. It has been affirmed that the firing of the French picquet of dragoons in the forest caused us to go too much to the left. On the contrary, we were moving directly towards the ford of Huerta on the Tormes.

An eye-witness account of the advance of the Light Division, published in the *United Service Journal* of March 1829, reads as follows:

> In the battle of Salamanca, the 43rd led the heavy column employed to drive back Foy's Division and seize the ford of Huerta, and on that occasion the Regiment made a very extraordinary advance in line for a distance of three miles under a cannonade, which, though not heavy was constant, with as clear and firm a line as at a review. What renders the march more remarkable is that it was made after dark; the Regiment kept its line simply by the touch to the centre; and the late General Shaw Kennedy, who commanded the left centre company on that occasion, declared that the line was so well kept as to have been able at any moment to fire a volley and charge with the bayonet. Major Napier rode during the whole time in front of the left centre company, and from time to time joked with Captain Shaw on the safety of the humble pedestrian compared with the lot of a mounted officer, as the round shot all flew over the heads of the men on foot.

End of the Battle 203

Captain Shaw-Kennedy had been ADC to General Craufurd, but on his general's death at Ciudad Rodrigo returned to the 43rd Light Infantry.

The Light Division's advance had progressed steadily in contact with Foy's division for 3 miles with the French steadfastly refusing to break, but having gained time for the rest of the army Foy seized an opportunity to halt von Alten's division and get away. Foy pinpoints this piece of favourable ground as follows: 'The enemy's pursuit stopped near Utero de Maria Ascensio':[10]

> I decided not to enter the wood but to take a position very nearby, behind a ravine,[11] in order to cover the retreat of the army. There was time; the victorious enemy was advancing towards Alba de Tormes between Calvarrasa and the wood, with two strong bodies of infantry, six cannon and 1,500 cavalry. I sent my skirmishers to delay their advance and they engaged them with artillery and musketry.

Napier, still commanding the leading battalion, believed that Foy had an impossible task as:

> The flanking brigades from the 4th Division having now penetrated between Maucune [sic, Ferey] and Foy, it seemed difficult for the latter to extricate his troops from the action; nevertheless, he did it with great dexterity. For

General Karl von Alten took command of the Light Division following the death of General Craufurd earlier in the year at Ciudad Rodrigo.

having increased his skirmishers on the last defensible ridge, along the foot of which run[s] a marshy stream, he redoubled his fire of musketry and made a menacing demonstration with his horsemen just as the darkness fell, whereupon the British guns immediately opened, a squadron of dragoons galloped forwards from the left, the infantry crossing the marshy stream with an impetuous pace gained the summit of the hill and a rough shock seemed at hand; but the main body of the French had gone into the thick forest on their own left during the firing, and the skirmishers fled swiftly after, covered by the smoke and darkness.

End of the Battle

Major William Napier of the 43rd Light Infantry led the pursuit of Foy's division.

Foy continued his own account:

> Night saved my division and those I was protecting; without it I would probably have been broken and the enemy would have arrived at Alba de Tormes before the remains of our seven broken divisions. For an hour after sunset the English cavalry continued its charges on my regiments formed alternately in line and *en masse*. I had the good fortune to have my division in hand at all times and maintain its good order, although many of the broken units coming onto our left threatened to carry disorder into our ranks.[12]

Through a combination of darkness and adroit handling of his veteran division General Foy was able to make a clean break from his pursuers. The flashes of fire and smoke from his battalion's muskets helped conceal the withdrawal into the darkness of the woods and escape. Foy concluded that his division 'found their way to Alba de Tormes where the army was gathered about 10 at night'.

The Light Division was directed on the Huerta where Wellington expected to secure the total destruction of the Army of Portugal, as he believed that the bridge at Alba de Tormes was held by a battalion of Spanish troops. General Carlos d'España had however, several days earlier ordered what he considered to be a dangerously isolated position to be abandoned, which allowed the majority of the French army to escape across the bridge. Wellington reported in his dispatch that 'When I lost sight of them in the dark I marched on Huerta and Encinas, and they went by Alba. If I had known there had been no garrison in Alba, I should have marched there and probably have had the whole.'

Sergeant Whitehead of Ross's RHA Troop, however, records that some French units did withdraw across the ford of Huerta and that they were engaged by the guns: 'Halted two hours and resumed the pursuit. At 4 o'clock came into action at 400 yards on the enemies [*sic*] rear as they were fording the Tormes.'[13]

The Light Division, without a local guide, had bivouacked at around midnight near Calvarrasa de Abajo. The 6th Division had been ordered to pursue, but they were so exhausted, disorganized and reduced in numbers that having reached the woods they came to a halt. If the Light Division had seen and been able to follow Foy, presumably the rearguard action would have continued, but in all reality the small Spanish garrison would already have been overwhelmed. The best that could have been hoped for would have been a modest increase in the number of prisoners.

The weapons of the Light Division: the 1806 New Land Pattern musket and the 1800 Pattern Short infantry rifle (not to scale).

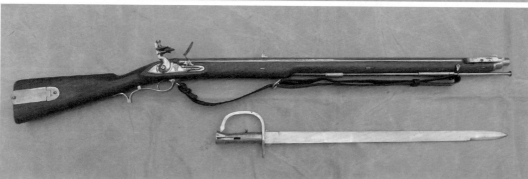

Escape

Though Foy may have got away in good order thanks to the skilful handling of his division, as Captain Lemonnier-Delafosse recorded, the rest of the Army of Portugal was in an advanced state of disorder:

> A shapeless mass of soldiery rolling down the road like a torrent – infantry, cavalry, artillery, wagons, carts, baggage-mules, the reserve park of artillery drawn by oxen, all mixed up. The men shouting, swearing, running, were out of all order, each one looking after himself alone – a complete stampede. The panic was inexplicable to one who, coming from the extreme rear, knew that there was no pursuit by the enemy to justify the terror shown. But alas! I know well that if the French have boldness and extreme impetuosity in attack, if they fail they are then shameless and irresponsible in flight. It is the fear of being captured that gives our soldiers wings. I had to stand off far from the road, for if I had got near it, I should have been swept off by the torrent in spite of myself.

The flight that night was not, however, unopposed. Beamish recounted a tale from the pursuit by the Light Brigade of the KGL (7th Division) during the night of 22/23 July:

> During the advance of the line battalions of the Legion at the close of the day, Serjeant Scheidemann, with twenty skirmishers of the 2nd Battalion, became separated from the rest of his company by the difficulties of the ground, and followed independently in pursuit. He drove before him a superior number of the enemy's infantry, and, falling in with a squadron of English dragoons, mainly contributed to the dispersion of another body, which had formed square in a wood. The serjeant now sought to rejoin his battalion and coming up with an officer's detachment of the Legion, also on its return, undertook to lead the way, marching with six men about a hundred paces in front. It was dark; the road led through a wood; after some time he found that his party was again isolated; and to increase his difficulties, eleven French infantry soldiers appeared in his front! – however, Scheidemann encouraging his men, attacked the enemy, and brought the whole in prisoners.[14]

With bodies of men, both friends and enemies, moving around the woods it was a tense night for the picquets posted by the various divisions. Among those out in front was General Sir Stapleton Cotton:

> Lord Wellington then desired Sir Stapleton to take a portion of the cavalry and patrol along the river in the direction of Alba. He did so, and after placing small posts of observation at different points on the banks, was returning, when he was fired at by a Portuguese picquet, who, in the darkness of the night, mistook his party for a body of the enemy.[15] By this unlucky volley Cotton's orderly was wounded, several horses struck, and he

208 Salamanca Campaign, 1812

The Military General Service Medal with four bars including the Battle of Salamanca in 1812.

himself received a bullet in the left arm, shattering one of the small bones. Though badly hurt, Sir Stapleton contrived to ride on to the village of Calvarrasa de Abajo. On arriving there he was carried from his horse into a miserable pillaged hovel, and placed in a pig trough, the most comfortable place that could be found. Soon after, Lord Wellington rode up to inquire into the nature of the accident, and on learning what had occurred sent for the surgeon of the 14th Dragoons. The latter advised immediate amputation, but Sir Stapleton steadily refused to consent to it until the opinion of the principal medical officer of the army – Dr. McGrigor – had been obtained.[16]

The battle that was the climax of weeks of marching and manoeuvring was over. No amount of dissembling by Marshal Marmont and his staff could conceal the scale of the reverse to French fortunes in the Peninsular inflicted on 21 July 1812. Even though Wellington followed up on his victory, the Anglo Portuguese army was still far smaller than that which the French could assemble should the marshals cooperate with King Joseph.

Regimental Lace and Uniform Distinctions

Every British regiment had a unique combination of facing colour, lace and layout of buttonholes. Here the 6th Division's five British battalions are used as examples.

A regimental coat of the Grenadier Company of the 11th Foot.

Facing colour: Wool material in the regimental colour was principally used for the collars and cuffs.
Regimental lace: 13mm worsted lace incorporating coloured stripes and/or shapes. Some regiments changed their lace in the 1812 dress regulations. The 95th Rifles did not have a regimental lace.
Buttonhole layout: Regimental lace was sewn around the buttonholes in 'square' or 'bastioned' style, either singly on the jacket or in pairs.
Officers: A further distinction for officers was the use of gold or silver lace, buttons and epaulets.
Sergeants: In line regiments they wore plain white worsted lace and in the Guards gold, otherwise they conformed to the layout of the buttonholes of their regiment.

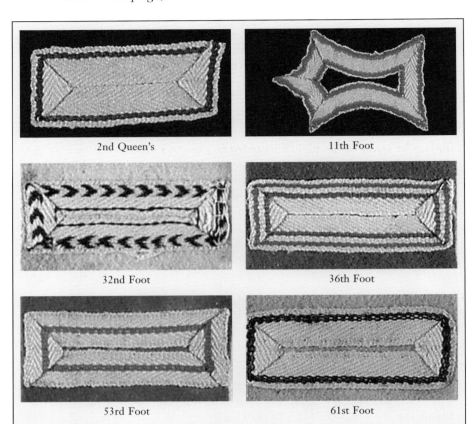

2nd Queen's

11th Foot

32nd Foot

36th Foot

53rd Foot

61st Foot

2nd Queen's: Blue facings with single square loops. Blue double worm chain woven near the outer edge of the lace.

11th Foot: Dark green facings, with bastioned loops in pairs. Lace had two red and two green stripes, with red stripes on the inner and outer edge. The narrow green stripes were adjacent to the red stripes.

32nd Foot: White facings, with square loops in pairs. Lace black worm and a black stripe. Narrow black stripe on inner edge and black v-worm on outer edge.

36th Foot: Mid-green facings, with square loops in pairs. One red and one green stripe, with the narrow green stripe centred on the lace and the narrow red stripe on the outer edge.

53rd Foot: Red facings, with square loops in pairs. The lace had a red stripe centred on it.

61st Foot: Buff facings, with single square loops. Lace had a blue stripe near the outer edge.

Chapter Ten

Pursuit and Garcihernández

'The mingled mass of fugitives fled to the woods and to the river for safety, and under cover of the night succeeded in gaining the pass of Alba over the Tormes. It was now ten o'clock at night: the battle was ended. At this point it had been confined to a small space, and the ground, trampled and stained deep, gave ample evidence of the havoc that had taken place. Lord Wellington, overcome as he was with fatigue, placed himself at the head of the 1st and Light Divisions and a brigade of cavalry, and following closely the retreating footsteps of the enemy ... and left the remnant of his victorious army to sleep upon the field of battle they had so hardly won.'

[Lieutenant William Grattan]

While Marmont's shattered and disorganized army marched east overnight through the woods and over the Alba de Tormes bridge, the equally exhausted allied divisions came to a halt around midnight. Back on the field of battle, Sergeant James Hale, a soldier in the 9th Foot of the 5th Division, recorded that

We remained on our ground that night and sent out our picquets as usual towards the enemy, and a little after ten o'clock there was silence on both sides. So then the first thing that was most necessary for us to do was to search for the wounded; but in consequence of it being dark, and among bushes, &c. many lay bleeding in their gore till next morning. It plainly appeared to us this day, that the enemy were supplied with a load of provisions for a long advance, just as if they were certain of driving us back into Portugal again; for in several places where they had been so closely pursued by our army, they left a great quantity behind, which fell into our hands: however, in the course of this day most of us got loaded with what they left behind; for some found small bags of biscuit, about ten or twelve pounds weight; some, small bags of flour, about the same weight; and some, joints of mutton and goat's flesh; all of which we found very acceptable, for at that time we were rather short of provisions. So when our camp was formed, and our picquets posted, the remaining part were soon very busily employed in providing for the belly: some making hard dumplings with the flour that we had found, some getting wood, and others searching for water for our cooking, which by chance was found at about one mile distance from our camp. Therefore, towards the middle of the night, we enjoyed ourselves over a most noble supper, and after a little conversation over what had passed during the day, we wrapped ourselves up in our blankets, with our accoutrements on,

Lieutenant Thomas Browne, 23rd and Wellington's headquarters staff.

and lay down in hopes of getting a few hours' good rest, for we were then getting very much fatigued for want of sleep.

Other British soldiers, probably those who remained halted short of the woods, recalled collecting French Charleville muskets for firewood and sitting up late into the night talking over the events of the day. Other soldiers and camp followers, as described by Lieutenant Browne, were active in the shadows of the night:

> All ideas of conduct or decency had disappeared – plunder & profligacy seemed their sole object, & the very Soldiers their Husbands evidently estimated them in proportion to their proficiency in these vices. They covered in number the ground of the field of battle when the action was over & were seen stripping & plundering friend and foe alike. It is not doubted that they gave the finishing Wow to many an Officer who was struggling with a mortal wound; & Major Offley of the 23rd Regiment, who lay on the ground, unable to move, but not dead, is said to have fallen victim to this unheard-of barbarity. The daring & enterprise of these creatures, so transformed beyond anything we have heard of in man, is not to be described.

Captain Ross-Lewin had been wounded during the 6th Division's attack on the Peña de Águeda ridge and made his way back to Arapiles for treatment. He was lucky, as he recalled:

> ... as it was already dusk, I wandered about, ignorant whether I was or was not taking the right direction for a village. I had walked for some time in this state of perplexity, when I suddenly heard the trampling of horses, and,

Stripping the dead. One of Goya's 'Disasters of War' sketches portraying the aftermath of battle speaks for itself.

on calling out to know who went there, I found, to my great satisfaction, that the party belonged to my own regiment, and that my batman was one of their number. They conducted me to the village of Arapiles, where we found the men breaking open the houses for the admittance of wounded officers, seven of whom were of my regiment. All the habitations and outhouses, even to the very pigsties, were speedily filled with wounded men, whose cries to have the dead taken away from them were incessant throughout the whole night.

Meanwhile, the French were streaming across the Alba de Tormes bridge. Colonel Girard, Maucune's chief of staff recalled in his memoirs:

In order to protect the passage, General Maucune and I – the only senior officers remaining! – had with great effort collected a thousand or 1,200 men and Blanzat's battery, now reduced to ten guns. Our advanced posts were so close to the enemy that we heard their voices. Wellington might, in the course of the night, have got some of his cavalry across the Tormes and attacked us simultaneously at both ends of the bridge. But fortunately, he did nothing. It was dawn before his advance guard prepared to attack us. Our army was safely across the river, but it had not had enough time to reform and be ready for battle.

General Maucune told me to cross the river and help rally the bulk of our troops. I asked to leave this until we had halted the enemy's advance by our volleys and artillery fire, and so forced him to deploy. We would still have time to disengage and retreat across the bridge, while our cannonade would alert the general that the enemy had begun their advance. Maucune accepted all my suggestions, and it turned out as I predicted.[1]

Once across the river, the French had but one simple aim: to put maximum distance between the main body of the Army of Portugal and their pursuers. To that end the wounded Clausel deployed his only intact division to hold the Alba de Tormes bridge and gave General Foy orders to deny it to the enemy until 0900 hours.

On the morning of 22 July, most of Wellington's divisions after a week of strenuous marching in the heat of the Iberian summer were left to rest, with General Bock's KGL dragoons and Anson's light cavalry brigades leading the pursuit, supported by Ross's and Bull's RHA troops. They were followed by the Light and 1st divisions, leaving the 7th Division and squadrons of cavalry scouring the woods west of the river and rounding up prisoners.

When the cavalry reached the Tormes some time before 0800 hours Foy's rearguard was still in place, but so fast had the French progress been, he could himself join the march east, gaining ground while the allied cavalry filed across the long, narrow Alba de Tormes bridge.

Wellington directed the pursuit on three routes in a generally easterly direction from the Tormes. General Bock's brigade of KGL dragoons on the left crossed the river by the fords and quickly found that there were only a handful of enemy troops out on this flank and no sign of the defeated army having passed

The bridge at Alba de Tormes.

that way en masse. Consequently, they turned south to where Wellington in person was forward with the squadrons of Anson's light cavalry brigade, leading them in the direction of Peñarandilla. The KGL dragoons arrived in time to see Wellington spot the enemy rearguard on a distinct ridge east of the village of Garcihernández and the Rio Camo.

Cavalry Action at Garcihernández

Having advanced out of contact with the enemy for some 6 miles, Anson's scouts finally came across French soldiers in Garcihernández and others filling canteens in the river. Beyond the Camo they could see a proper rearguard made up of squadrons of Curto's chasseurs, a brigade of Foy's division and an artillery battery.

When Wellington came up to the front, he could only see the chasseurs formed on one of the rounded tops. What, however, he could not see were four infantry battalions,[2] which were making their way up the ridge by the easiest route, via a shallow valley. Consequently, rather than wait for the Light Division, which was toiling along in the wake of the cavalry, Wellington ordered Anson's men forward. Lieutenant Tomkinson of the 16th Light Dragoons recorded in his

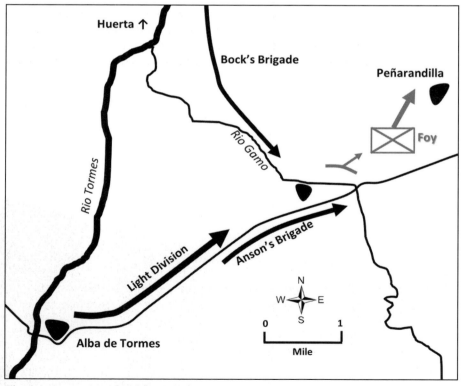

The pursuit, morning of 23 July 1812.

diary 'We charged the cavalry, with two squadrons from the 11th and 16th, which fled.' With the squadrons of chasseurs on the left seen off, the two squadrons of the French right wing withdrew slightly but remained on the high ground in support of the French infantry.

Meanwhile Wellington, on seeing General Bock's brigade appearing to his left, sent Colonel May, a senior gunner officer on his staff, with orders for the heavy dragoons to join the action, presumably as the French cavalry outnumbered Anson's men. Having accepted the order to charge, the short-sighted Bock asked: 'But you will be good enough to shew us the enemy':

> To this request Colonel May readily assented, and gallantly accompanied and led the first squadron in the charge, where he was severely wounded. When afterwards relating the circumstance, the gallant colonel was wont jestingly to reply to all: 'That was what I got by playing the dragoon and leading the Germans.'[3]

What happened was that the 1st Squadron, 1st Dragoons KGL under *Hauptmann* von Haltorff along with General Bock, the field officers of the regiment and Lieutenant Colonel May 'dashed on without waiting for the remaining squadrons and made straight for the enemy's cavalry'. As the dragoons passed the bottom of the valley, unbeknown to them they crossed the field of fire of a battalion of the 76th *Ligne* that was already deployed in square. The volley fired by the company on the face of the square nearest the dragoons was at a range of about 80 yards and according to Beamish it resulted in 'Colonel May and several men and horses being wounded, and the pursuit was discontinued':

> *Hauptmann* Gustavus von der Decken, who commanded the 3rd or left squadron of the regiment, seeing that if he advanced according to the order given, his flank would be exposed to the fire of a dense infantry square, formed the daring resolution of attacking it with his single squadron.
>
> This square stood on the lower slope of the heights, and obedient to the signal of their chief, the German troopers advanced against it with order and determination, while a deafening peal of musketry from the enemy greeted their approach. Arrived within a hundred yards of the point of attack, the gallant squadron officer, struck by a ball in the knee, fell mortally wounded, and *Leutnant* von Voss, with several men and horses, were killed; but instantly, *Hauptmann* von Uslar Gleichen, who commanded the left troop, dashing forward, placed himself at the head of the squadron, and re-animating his followers by words and example, while another shower of bullets carried destruction among their ranks, the intrepid soldiers forced onward, and bringing up their right flank, appeared before the enemy's bayonets on two sides of the square.

Facing the dragoons was the square's normally impregnable hedge of steel bayonets onto which horses simply wouldn't hurl themselves. The hitherto steady square was, however, undone by one of those accidents of war: a horse was shot, and its momentum or pain sent it crashing into and flattening the three-deep ranks and creating a gap in one face of the square. Seeing the gap, other troopers urged their horses on and, leaping the carnage, were in the centre of the French square. With cavalry in among them sabring the tightly-packed and increasingly disorganized ranks the square broke, with the far-face companies running for the shelter of their compatriots further up the valley. Beamish continued: '*Hauptmann* von Reitzenstein, who commanded the 2nd Squadron, seeing the success which had attended the daring onset of his comrades on the left, and being also impeded in his forward movement by the difficulties of the ground, decided upon following up the discomfiture of the infantry.'

The next target was the two battalions of the 6th *Légère*. The two infantry battalions were heading as fast as possible for the safety of steep ground on the flank of the valley, which would be difficult terrain for the dragoons, but the KGL squadrons were moving too fast. The battalion in column furthest down the valley did not have time to form square, but its rear companies faced about and fired. *Hauptmann* von Reitzenstein's squadron:

> was received with a steady and destructive fire, by which *Leutnant* Heugel was killed, and *Leutnant* Tappe severely wounded; but the moral force of the French infantry had been shaken by the fearful overthrow which they had

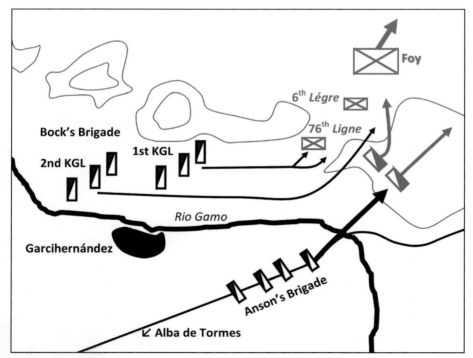

Cavalry action at Garcihernández.

just witnessed, and some timid individuals leaving their ranks, Reitzenstein rushed in with his ready followers; the square [*sic*] broke, and the greater part of the battalion was cut down or captured.

Towards the top of the valley the second battalion of the 6th *Légère*, supported by the remaining chasseurs, had managed to form a square of sorts along with those who had escaped from the destruction of their sister battalion. By now the 2nd KGL dragoons had arrived and Baron Marschalck's 3rd Squadron was joined by the left troop of the 2nd Squadron under Lieutenant Fumetty. As their first move, they charged 300 yards uphill and dispersed the squadrons of chasseurs without physically coming into contact with them. The final phase was to turn on the nearby poorly-formed square of the 6th *Légère* with gaps in its ranks, which were promptly exploited and the French infantry were cut down. Further up the hill:

> The wreck of the routed battalions now rallied and attempted to make a stand on a rising ground near the high road to Peñarandilla [alongside the 69th *Ligne*], where they again formed a connected body. Marschalck and Fumetty led their troopers a second time to the charge, but their little force had become too much reduced and the horses were too fatigued to admit of any impression being made upon the enemy. The French received the attack as well with a heavy fire ... to which they now had recourse; *Hauptmann* von Uslar was killed, *Leutnant* Fumetty was wounded, and several men and horses were struck down. No farther attempt was made by the dragoons, and the enemy resumed their retreat.

KGL dragoons in action against soldiers of the 76th *Ligne* at Garcihernández.

This was the end of a remarkable action that had seen a cavalry force and a brigade of infantry dispersed by vigorous action, one that Oman calculated had cost the French 1,100 dead, wounded and prisoners. The bill had, however, been significant for the KGL dragoons who lost 127 out of a strength of approaching 800 officers and troopers.

Lieutenant Ingilby recalled how his battery (Gardiner's company), which was normally attached to 1st Division, found itself acting as horse artillery as Wellington and the advance guard resumed the pursuit of Foy's battalions:

> We kept pace with the dragoons, mounting the gunners of the gun-carriages and, outstripping the infantry, came up with their rear-guard again. The French squadrons threatened to charge, the Commander-in-Chief dismounted, threw himself amongst our guns, and directed our fire personally. Had the French known the circumstance, it was not difficult to have captured him, but they stopped short at grape shot distance, and in the meanwhile our infantry and more squadrons arrived.[4]

Ingilby concluded by saying that 'The French retired with great rapidity', but this was one of many occasions, in this case twice in two days, when the army was very nearly deprived of Wellington's leadership.

General Foy overall conducted an excellent rearguard action after the battle.

Another of Goya's sketches depicting the horrors of the Peninsular War, this one illustrating the fate of many a wounded or straggling French soldier.

Corporal John Douglas of the 1st Royals, 5th Division crossed the Tormes during the 23rd and the following day marched past the scene of the action at Garcihernández on their way east:

> On the 24th we passed through the town and reached the heights of Peñaranda. Here the French rearguard, consisting of three regiments, formed square against the cavalry, and if I may be allowed to form an opinion, defended themselves bravely, as the number of men and horses which lay on the spot told in language not to be mistaken they had done their duty; and the exactness of the squares, which was very visible by the sight of the Frenchmen and firelocks as they lay, no less a proof of the superior bravery of the British cavalry that had conquered them. We continued the pursuit but the weather, which was intensely warm, rendered our march very fatiguing. Some days marching through pine forests, where not a breath of air could reach us, while the black sand stirred into dense clouds with such a number of troops and the ever attendant followers of an Army, rendered it nearly suffocating.

The Army of Portugal, unencumbered by a cavalcade of followers and baggage, had, however, easily been able to put distance between them and the allied army, but following in the wake of the French was not a pleasant experience. Lieutenant Cooke of the 43rd recorded the fate of many of the French wounded:

> As we passed onwards, lying by the side of the road were numerous objects to remind us of the miseries of war in all its horrors: many French soldiers lay dead. The scorching rays of the sun had so blistered their faces and swelled their bodies that they scarcely represented human forms; they looked like huge and horrible monsters.
>
> It is impossible to convey an adequate idea of such spectacles. These now inanimate objects had marched over sandy plains ... Crowding into the battle under a scorching sun, covered with dust, they had received severe wounds. Enduring excruciating torture, they were finally dragged, or carried from the scene of action on rudely-constructed bearers, then left to perish by the side of the road, or on stubble land, with their parched tongues cleaving to the roof of their mouths. And then, before breathing their last sigh, they would behold ... the uplifted hand of a Spanish assassin, armed with a knife to put an end to their existence. These dreadful fates awaited the defeated French soldiers in Spain.

The March to Madrid

Within several days of the battle Wellington was informed of the nature and extent of Marmont's wounds, but a couple of sentences from Major William Napier's letter home exemplify the rumours that abounded across the army as to the marshal's fate:

> Marmont lost his arm and had two or three wounds. The people of Tudela say he died three days ago. He was a brave fellow and a good officer and had the best of the business until the 22nd, when he extended his left wing too much, and Lord Wellington seized the opportunity like a hawk.

Such notes are to be found in virtually all contemporary letters and diaries in the aftermath of the battle. What Wellington was less certain about were French intentions following their defeat.

As General Foy marched away with his battered rearguard he met up with Caffarelli's meagre reinforcement from the Army of the North, just 800 light cavalry[5] and a battery of guns, but the sight of this was enough to keep Anson's four squadrons following at a respectable distance. The Light and 1st divisions were still some distance behind, and Bock's brigade was halted reorganizing after their mounted action. Consequently, a classic pursuit by the allies was not possible. Any effort to catch and harry the Army of Portugal, which had covered 40 miles in thirty-six hours, would inevitably cost Wellington casualties in addition to those he had already suffered in the battle. What must have been in his mind was the habit of the independently-minded French marshals and generals of finally putting aside their self-interest in times of crisis and the likelihood of having to face a far larger army. This, however, would not be for some time as intercepted dispatches indicated that King Joseph's commanders had all found pressing reasons for not leaving their fiefdoms or, as in the case of Caffarelli, making a token contribution.

In his dispatch to King Joseph, Marshal Marmont had covered up the extent of his defeat, but General Clausel writing to Joseph revealed the true extent of the disaster, stating that he only had 22,000 badly shaken men in hand with the army. Many French soldiers were of course still dispersed and yet to find their regiments, and over the following days numbers grew. Unaware of the king's approach from Madrid with 14,000 men, Clausel decided to march to Valladolid some 65 miles north-east and a further 80 miles on to Burgos. Wellington, amid some enduring criticism over the lack of hard pursuit, followed in six easy marches across familiar country, his aim being to manoeuvre the Army of Portugal away from juncture with the king's Army of the Centre.

Reluctant to give up resources, Clausel left a number of French garrisons in, for example, Tordesillas, Zamora, Torà and Benavente. These were invariably small and vulnerable and were to be dealt with by Spanish and Portuguese forces aided by guerrilla bands which would in the first instance invest these places.

Meanwhile, on 30 July, the allied headquarters had reached Boecillo from where Wellington rode with several staff officers and an escort of two squadrons of cavalry:

> to Valladolid, a distance of 3 leagues.[6] The French had abandoned the city, leaving behind them 800 sick, 17 pieces of cannon and 20,000 shot and shell.

The march to Madrid.

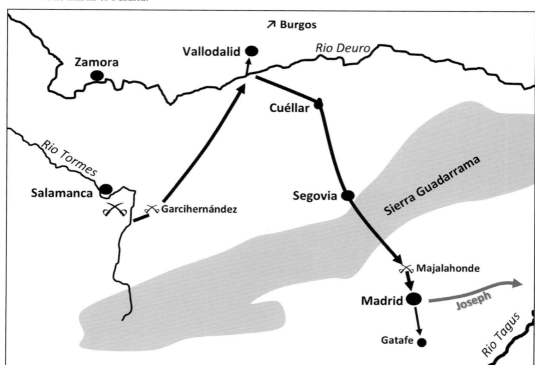

After giving some direction relative to the sick and wounded French, & also establishing the military police of the town, Ld. Wellington rode back to Boecillo; & it plainly appearing that there was little chance of overtaking the enemy.[7]

Having crossed the Duero and arrived at Valladolid, the allied army found in addition to the artillery and ammunition, which the French could not take away for a want of draft horses, there were plenty of shoes and clothing, which were distributed to the army.[8] In all, this represented a significant boost as Wellington was now more than 100 miles from his forward magazine at Ciudad Rodrigo. In short, he had for the time being reached the practical extent of his lines of communication. It was not only marching into danger to follow the French to Burgos, but also logistically unsustainable.

After a pause of five days,[9] leaving two divisions to secure the line of the Duero, Wellington turned south, having heard from General D'Urban's patrols that King Joseph was within striking distance. Now there was no danger of the armies of the Centre and Portugal joining forces, according to Lieutenant Browne he '... decided on a rapid movement against them & on the 6th [August] moved on Mozoncillo, 5 leagues. On arrival there he found that King Joseph having got intelligence of this advance against him abandoned Segovia.'

From Segovia, Madrid was an objective that would force the French to concentrate and abandon much of their conquered territory, which would provide the Spanish armies time and space to regenerate into a more effective fighting force. En route to Madrid Wellington was forced to leave the whole of the 6th Division at Cuéllar, not only because of their losses in battle but because of growing rates of sickness. Five of their battalions had fought in the ill-fated 1809 expedition in the Low Countries and were either suffering from the lingering effects of Walcheren fever or were simply not fully acclimatized to the peninsula. Not only were the hospitals filling with 6th Division soldiers, but with the army's most newly-arrived reinforcements as well. The long march, sketchy rations and the Iberian summer heat had rendered them liable to a variety of illnesses. Consequently, there were hospitals and convoys of sick stretching back down the army's line of communication to Lisbon and the hospital and depot at Belém. For example, the Light Division was expecting a significant draft of some 216 men: both men fresh from England and those recovered from wounds received at Ciudad Rodrigo and Badajoz. In the event only twenty-six soldiers arrived with the division during August, but this number, now including Salamanca casualties, had increased to some 200 by the end of September 1812.

The Affair at Majadahonda[10]

As the allies marched south over the Sierra Guadarrama, via the Pass of Navacerrada, they encountered minor opposition; it did not seriously disrupt progress towards Madrid but as they descended from the passes they met more determined resistance. Without Soult coming to his aid as ordered, King Joseph

The Sierra de Guadarrama Mountains were a pleasant relief from the heat of the plains around Salamanca, but the steep ascents were still a challenge to many undernourished soldiers.

was preparing to abandon his capital, which was in turmoil. In order not to be seen making a precipitous flight at the first sight of the enemy and to buy time, he ordered elements of the Army of the Centre to check Wellington's advance. Consequently, on 11 August the allied column led by General D'Urban's Portuguese cavalry and the 7th Division were attacked less than 10 miles from Madrid.

The previous evening D'Urban's Portuguese dragoons of the advanced guard came up against the cavalry outposts of Joseph's army provided by General of Brigade de Reiset's 13th and 18th dragoons on the Arroyo del Zújar, north of the village of Las Rozas. At dawn D'Urban ordered his regiments forward supported by Major Macdonald's E Troop RHA, with Bock's KGL brigade following some distance behind them.

Advancing with two of his regiments, D'Urban turned the French flank with the third, supported by two of the guns, whose fire forced the French to retire to the village of Las Rozas, where they made a stand. When they were again outflanked, the French cavalry withdrew a mile to the village of Majadahonda, which took D'Urban to within 7 miles of Madrid. Here he awaited orders from Wellington, who arriving in the village confirmed an advance towards Madrid, but he instructed his brigade to water the horses and prepare their lunch while the rest of the advance guard closed up.

In a short while, General Bock's brigade of dragoons occupied Las Rozas and took the opportunity to unsaddle for the first time in three days, feed the horses and men and rest while the 7th Division caught up. The leading battalion of the

Pursuit and Garcihernández 225

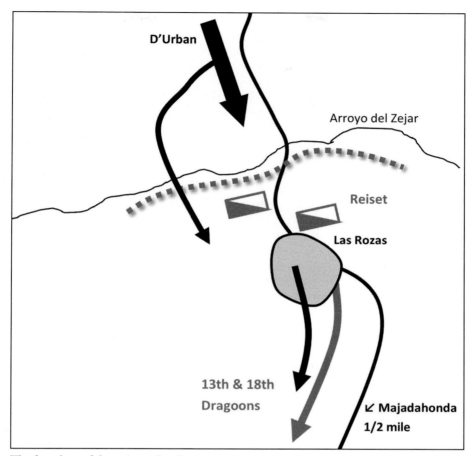

The first phase of the action at Las Rozas.

division, the 1st Light Battalion KGL, arrived after several hours and they soon also had their equipment and coats off, secure in the knowledge that D'Urban's brigade was a mile ahead of them and that as over the previous days, the enemy were falling back.

All was quiet while the allies waited for the heat of the day to abate, but at about 1600 hours a forty-strong KGL dragoon picquet under Lieutenant Kuhls, which had earlier successfully followed the French was seen galloping towards Majadahonda. The KGL's historian wrote:

> Kuhls tracked the enemy for four miles ... and charging boldly in front of a defile, killed and wounded several of the rear guard; but about three o'clock in the afternoon, the French horsemen returned, reinforced by a battalion of infantry and some guns, and the Germans fell back upon a Portuguese picquet.[11]

Hot on the heels of the picquet were General Treillard's cavalry,[12] some 2,000 strong, advancing from the woods. The three French brigades were initially deployed in lines one behind the other, and were closing at speed, clearly determined to attack with the benefit of surprise. The Portuguese rushed to assemble in line in front of Majadahonda, while Captain Dyneley, the battery captain, got a section of 6-pounders limbered and the drivers mounted. He wrote: 'As soon as I got two guns ready, my friend Harding and I went away with them at speed to the front and directed the rest to follow me.'

Despite outnumbering him three to one, D'Urban, full of confidence in his dragoons following their action at Salamanca, decided to fight the French cavalry rather than retire on his supports at Las Rozas. He did, however, summon the KGL dragoons to his assistance.

D'Urban deployed one squadron in a mounted skirmish screen, with the remainder of the 1st and 12th regiments in line. His final squadron was refused on his left flank, where along with Kuhls' KGL patrol, it could defend the guns. The presence of E Troop's guns was of course another reason for the French to close with the Portuguese as quickly as possible, particularly as their own artillery was still some way to the rear. Such was the speed of advance that Dyneley only had time to fire three or four rounds before the opposing bodies of cavalry closed on each other. D'Urban ordered a counter-charge by his dragoons, but as he later

Colonel Reiset commanded the leading French brigade of dragoons at Majadahonda.

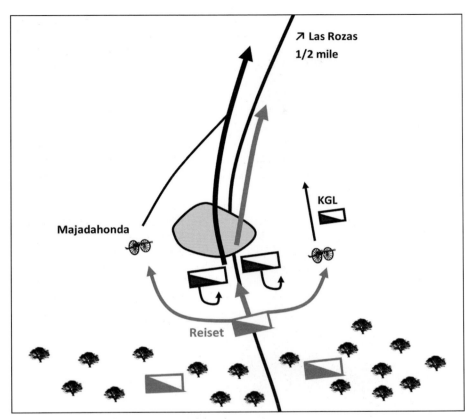

The second phase of the action at Majadahonda.

wrote: 'At Salamanca they followed me into the enemy's ranks like British dragoons; yesterday they were so far from doing their duty that in the first charge they just went far enough to land me in the enemy's ranks.' Dyneley noted:

> ... then I saw how the thing was to go with us. The Portuguese wavered, and I turned to Harding and said, 'They'll most certainly turn our right flank, I hope the guns on the right will be able to get away.' By this time, the French cavalry gained march upon us ... we, of course, limbered up and away we went at speed ... we had galloped about 3 or 4 hundred yards, the confusion became very great ... I was at the time galloping about half a dozen yards in the rear of the last gun ... when my horse making a trip ... I came head over heels ... I was hurt a little and had one of my shoes nearly torn off my foot.[13]

Of Macdonald's four guns, only one got away; of the others one broke a wheel at speed on rough ground and two had their drivers cut down as they pulled away. Captain Dyneley and fourteen gunners were captured in the pursuit along with

Hamilton Smith's depiction of a mounted gunner of the Royal Horse Artillery.

two guns. This was despite Lieutenant Kuhls' Germans bravely attempting to save the guns. In the meantime, the German dragoons in Las Rozas were, according to Beamish:

> quietly occupied with their stable duties in various parts of the village, many of the men in their shirts and trousers. Kuhls had sent in several reports of the enemy's movements, but Colonel de Jonquières ... made no preparations to meet an attack, and the brigade was completely surprised. The alarm was sounded; two companies of the light battalion which were stationed in

the lower part of the village, soon stood to their arms; the dragoons hastened to saddle, and every exertion was made on the part of the officers to receive the threatened onset.

The KGL troopers were, however, too dispersed to be quickly assembled, but *Hauptmann* von Reitzenstein and *Hauptmann* Marschalck with great 'presence of mind' brought together groups of troopers and faced the mass of French cavalry at the entrance to the village, but they were inevitably overpowered by sheer numbers. Beamish continued:

> ... the elated enemy, following up their successes at a rapid rate, crowded into the place [Las Rozas], and appeared suddenly in an open space which divided the upper from the lower part of the village. Here the main body of the 1st Light Battalion, together with the baggage of the whole was stationed, and the French riding wildly about, caused great confusion, took some prisoners, and wounded seven men of the battalion; but the companies quickly formed in the open space and drove back the horsemen.

The part played by the riflemen of the 1st Light Battalion's companies who fired from the cover of the houses is not to be ignored. They significantly contributed to driving the French dragoons out of the village and keeping the next wave back long enough for the KGL dragoons to mount, but many fought bareback in their shirtsleeves and watering caps.

With Reiset's dragoons ejected from the village, the two regiments of the KGL brigade now properly formed and D'Urban's Portuguese rallied, a counter-attack was launched on the disordered dragoons of the leading French brigade. The Portuguese brigade was to the left of the KGL, formed in echelon having the left squadron forward. The allies were only just deployed when two French squadrons advanced 'at a slow pace', bringing forward their right flank to attack the Portuguese and the French opened fire with the three guns brought up with Chassé's infantry brigade![14]

> The allies rode out bravely to meet the threatened attack, but just when the pace had been increased to the charge, and the Portuguese brigade had arrived within twenty or thirty paces of the enemy, they again deserted their officers, wheeled about, and fled back to the village!

D'Urban was again lucky to escape and confirmed that 'In the second [charge], which (having got them rallied) I rashly attempted, I could not get them within 20 yards of the enemy – they left me alone and vanished before the French helmets like leaves before the autumn wind.'

This left the KGL dragoons again outnumbered, with the left flank exposed to the enemy. Consequently, they were in danger of being surrounded and destroyed and had no alternative but to make a rapid retreat, which they did in column of squadrons. The French followed, taking prisoners from the rear sections; among them was Colonel de Jonquières.

230 *Salamanca Campaign, 1812*

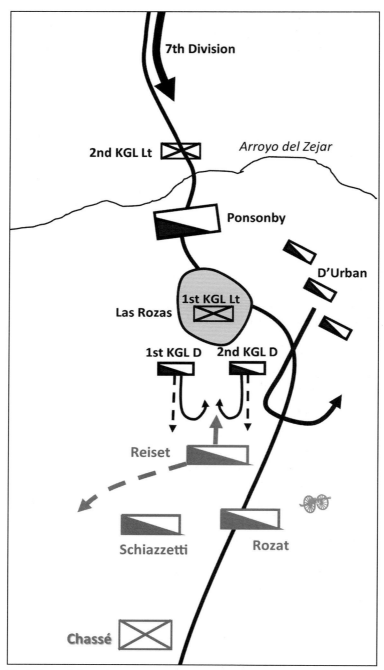

Final phase of the action.

With the French now strung out, the KGL dragoons halted and formed near the village and the leading squadron of the 2nd Regiment under *Hauptmann* Friesland, joined by the picquet under Kuhls, impetuously charged and, as soon as his squadron was formed, *Hauptmann* von Lenthe advanced to the charge. As the Germans approached the French dragoons, an officer rode forward and called on Lenthe to surrender, but a trooper dashed from the ranks and 'cut the haughty captain from his horse'. With that, the French squadron turned and withdrew. At this stage the action was brought to a halt as the 7th Division and General Ponsonby's heavy cavalry brigade were coming into sight and the French withdrew to Majadahonda.

The bold action by General Treillard's cavalry had bought some hours for Joseph, but above all it had restored some dignity to French arms. Wellington was, however, furious at the reverse and even though there were various proposals to retrain or shame the Portuguese dragoons, he wrote:

> As for sending the cavalry to the rear that is impossible at the present. We have still a good deal upon our hands, and we are worse provided with cavalry than our neighbours; and a body commanded by such a man as D'Urban, even though they will not fight, are better than none. In fact, they behaved infamously, and they must not be employed again alone, or with our cavalry, who gallop too fast for them.[15]

By the following morning the French had vacated Majadahonda and the allied advance continued. E Troop's two captured guns were found abandoned, with the French having attempted to burn and otherwise damage the carriages, thus going some way to preserving Wellington's reputation for never having lost a gun!

Madrid

The 7th Division led the way towards Madrid, but having not always been welcomed by the Spanish rural population, many of whom were suspicious of their former enemy, the officers and men of the army were unsure of the reception they would receive in the city as 'protestant heretics'. However, they need not have worried as Lieutenant Browne who was riding with Wellington's staff and one of the first into the city confirms:

> The army immediately moved on to Madrid & took possession of the capital. When Ld. Wellington approached with his staff, in the group of which I rode, a deputation of the principal Authorities & inhabitants came out to meet him, amidst loud & continued acclamations from thousands who had joined this procession.

Following a short distance behind was the column of troops led by the 68th Light Infantry. Private Green recalled that their reception was no less effusive:

> The 12th, we moved off early, and suffered much from the paved roads. This day Lord Wellington passed our division on his way to the capital: when we

were within five miles of Madrid, the people came out in great numbers to meet us: the day being very hot, some of our men fainted, but the Spaniards immediately took them under their care, giving them wine or spirits; a great number of melons were also distributed to the men in the ranks. The people shouted and rejoiced as we marched along, and the bands of the different regiments enlivened the scene by frequently playing the 'Downfall of Paris', the colours were displayed, and we frequently gave three cheers: indeed, there was little else but shouts and bursts of approbation for the last two miles. When at length we arrived at the gates; the streets were crowded with the populace, and the windows occupied by ladies; the tops of the houses near the gate were also crowded. We marched along the streets amidst the rending and exulting shouts of *'Viva los Ingleses!'* or 'Long live the English'; the bells of the different churches rang, the ladies waved their handkerchiefs from the windows, and every countenance beamed with joy, welcoming their deliverers: in some instances, the Spaniards embraced the soldiers. We halted in front of the new palace: here we shouted and cheered the people in return. Ours was the first regiment of British infantry that entered Madrid: after waiting a few minutes, the whole of our division marched into a convent, which was the largest I ever saw, affording room and convenience for nine regiments; and in the centre of the square stood a fountain which nearly supplied the whole with good water.

There was plenty of food for the 7th Division's soldiers, including the large goldfish in the ornamental ponds in the gardens of the royal palace, but of those soldiers who caught them many were sick. Private Wheeler recorded that they turned their 'attention to the delicious fruit with which the garden abounded. We soon provided ourselves with some of the choicest luxuries that were intended to grace the table of King Joseph.'

Captain Leach of the 95th Rifles wrote in his memoirs that the following day when the Light Division marched into the city the reception was undiminished:

Old and young, men, women, and children, in tens of thousands, filled the streets, embracing the officers and soldiers, kissing the colours of the regiments, and the happy ensigns who carried them. They cried, laughed, sung, and danced with joy, so that it was impossible to doubt their sincerity. Few of us were ever so caressed before, and most undoubtedly never will be again. The windows and balconies were crowded with elegantly dressed females, all joining in the enthusiasm of the moment. The French had been four years in possession of Madrid, and at length they witnessed their departure.[16]

When the leading elements of the army entered Madrid, the king and his chief of staff Marshal Jourdan had already abandoned the capital. They had, however, left a nominal garrison of 2,000 conscripts[17] along with 500 sick in the fortification on El Retiro hill on the eastern outskirts of the city. Lieutenant Browne explained that 'Immediately on our entrance, Ld. Wellington invested El Retiro with a

Joseph Bonaparte had been placed on the usurped throne of Spain by his brother Napoleon.

sufficient force, & began works against it.' Two British battalions were detailed to assault the place. Private Green of the 51st Light Infantry recalled:

> As soon as it was dark, we entered the Royal Gardens under a smart fire of musketry that done us no harm. We soon got under cover of a long wall close under the forts. Through this wall the chasseurs [*Britanniques*] were employed in making a breach which they had completed by daylight, sufficient for a subdivision to march through.[18] The noise in making this breach drew a sharp fire from the enemy that continued all night without doing much mischief, as the wall protected us.
>
> Daylight shewed us the forts and we were expecting every moment to march through the breach in the wall to storm the works, but the enemy surrendered and before noon the whole of the forts were in our possession.

Browne described the end of the short-lived 'siege' and its aftermath:

> ... the French sent out a flag of truce & agreed to capitulate. We took possession on the following day, finding immense stores, 180 pieces of cannon,

20,000 Muskets, & one Eagle;[19] the number of prisoners was about 2,000. Permission had been given to the garrison to march out with the honours of war, but they were to deposit their arms & accoutrements on the glacis. Here I saw them assembled for that purpose, rage was strongly depicted on their countenances, & many were beginning to knock off the butt-end of their muskets, by striking them violently against the ground. This was not put an end to without considerable difficulty. They were marched thro' the streets of Madrid, under a strong escort of Spanish Guerrillas, a compliment purposely paid to the nation. The French were all the time, imploring to be taken out of the custody of these Spaniards, & that a British escort should be given them to Bilbao, the place of their embarkation for England. They seemed perfectly well aware of the ill treatment and cruelty to which they would be subject in Spanish hands; possibly feeling that they had well deserved it.

Their fear was not misplaced. Wellington had to stop prisoners being killed at the least excuse by their escort. Meanwhile, as the allies were completing the liberation of Madrid, Joseph marched to join Marshal Suchet in Valencia, along with his small Central Army and those citizens who had supported him on his throne. These *afranceados*, facing retribution for what was seen as treasonous collaboration, had very little choice but to follow the king. Whole families took to the road with whatever of their portable wealth they could carry with them. This unwieldy convoy of 10,000 souls and nearly 2,000 vehicles, laden with the riches of the city, was strung out on the road south and repeatedly fell prey to the people of the villages through which they passed. Not only that, there were also the soldiers of Joseph's army who pillaged them unmercifully and the guerrillas, many of whom were not only patriots but, as Goya characterized them, brigands as well.

Back in the city, those members of the allied army who had money, for the pay of the army was months in arrears, were not to enjoy its delights for long.

The Burgos Campaign

Having won a significant victory and liberated Madrid but with the French far from driven from Spain, Wellington's future course of action depended on that of the enemy, particularly the Army of the South. Soult, as already noted and as Wellington predicted, was reluctant to leave his virtually independent fiefdom of Andalucía and its wealth, which he had enjoyed for two and a half years. He argued that removing troops to join Joseph would lead to a loss of territory to the various Spanish generals lurking on the periphery of his area and instead proposed fanciful alternative plans that would not involve his army. By the middle of August 1812, however, the situation was such that he had to comply with Joseph's demands and began a phased evacuation of Andalucía, concentrating his army between Córdoba and Granada prior to marching east to join the king and Suchet in Valencia.

An unknown officer of the 52nd Light Infantry.

By the end of the month Wellington was still unsure of Soult's intentions, but to his surprise a rejuvenated Army of Portugal reoccupied Valladolid and was rescuing other isolated garrisons. With the British expeditionary force operating belatedly on Spain's Mediterranean coast and General Hill marching up the Guadiana valley towards Madrid, the allied army was again in motion north to confront General Clausel. To secure Madrid, however, Wellington left almost half his force behind under the command of General Karl von Alten. This included the 3rd and Light divisions and part of the cavalry who were located just south of the city around Getafe to observe the Rio Tagus. At some 30,000 strong, Wellington's force had Clausel withdrawing east, with no intention of offering battle; the allies followed and arrived before Burgos on 19 September.

236 Salamanca Campaign, 1812

The fortress of Burgos stands on the northern bank of the Rio Arlazón, guarding the point where one of the great roads to France crossed the river and was held by a garrison of 2,000 men under General Dubreton. Wellington hoped to take the fortress quickly, in the manner in which he had taken Ciudad Rodrigo eight months earlier. The siege started well with the storming of the unfinished San Miguel hornwork by the 42nd Highlanders and some of the 1st Division's light companies, at the not insignificant cost of 400 casualties. Entrenching to produce the parallels and batteries to take on the outer defences of the main fortification began, but being dominated by French guns digging in was as costly as the approach to Badajoz had been. On 23 September under time pressure Wellington ordered an escalade of the castle's outer walls but this failed, and he had to resort to conventional breaching. With just eight siege guns and limited ammunition it was soon apparent that battering the walls to create a ramp of rubble for an assault was virtually impossible. Consequently, he turned to tunnelling to undermine the walls to create a breach, but the engineers encountered what proved to be the foundations of an old outer wall. As a result, when the mine was fired it only produced a partial collapse and the assault timed to coincide with the detonation failed. On 4 October a second more successful mine breached the outer wall and the Highlanders of the 2nd 42nd successfully stormed this defence. Sapping towards the castle's inner wall continued with virtually all the handful of engineers becoming casualties, and General Dubreton launched two sallies which

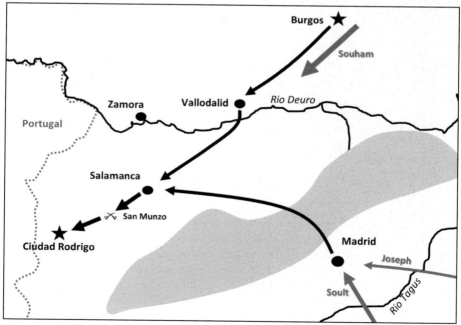

The retreat to Ciudad Rodrigo.

delayed work. Despite the advice of Lieutenant Colonel Burgoyne of the Royal Engineers that the breaches were not practicable, the fortress was stormed on 18 October and at several points the stormers secured lodgements, but they were insufficiently strong to either hold them or exploit into the castle.

By now the Army of Portugal, now under the command of General Souham, was approaching and on 20 October Wellington was forced to abandon the siege. Not only that, General Drouet's army was coming down from the north-east and Soult and the king were now finally approaching Madrid on separate routes

General Joseph Souham.

with a total of 60,000 men from the south. Consequently, with the enemy commanders now co-operating and united in their aim, Wellington was forced to fall back to the Rio Duero and Hill to abandon Madrid and march to rejoin the army.

Facing 53,000 men of the armies of Portugal and the North with just 30,000 men, Wellington's well-calculated attempts to hold the line of the Duero in a series of actions known as the Battle of Tordesillas failed when the French captured the bridge. The two wings of the army were united at Alba de Tormes, where Marshal Soult took command of the pursuit from Salamanca. The retreat in increasingly bad weather back to Ciudad Rodrigo was terrible for both sides and sorely tested the Light Division that provided the army's rearguard. The action on the Rio Huerta at San Muñoz on 17 November and a final failed attempt to outflank the Light Division the following day saw the French at the end of their tether. Having outrun their supplies and unopposed, the allied army limped back to winter quarters in the same area they had left five months earlier.

Wellington's 'year of victories' had ended with another painful and humiliating retreat, this time back to the borders of Portugal and Spain, but the 1812 campaign in Iberia had shown that the small allied army could take on the might of the French army and win an offensive battle. Wellington always said that it was not his job to win the war on his own and in that respect, the greatest and lasting impact of the Salamanca campaign was in forcing Soult to abandon Andalucía. This liberated about a third of Spain and provided time, money and opportunity for the Spanish army to regenerate for the liberation of most of the remainder of their country in 1813.

The stone bridge over the Duero at Tordesillas which the French captured intact.

Appendix I

Order of Battle

Allied Army
(Lieutenant General Viscount Wellington)

1st Division (Major General Campbell)
  1st Brigade (Colonel Fermor): 1st Coldstream Guards, 1st/3rd Guards, 1 company 5th/60th Rifles
  2nd Brigade (Major General Wheatley): 2nd/24th Foot, 2nd/42nd Foot, 2nd/58th Foot, 1st/79th Foot, 1 company 5th/60th Rifles
  3rd Brigade (Major General Howard): 1st/50th Rifles, 1st/71st Foot, 1st/92nd Foot, 1 company 5th/60th Rifles
  4th Brigade (Major General Baron Löwe): 1st, 2nd, 5th Line Battalions, King's German Legion

3rd Division (Major General Pakenham)
  1st Brigade (Colonel Wallace): 1st/45th Foot, 1st/74th Foot, 1st/88th Foot, 3 companies 5th/60th Rifles
  2nd Brigade (Major General Campbell): 1st and 2nd/5th Foot, 2nd/83rd Foot, 94th Foot
  Portuguese Brigade (Colonel Power): 1st and 2nd/9th, 1st & 2nd/21st Portuguese Line Regiments, 12th Caçadores

4th Division (Major General Cole)
  1st Brigade (Major General Anson): 27th Foot, 40th Foot, 1 company 5th/60th Rifles
  2nd Brigade (Colonel Ellis): 1st/7th Fusiliers, 1st/23rd Fusiliers, 48th Foot, 1 company Brunswick Oels
  Portuguese Brigade (Colonel Stubbs): 1st and 2nd/11th, 1st & 2nd/23rd Portuguese Line Regiments, 17th Caçadores

5th Division (Major General Leith)
  1st Brigade (Colonel Hay): 3rd/1st Foot, 1st/9th Foot, 1st and 2nd/38th Foot, 1 company Brunswick Oels
  2nd Brigade (Major General Dunlop): 1st and 2nd/4th Foot, 2nd/30th Foot, 2nd/44th Foot, 1 company Brunswick Oels
  Portuguese Brigade (Brigadier General Spry): 1st & 2nd/3rd, 1st & 2nd/15th Portuguese Line Regiments, 8th Caçadores

6th Division (Major General Clinton)
  1st Brigade (Colonel Hulse): 1st/11th Foot, 2nd/53rd Foot, 1st/61st Foot, 1 company 5th/60th Rifles
  2nd Brigade (Colonel Hinde): 1st/2nd Queens, 1st/32nd Foot, 1st/36th Foot, 1 company 5th/60th Rifles

Portuguese Brigade (Brigadier General Rezende): 1st & 2nd/8th, 1st & 2nd/12th Portuguese Line Regiments, 9th Caçadores

7th Division (Major General Hope)
1st Brigade (Colonel Halket): 1st and 2nd Light Battalions KGL, 7 companies Brunswick Oels
2nd Brigade (Major General Bernewitz): 2nd/51st Light Infantry, 85th Light Infantry, Chasseurs Britanniques
Portuguese Brigade (Colonel Collins): 1st & 2nd/7th, 1st & 2nd/19th Portuguese Line Regiments, 2nd Caçadores

Light Division (Major General Karl von Alten)
1st Brigade (Lieutenant Colonel Barnard): 1st/43rd Foot, 2nd & 3rd/95th Rifles, 1st Caçadores
2nd Brigade (Major General Vandeleur): 1st/52nd Foot, 1st/95th Rifles, 3rd Caçadores

Independent Brigades
Portuguese Brigade (Colonel Pack): 1st & 2nd/1st, 1st & 2nd/16th Portuguese Line Regiments, 4th Caçadores
Portuguese Brigade (Brigadier General Bradford): 1st & 2nd/13th and 1st & 2nd/24th Portuguese Line Regiments, 5th Caçadores

Spanish Division (General Carlos D'España): 2nd Battalion, Regiment Princesa, Tiradores de Castilla, Caçadores de Castilla, 2nd Battalion, Juan Regiment, 3rd Battalion, 1st Seville Regiment, 1 battery 6-pounders

Cavalry
Le Marchant's Brigade: 5th Dragoon Guards, 3rd and 4th Dragoons
Anson's Brigade: 11th, 12th, 16th Light Dragoons
Von Alten's Brigade: 14th Light Dragoons, 1st Hussars KGL
Bock's Brigade: 1st and 2nd Dragoons KGL
D'Urban's Brigade: 1st and 11th Portuguese Dragoons

Artillery (Colonel Framingham) (54 guns)
Ross's, Bull's, McDonald's troops, Royal Horse Artillery
Lawson's, Gardiner's, Green's, Douglas's, May's companies Royal Artillery
Sympher's Company King's German Artillery
Arriga's Battery Portuguese Artillery

Army of Portugal
(Marshal Marmon Duc d'Dalmatia)

Foy's Division
Chemineau: 2 bns 6th *Légère*, 2 bns 69th *Ligne*
Desgraviers-Berthelot: 2 bns 39th and 2 bns 76th *Ligne*

Clausel's Division
Berlier: 3 bns 25th *Légère*, 2 bns 27th *Ligne*
Barbot: 2 bns 50th and 2 bns 59th *Ligne*

Ferey's Division
Menne: 2 bns 31st *Légère*, 2 bns 26th *Ligne*
?: 3 bns 47th and 2 bns 70th *Ligne*

Sarrut's Division
  Fririon: 3 bns 2nd *Légère*, 3 bns 36th *Ligne*
  ?: 3 bns 4th *Légère*
Macune's Division
  Arnaud: 3 bns 15th and 2 bns 66th *Ligne*
  Montfort: 2 bns 82nd and 2 bns 59th *Ligne*
Brenier's Division
  Taupin: 3 bns 17th *Légère*, 3 bns 65th *Ligne*
  ?: 3 bns 22nd and Prussian Regiment (-)
Thomières' Division
  Bonté: 3 bns 1st and 2 bns 62nd *Ligne*
  ?: 23 bns 50th *Ligne*
Bonet's Division
  Gautier: 3 bns 11th and 3 bns 119th *Ligne*
  Barbot: 3 bns 120th and 3 bns 122nd *Ligne*
Curto's Light Cavalry
  ?: 3rd Hussars, 2 squadrons, 22nd Chasseurs, 2 squadrons, 26th Chasseurs,
    2 squadrons, 28th Chasseurs, 1 squadron
  ?: 13th Chasseurs, 5 squadrons, 14th Chasseurs, 4 squadrons,
    1 march squadron
Boyer's Dragoons
  ?: 6th Dragoons, 2 squadrons, 11th Dragoons, 2 squadrons
  ?: 15th Dragoons, 2 squadrons, 25th Dragoons, 2 squadrons
Artillery (78 guns)

Goya's portrait of Wellington was begun in Madrid in 1812 but revised and updated with subsequent awards in 1814. In the aftermath of the Battle of Salamanca, Wellington was immediately elevated in the British peerage from Viscount to Marquis, and in early 1813 he was similarly promoted from Knight of the Bath to Knight Grand Cross of the Bath.

Appendix II

Wellington's Salamanca Dispatch
General the Earl of Wellington, K.B., to the Earl Bathurst, Secretary of State

Flores de Avila, July 24, 1812.

My Lord

My aide-de-camp, Captain Lord Clinton, will present to your lordship this account of a victory which the allied troops under my command gained in a general action fought near Salamanca on the evening of the 22nd inst. which I have been under the necessity of delaying to send till now, having been engaged ever since the action in the pursuit of the enemy's flying troops.

In my letter of the 21st I informed your lordship, that both armies were near the Tormes; and the enemy crossed that river with the greatest part of his troops in the afternoon by the fords between Alba de Tormes and Huerta, and moved by their left towards the roads leading to Ciudad Rodrigo.

The allied army, with the exception of the 3rd Division and General D'Urban's cavalry, likewise crossed the Tormes in the evening by the bridge of Salamanca, and the fords in the neighbourhood; and I placed the troops in a position of which the right was upon one of the two heights called Los Arapiles, and the left on the Tormes below the ford of Santa Marta.

The 3rd Division and Brigadier General D'Urban's cavalry were left at Cabrerizos, on the right of the Tormes, as the enemy had still a large corps on the heights above Babilafuente, on the same side of the river; and I considered it not improbable, that finding our army prepared for them in the morning, on the left of the Tormes, they would alter their plan, and manoeuvre by the other bank.

In the course of the night of the 21st I received intelligence, of the truth of which I could not doubt, that General Scovell had arrived at Pollos on the 20th, with the cavalry and horse artillery of the Army of the North, to join Marshal Marmont; and I was quite certain that these troops would join him on the 22nd or 23rd at the latest.

There was no time to be lost therefore, and I determined that if circumstances should not permit me to attack him on the 22nd, I would move towards Ciudad Rodrigo without further loss of time, as the difference of the numbers of cavalry might have made a march of manœuvre, such as we have had for the last four or five days, very difficult, and its result doubtful.

During the night of the 21st the enemy had taken possession of the village of Calvarrasa de Arriba, and of the height near it called Nuestra Señora de la Peña, our cavalry being in possession of Calvarrasa de Abajo; and shortly after daylight detachments from both armies attempted to obtain possession of the more distant from our right of the two hills called Los Arapiles.

The enemy, however, succeeded, their detachment being the strongest, and having been concealed in the woods nearer the hill than we were, by which success they strengthened materially their own position, and had in their power increased means of annoying ours.

In the morning, the light troops of the 7th Division, and the 4th [2nd] Caçadores belonging to General Pack's brigade, were engaged with the enemy on the height called Nuestra Señora de la Peña; on which height they maintained themselves with the enemy throughout the day. The possession, by the enemy, however, of the more distant of the Arapiles rendered it necessary for me to extend the right of the army la potence to the heights behind the village of Arapiles, and to occupy that village with light infantry; and here I placed the 4th Division, under the command of the Honourable Lieutenant General Cole; and although, from the variety of the enemy's movements, it was difficult to form a satisfactory judgement of his intentions, I considered that, upon the whole, his objects were upon the left of the Tormes; I therefore ordered the Honourable Major General Pakenham, who commanded the 3rd Division, in the absence of Lieutenant General Picton, on account of ill health, to move across the Tormes with the troops under his command, including Brigadier General D'Urban's cavalry, and to place himself behind Aldeatejada; Brigadier General Bradford's brigade of Portuguese infantry, and Don Carlos D'España's infantry having been moved up likewise to the neighbourhood of Las Torres, between the 3rd and 4th divisions.

After a variety of evolutions and movements, the enemy appears to have determined upon his plan about two in the afternoon; and under cover of a very heavy cannonade, which, however, did us but very little damage, he extended his left, and moved forward his troops, apparently with an intention to embrace, by the position of his troops, and by his fire, our post on that of the two Arapiles which we possessed, and from thence to attack and break our line; or at all events to render difficult any movement of ours to our right.

The extension of his line to his left, however, and its advance upon our right, notwithstanding that his troops still occupied very strong ground, and his position was well defended by cannon, gave me an opportunity of attacking him, for which I had long been anxious. I reinforced our right with the 5th Division, under Lieutenant General Leith, which I placed behind the village of Arapiles, on the right of the 4th Division; and with the 6th and 7th divisions in reserve; and as soon as these troops had taken their stations, I ordered the Honourable Major General Pakenham to move forward with the 3rd Division, and General Durban's cavalry, and two squadrons of the 14th Light Dragoons, under

Lieutenant Colonel Hervey, in four columns, to turn the enemy's left on the heights, while Brigadier General Bradford's brigade, the 5th Division, under Lieutenant General Leith, the 4th division, under the Honourable Lieutenant General Cole, and the cavalry, under Lieutenant General Sir Stapleton Cotton, should attack them in front, supported in reserve by the 6th Division, under Major General Clinton, the 7th Division, under Major General Hope, and Don Carlos D'España's Spanish division, and Brigadier General Pack should support the left of the 4th Division, by attacking that of the Los Arapiles, which the enemy held. The 1st and Light divisions occupied the ground on the left and were in reserve.

The attack upon the enemy's left was made in the manner above described, and completely succeeded. Major General the Honourable Edward Pakenham formed the third division across the enemy's flank and overthrew everything opposed to him. These troops were supported in the most gallant style by the Portuguese cavalry under Brigadier General D'Urban, and Lieutenant Colonel Hervey's squadrons of the 14th, who successfully defeated every attempt made by the enemy on the flank of the 3rd Division.

Brigadier General Bradford's brigade, the 5th and 4th divisions, and the cavalry under Lieutenant General Sir Stapleton Cotton, attacked the enemy in front, and drove his troops before them from one height to another, bringing forward their right, so as to acquire strength upon the enemy's flank, in proportion to the advance. Brigadier General Pack made a very gallant attack upon the Arapiles, in which, however, he did not succeed, except in diverting the attention of the enemy's corps placed upon it, from the troops under the command of Lieutenant General Cole, in his advance.

The cavalry under Lieutenant General Sir Stapleton Cotton made a most gallant and successful charge against a body of the enemy's infantry, which they overthrew and cut to pieces. In this charge Major General Le Marchant was killed at the head of his brigade; and I have to regret the loss of a most able officer.

After the crest of the height was carried, one division of the enemy's infantry made a stand against the 4th Division, which, after a severe contest, was obliged to give way, in consequence of the enemy having thrown some troops on the left of the 4th Division, after the failure of Brigadier General Pack's attack upon the Arapiles, and the Honourable Lieutenant General Cole having been wounded.

Marshal Sir William Beresford, who happened to be on the spot, directed Brigadier General Spry's brigade of the 5th Division, which was in the second line, to change its front, and to bring its fire on the flank of the enemy's division; and I am sorry to add, that while engaged in this service, he received a wound, which I am apprehensive will deprive me of the benefit of his counsel and assistance for some time. Nearby, about the same time Lieutenant General Leith received a wound, which unfortunately obliged him to quit the field. I ordered up the 6th Division under Major General Clinton, to relieve the 4th, and the battle was soon restored to its former success.

The enemy's right, however, reinforced by the troops which had fled from his left, and by those which had now retired from the Arapiles, still continued to resist; and I ordered the 1st and Light divisions, and Colonel Stubbs' Portuguese brigade of the 4th Division, which was re-formed, and Major General William Anson's brigade, likewise of the 4th Division, to turn the right, while the 6th Division, supported by the 3rd and 5th, attacked the front. It was dark before this point was carried by the 6th Division, and the enemy fled through the woods towards the Tormes. I pursued them with the 1st and Light divisions, and Major General William Anson's brigade of the 4th Division, and some squadrons of cavalry under Lieutenant General Sir Stapleton Cotton, as long as we could find any of them together, directing our march upon Huerta and the fords of the Tormes, by which the enemy had passed on their advance; but the darkness of the night was highly advantageous to the enemy, many of whom escaped under its cover, who must otherwise have been in our hands.

I am sorry to report that owing to this same cause, Lieutenant General Sir Stapleton Cotton was unfortunately wounded by one of our own sentinels, after he had halted.

We renewed the pursuit at break of day in the morning with the same troops, and Major General Bock's, and Major General Anson's brigades of cavalry, which joined during the night; and having crossed the Tormes we came up with the enemy's rearguard of cavalry and infantry, near La Serna; they were immediately attacked by the two brigades of dragoons; and the cavalry fled, leaving the infantry to their fate. I have never witnessed a more gallant charge than was made on the enemy's infantry by the Heavy Brigade of the King's German Legion, under Major General Bock, which was completely successful, and the whole body of infantry, consisting of three battalions of the enemy's first division were made prisoners.

The pursuit was afterwards continued as far as Peñaranda last night; and our troops are still following the flying enemy.

Their headquarters were in this town, not less than ten leagues from the field of battle, for a few hours last night; and they are now considerably advanced on the road towards Valladolid by Arévalo. They were joined yesterday on their retreat by the cavalry and artillery of the Army of the North, which have arrived at too late a period, it is to be hoped, to be of much use to them.

It is impossible to form a conjecture of the enemy's loss in this action; but from all reports it is very considerable. We have taken from thus eleven pieces of cannon,* several ammunition waggons, two eagles, and six colours; and one general, three

---

*The official returns only account for eleven pieces of cannon, but it is believed that twenty have fallen into our hands.

colonels, three lieutenant colonels, 130 officers of inferior rank, and between six and seven thousand soldiers are prisoners;† and our detachments are sending in more every moment. The number of dead on the field is very large.

I am informed that Marshal Marmont is badly wounded and has lost one of his arms; and that four general officers have been killed, and several wounded.

Such an advantage could not have been acquired without material loss on our side; but it certainly has not been of a magnitude to distress the army, or to cripple its operations.

I have great pleasure in reporting to your lordship, that, throughout this trying day, of which I have related the events, I had every reason to be satisfied with the conduct of the general officers and troops.

The relation which I have written of its events, will give a general idea of the share which each individual had in them; and I cannot say too much in praise of the conduct of every individual in his station.

I am much indebted to Marshal Sir William Beresford for his friendly counsel and assistance, both previous to and during the action; to Lieutenant Generals Sir Stapleton Cotton, Leith and Cole, and Major Generals Clinton, and the Honourable Edward Pakenham, for the manner in which they led the divisions of cavalry and infantry under their command respectively; to Major General Halle, commanding a brigade in the 6th Division; Major General G. Anson, commanding a brigade of cavalry; Colonel Hinde, Colonel the Honourable William Ponsonby, commanding Major General Le Marchant's brigade, after the fall of that officer; to Major General William Anson, commanding a brigade in the 4th Division; Major General Pringle, commanding a brigade in the 5th Division, and 5th Division after Lieutenant General Leith was wounded; Brigadier General Bradford; Brigadier General Spry, Colonel Stubbs, and Brigadier General Power of the Portuguese service: likewise to Lieut. Col. Campbell of the 94th, commanding a brigade in the 3rd Division; Lieutenant Colonel Williams of the 60th Foot; Lieutenant Colonel Wallace of the 88th, commanding a brigade in the 3rd Division; Lieutenant Colonel Ellis of the 23rd, commanding General the Hon. Edward Pakenham's brigade in the 4th Division, during his absence in the command of the 3rd Division; the Honourable Lieutenant Colonel Grenville of the 38th Regiment, commanding Major General Hay's brigade in the 5th Division, during his absence on leave; Brigadier General Pack; Brigadier General the Conde de Rezende, of the Portuguese service; Colonel Douglas of the 8th Portuguese Regiment; Lieutenant Colonel the Conde de Ficalho, of the same regiment; and Lieutenant Colonel Bingham, of the 53rd Regiment; likewise to Brigadier General D'Urban, and Lieutenant Colonel Hervey, of the 14th Light Dragoons; Colonel Lord Edward Somerset, commanding the 4th Dragoons;

† The prisoners are supposed to amount to seven thousand, but it has not been possible to ascertain their numbers exactly, from the advance of the army immediately after the action was over.

and Lieutenant Colonel the Honourable Frederick Ponsonby, commanding the 12th Light Dragoons.

I must also mention Lieutenant Colonel Woodford, commanding the light battalion of the Brigade of Guards who supported by two companies of the fusiliers, under the command of Captain Crowder, maintained the village of Arapiles against all the efforts of the enemy, previous to the attack upon their position by our troops.

In a case in which the conduct of all has been conspicuously good, I regret that the necessary limits of a dispatch prevents me from drawing your lordship's notice to the conduct of a larger number of individuals; but I can assure your lordship, that there was no officer of corps engaged in this action who did not perform his duty by his sovereign and his country.

The royal and German artillery under Lieutenant Colonel Framingham, distinguished themselves by the accuracy of their fire, wherever it was possible to use them; and they advanced to the attack of the enemy's position with the same gallantry as the other troops.

I am particularly indebted to Lieutenant Colonel De Lancey, the Deputy Quartermaster General, the head of the department present in the absence of the Quartermaster General, and to the officers of that department, and of the staff corps, for the assistance I received from them, particularly the Honourable Lieutenant Colonel Dundas, and Lieutenant Colonel Sturgeon of the latter, and Major Scovell of the former; and to Lieutenant Colonel Waters, at present at the head of the Adjutant General's department at headquarters, and to the officers of that department, as well at headquarters as with the several divisions of the army; and Lieutenant Colonel Lord Fitzroy Somerset, and the officers of my personal staff. Among the latter I particularly request your Lordship to draw the attention of his Royal Highness the Prince Regent to his Serene Highness the hereditary Prince of Orange, whose conduct in the field, as well as upon every other occasion, entitles him to my highest commendation, and has acquired for him the respect and regard of the whole army.

I have had every reason to be satisfied with the conduct of the Mariscal de Campo Don Carlos d'España, and of Brigadier Don Julián Sánchez, and with that of the troops under their command respectively; and with that of the Mariscal del Campo Don Miguel Álava, and of Brigadier Don Joseph O'Lawlor, employed with this army by the Spanish government, from whom, and from the Spanish authorities, and people in general, I received every assistance I could expect.

It is but justice likewise to draw your lordship's attention, upon this occasion, to the merits of the officers of the civil departments of the army. Notwithstanding the increased distance of our operations from our magazines, and that the country is completely exhausted, we have hitherto wanted nothing, owing to the diligence and attention of Commissary General Mr Bisset, and the officers of the department under his direction.

I have likewise to mention that by the attention and ability of Doctor McGrigor, and of the officers of the department under his charge, our wounded, as well as those of the enemy left in our hands, have been well taken care of; and I hope that many of these valuable men will be saved to the service.

Captain Lord Clinton will have the honour of laying at the feet of his Royal Highness the Prince Regent, the eagles and colours taken from the enemy in this action.

I enclose a return of the killed and wounded.

By letters received from Lieutenant Colonel Sir Howard Douglas, I learn that General Santocildes had left 8,000 men to carry on the siege of Astorga, and had joined General Cabrera's division at Benavente with about 3,000; and that the whole 7,000 were on their march along the Esla towards the Duero.

I have the honor to be, &c. WELLINGTON.

	Killed	Wounded	Missing
Officers	41	252	1
Serjeants	28	178	1
Rank and File	625	3,840	254
Horses	114	133	44
Total	694	4,270	256
British	388	2,714	74
Portuguese	304	1,552	182
Spanish	2	4	–

An officer, Sergeant and soldiers of a centre company of the 44th East Essex Regiment. They wear the 1806 'stovepipe' regimental cap and the officer the bicorn, both of which were eventually replaced with the issue of the new uniform.

Notes

Chapter One: The Situation in Spring 1812

1. Saunders, Tim, *Masséna at Bay* (Pen & Sword, 2021).
2. Grattan, William, *Adventures of the Connaught Rangers* (London, H. Colborne, 1847).
3. Wellington, 2nd Duke (ed.), *Supplementary Dispatches, Correspondence and Memoranda* (London, 1871).
4. Half the battalion, which was in this case four companies.
5. General Drouet, Comte d'Erlon.
6. See Saunders, *Masséna at Bay* (Pen & Sword, 2021).
7. These would have been line infantry grenadiers wearing bearskins, red plumes and epaulets similar to those of the grenadiers of the Imperial Guard.
8. The operation beyond the reprovisioning of Ciudad Rodrigo has often been characterized as a 'reconnaissance' but it was almost certainly more than that and revealed Marmont's tendency to hesitate at crucial moments.
9. See Saunders, *The Sieges of Ciudad Rodrigo 1810 and 1812* (Pen & Sword, 2018).

Chapter Two: Plans and Preparations

1. The decision to campaign in the north was at least in part based on a desire not to lose Ciudad Rodrigo which was, despite Wellington's complaints to the Spanish Junta, still not properly repaired or provisioned.
2. The strategic importance of a bridge at Almaraz is that it reduced the distance for Wellington's troops to march to the aid of Beresford by 150 miles, but added more than 300 miles for Marmont and Soult. Ferries existed, but they were not practical for major troop movements.
3. The Staff Corps were engineers under the control of the Horse Guards, while the Royal Engineers and the sappers and miners were under the Ordnance Board. Following the inadequacy of engineering in the peninsula revealed in 1812, all three were brought together in the Royal Engineers.
4. The losses during the Walcheren Expedition of 1809 and the lingering effects of malarial dysentery also served to reduce the availability of reinforcements.
5. Gurwood, *Dispatches*, Vol. 9.
6. Operating in the border lands among familiar villages and alongside Sánchez, the Light Division initially did very well in recruiting Spanish volunteers.
7. The French assumed that an Irish Catholic would have little sympathy with the British and Curtis even dined with Marmont, passing on details of their conversation.
8. On Grant's return to Wellington's headquarters he was promoted to lieutenant colonel and took command of the Corps of Guides and was appointed as head of intelligence.
9. Marmont was under no illusions about the importance of Grant who was escorted to France by 300 dragoons.
10. Napier, William, *History of the War in the Peninsula* (Constable, 1995).
11. As an indication of the volumes of food imported, during the period 1810 to 1811, in addition to American wheat, more than a million barrels of flour were shipped to the peninsula.
12. Leno's logistic paradox.
13. Buckley (ed.), *The Napoleonic War Journal of Captain Thomas Henry Browne 1807–1816* (Army Record Society, 1987).

14. The advance into Spain was further delayed by the need to victual Ciudad Rodrigo due to the Spanish Junta's inability to do so.
15. Both Picton and Graham would be forced to leave the army within days: the former as his Badajoz wound reopened and the latter due to failing eyesight. On top of this Wellington's trusted quartermaster general was not to return to the army but take up a post in Ireland.
16. Delayed from 12 June because of the late arrival of three 18-pound cannon.

Chapter Three: The Opening Moves

1. Cooke, *Memoirs of the Late War* (Colburn & Bentley, 1831).
2. The companies paraded in the order 1 to 10, with No. 1 on the right flank and No. 10 on the left. The battalion on the march could be led ('in front') by either the left or right flank.
3. Tomkinson still held a commission in the 60th Regiment, but confirmation of the gazetting of his purchase into the 16th Light Dragoons was pending.
4. An English league is equal to 3 miles.
5. Tomkinson, Lieutenant Colonel William, *The Diary of a Cavalry Officer* (Spellmount, 1999).
6. Hay, Captain Andrew Leith, *Narrative of the Peninsular War* (Edinburgh, 1831).
7. Jones, General Sir John, *Journal of Sieges*, Vol. 1 (London, 1846).
8. Ibid.
9. Spherical case was otherwise known as 'shrapnel' after its creator.
10. Carcases were metal cages packed with combustible materials that could be fired from cannon and thrown or dropped from walls. They could be used to start fires, or at night illuminate the attackers.
11. The 68th joined Bernewitz's brigade, 7th Division, replacing the 85th which had lost heavily at Fuentes de Oñoro and at Badajoz and sent back to England to recruit.
12. The 7th Division's artillery was I Troop RHA, with five 6-pounders and a 5.5in iron howitzer.
13. According to Oman the composition was 28,000 British, 17,000 Portuguese and 3,000 Spanish troops.
14. Stanhope, Colonel James (ed. Glover), *Eyewitness to the Peninsular War and the Battle of Waterloo* (Pen & Sword, 2010).

Chapter Four: To the Duero and Back

1. Leach, Jonathan, *Rough Sketches of the Life of an Old Soldier* (London, Longman, 1831).
2. The actual number of guns once Bonet had arrived was seventy-eight.
3. The French soldier was more than capable of harvesting and grinding grain, as long as it lasted, which gave them unrivalled manoeuvrability but a finite period of concentration before needing to disperse to avoid starvation.
4. The 2nd Battalion, 5th Regiment of Foot and the 1st 36th had arrived by the time of Salamanca and joined the 3rd and 6th divisions respectively.
5. Warre, William (ed. Edmond Warre), *Letters from the Peninsula 1808–1812* (Leonaur reprint, 2019).
6. General George Anson's brigade consisted of the 11th, 12th and 16th light dragoons.
7. Four guns from Major Ross's troop had been sent forward when Bull's guns were outmatched and running low on ammunition. Ross's other two guns remained in the valley with the Light Division (Sergeant Whitehead's diary).
8. Kincaid, Captain Sir John, *Tales from the Rifle Brigade* (Pen & Sword, Barnsley, 2007).
9. Cooke, John, *With the Light Division* (Leonaur Ltd, 2007).
10. The section of guns was commanded by Captain Jenkinson RHA.
11. Simmons, Lieutenant George (ed. David Rogers), *Previously Unpublished Letters of G. Simmons* (*The Waterloo Journal*, Autumn 2016).
12. The 1st Brigade at this time consisted of the 1st 43rd Light Infantry, the 1st Caçadores and two companies of the 3rd 95th Rifles.
13. The fur caps were the colpacks worn by the elite companies of the chasseurs.

14. Both of the 'von Alten' general officers of the KGL were on the field at Castrejón. Victor Alten commanded the light dragoons that Kincaid is referring to here. His own divisional commander was Major General Carl von Alten.
15. On this occasion, as the threat posed by the enemy's cavalry was not as immediate as it had been at Fuentes de Oñoro. Consequently, they were able to loosen into open column of companies from which a proper square could be formed and the greater distance between companies meant that they suffered fewer casualties from enemy artillery fire.
16. Whitehead, Sergeant T., 'Record of the Service of The Chestnut Troop RHA', quoted in Lipscombe, *Wellington's Guns* (Osprey, 2013).
17. Open columns at 'wheeling distance' would permit the battalion to form square quickly or wheel to a flank and reduce casualties from artillery fire.
18. Vere, Charles, *Movements and Marches of the 4th Division* (Ipswich, 1841).
19. Botflower, Charles, *The Journal of an Army Surgeon during the Peninsular War* (Manchester, 1912).

Chapter Five: The Approach to Battle

1. According to Masséna and Marin, to facilitate wheeling into line of battle the battalions of both armies marched in open column of companies.
2. It is noted that some French officers who had earlier had their horses taken for dismounted cavalrymen were later that day seen riding dock-tailed English cavalry horses.

Chapter Six: Morning, 22 July 1812

1. Sergeant Hale of the 1st 9th Norfolks also wrote: 'This evening [21 July], the commander-in-chief of the French army sent a message to the governor of Salamanca, requesting him to make preparations for the staff of his army, for they should enter the town at such an hour next morning; this put the inhabitants rather in confusion.'
2. Wellington, *Supplementary Dispatches*, Vol. 14 (John Murray, 1872).
3. Fifty each from the four strongest regiments of Curto's light cavalry division.
4. Parquin, Denis Charles, *The Adventures of Captain Parquin* (Leonaur reprint, 2014).
5. The 14th Light Dragoons and 1st KGL Hussars.
6. In his dispatch Wellington states it was the 4th Caçadores, but that battalion was in Pack's brigade, which at this stage in the battle was more than 1.5 miles to the west. The 2nd Caçadores were the light battalion in Collin's Portuguese brigade in the 7th Division and therefore the most likely battalion to have been committed alongside the 68th.
7. The picquet was of a size to use the Lesser Arapile for observation rather than to defend it.
8. Lieutenant Colonel Charles Gordon-Lenox, 5th Duke of Richmond was an officer on Wellington's staff.
9. William Anson who commanded an infantry brigade in the 4th Division is not to be confused with George Anson who commanded a light cavalry brigade.
10. Beamish, Ludlow, *History of the King's German Legion*, Vol. II (London, 1837).
11. Dyneley, Captain, letter quoted by Lipscombe in *Wellington's Guns* (Osprey, 2013).
12. Anon, *Maxwell's Peninsular Sketches*, Vol. 1 (N and M reprint, 2002).
13. Hay, Captain Andrew Leith, *Narrative of the Peninsular War* (Edinburgh, 1831).
14. Also known as the Teso de Aldeatejada.
15. Lieutenant Tomkinson describes Wellington's change of heart as 'singular', remarking that regarding decisions, he 'is so little influenced, or allows any person to say a word'. Lieutenant Colonel Gordon, a member of Wellington's personal staff or 'family', however, wrote home that 'I assure you in the field I had more to say than anyone, and in the battle created much jealousy among family.'
16. Quoted by Edwards in *Wellington's Year of Victory* (Praetorian Press, 2013).
17. Grenville, Charles, *The Grenville Memoirs*, Vol. I (Longmans, 1885).
18. *Historical Record of the 94th (Scotch Brigade)*.

19. Marmont claims that if he had not been wounded, he would have been able to stop Thomières before he became dangerously extended. Foy and other senior French commanders disagreed.

Chapter Seven: The Right Wing

1. Grattan, William, *Adventures with The Connaught Rangers 1809–1814* (London, Edward Arnold, 1902).
2. Grattan was counting the division's two Portuguese regiments as single battalions. They actually consisted of two weak battalions each.
3. Rarely were both the 1st and 2nd battalions in the peninsula for long. Usually the 2nd Battalion had its effectives transferred to bring the 1st Battalion up to strength and was sent home with the 'broken down' and the sick to recruit. By September 1812 the 2nd/38th had indeed been ordered home.
4. Campbell, Lieutenant Colonel James, *The British Army: As it was and ought to be* (London, Boone, 1840).
5. General Montbrun, the long-time French cavalry commander had gone to Russia. Captain Parquin commented that 'The only commander left to lead our cavalry was General Curto, a good enough officer on the parade ground, but without that presence which wins the unhesitating confidence of soldiers.'
6. Arroyo de Azan.
7. *D'Urban papers*. Quoted by Oman.
8. There is some debate as to the extent to which the square was formed (Townsend, 14th Light Dragoons; Napier). Given the apparent ease with which the battalion was broken, it would appear that it was probably only partly formed.
9. Donaldson, Joseph, *Recollections of the Eventful Life of a Soldier* (Edinburgh, 1852).
10. As will be seen, not engaging in a fire-fight is in contrast with the 6th Division at a later stage in the battle.
11. In British infantry companies the captain was normally positioned at the right of the line and the senior lieutenant on the left. The third officer, if present, would be in the supernumerary rank to the rear.
12. At rest is a practical version of the Support Arms for the musket, where the lock is rested in the crook of the left arm and when on the march, the right hand is brought across and supports the weapon with a grip around the small of the stock. It is a comfortable and stable method of carriage when marching at speed.
13. Thomières' division numbered 4,350 men (Oman) and in three ranks would probably have been able to bring a maximum of 3,000 men to bear, but as the French column was well spread out along the ridge the number would have been much lower.
14. The casualty figures for the whole action (88th 138; 45th 55; the 74th 49) indicate that the Connaught Rangers bore the brunt of the enemy volley.
15. This was a significant achievement by the allied cavalry with no more than 1,000 sabres versus up to 1,700 chasseurs. The sight of the French infantry defeated and the low quality of their horses no doubt contributed to Curto's poor performance.
16. Lieutenant Pratt's parent regiment was the 30th Foot and Cruikshank the 38th. Some claim the 88th captured the Eagle of the 101st, but there was no mention of its capture in dispatches and it never arrived in London. It was almost certainly a 'Jingling Johnny' instrument.
17. Hay, Captain Andrew Leith, *Narrative of the Peninsular War* (Edinburgh, 1831).
18. The 3rd Battalion, 1st Royal Regiment of Foot, later the 1st Royal Scots.
19. Arrogant and boastful.
20. It is probable that being in the ascendancy and even possible that they could drive Maucune's first line back on their own, the light companies were reluctant to get out of the way of Grenville's volley and charge.
21. This stream bed (dry in high summer) is the Arroyo de Azan, which runs through Miranda de Azan, south of the Monte Azan Plateau under the motorway and the N-630 and on towards the

Camino a Arapiles. It is useful in pinpointing the action of the 5th Division, which is complemented by archaeological evidence of the line of the cavalry charge.
22. Cannon, Richard, *Historical Record of the Ninth, or The East Norfolk Regiment of Foot* (London, Parker, Furnivall & Parker, 1848).
23. Cotton, the overall cavalry commander, apparently exchanged 'strong words' with Le Marchant; the two did not get on!
24. The order in which companies would rapidly form square from line.
25. 'AZ', *Heavy Cavalry at Salamanca* (*United Services Journal*, 1833).
26. One of Brenier's brigades.
27. *Serrée en Masse* or close column of divisions of companies. In this formation infantry were closed up one behind the other, with minimal gaps between them. If steady, they could resist cavalry simply by the men on the flanks and rear of the column facing outwards. Among other reasons for the failure of defence could be that in a wooded situation there may have been gaps in the wall of bayonets which the dragoons could have exploited.
28. Colonel Elly, late of the light dragoons, was General Cotton's assistant adjutant general.
29. Lieutenant Gregory's troop.
30. Le Marchant, Denis, *Life of Le Marchant* (London, 1841).
31. The 11th, 12th and 16th light dragoons had been following Le Marchant.

Chapter Eight: The Centre

1. Bonet was by now commanding the army following Marmont's wounding. To avoid confusion, not least in the author's brain, I have continued referring to this division as 'Bonet's'. The same applies when Clausel succeeded to command of the army.
2. Vere, Colonel, *Movements, Marches and Operations of the 4th Division* (Ipswich, 1841).
3. Wheater, W., *Historical Record of the 7th or Royal Regiment of Royal Fusiliers* (Leeds, 1875).
4. British staff officers in Portuguese service also wore the uniform of that country rather than the red, silver-laced staff coat of their own army.
5. Synge, Charles, *The Twentieth Century*, Vol. 72 (Nineteenth Century and Afterwards, 1912).
6. Major J.W. Beattie, later Colonel, received the Peninsular Gold Medal.
7. It is generally accepted that when approaching close contact with bayonets fixed, one side or the other would usually break before bayonets drew blood.
8. Wellington always strove to retain campaign-hardened veterans and, in this case, when the battalion was sent home to recruit, four companies remained in the peninsula brigaded with four of the 2nd Queen's in a provisional battalion under the command of Colonel Bingham.
9. The then Captain Bingham had been one of the officers provided by the 81st Foot to the Experimental Corps of Riflemen, but having gained a majority in the 82nd he did not return when the Rifles were properly established in 1801.
10. McGuffie, T.H., *The Bingham Manuscripts: 2nd 53rd in the Peninsular War, 1809–10 and 1812–13* (*Journal of the Society for Army Historical Research*, Vol. 26, No. 107, 1948).
11. Newman, quoted in Bruce, *Life of Sir William Napier* (London, John Murray, 1864).
12. The 61st Regimental Digest.
13. Newman, Fredrick, letter quoted in Bruce's *Life of Napier*.

Chapter Nine: End of the Battle

1. Sources disagree over the number of guns: some say twelve and others fifteen. French foot artillery batteries at full establishment consisted of six guns and two howitzers.
2. 'Serjeant' is the old spelling of the rank, which in most regiments was only superseded by order in the twentieth century but is still used by the 11th's modern-day successors.
3. Unlike the French, the British did not have an equivalent of the *Pas de Charge*, just rolls for 'prepare to fire' and 'cease fire'. Bugles, with their wider range of calls, were increasingly being used, not just by the light companies, and in battle most of the drummers were employed in carrying casualties to the rear.

256 *Salamanca Campaign, 1812*

4. Newman quoted in Bruce, *Life of Sir William Napier* (London, John Murray, 1864).
5. If that battalion was, for instance, with Napoleon in Russia, battalions of that regiment serving in the peninsula would not have an eagle. A number of junior battalions had been specifically raised for the peninsula.
6. In the standardization of 1812, the colours of battalion fanions were 2nd Battalion white, 3rd red, 4th blue, 5th green, 6th yellow, 7th violet and 8th sky-blue. These are not to be confused with the much smaller company *fanions d'alignement*, the rough equivalent of British camp colours.
7. The 11th earned the nickname 'The Bloody Eleventh' and were offered the honour of being converted to light infantry. The regiment, however, preferred the option of becoming fusiliers, but in the event neither happened.
8. Quoted in Edwards, Peter, *Salamanca 1812: Wellington's Year of Victories* (Praetorian Press, 2013).
9. It is not known who formed the second line. The Portuguese brigade could have attacked on a frontage of two battalions with two in support, or it could have been a part of the 4th Division that had not made it as far as the left flank or indeed the 53rd, but that would have been a very short line.
10. A farmhouse in the Arroyo del Valle watercourse just over 1 mile east of the modern Urbanización Los Cisnes.
11. The Arroyo del Valle is far from a ravine in the area; just shallow stream valleys.
12. Girod de l'Ain, *Vie Militaire du Général Foy* (Paris).
13. Whitehead, Sergeant T., *Record of the Service of The Chestnut Troop RHA*, quoted in Lipscombe, *Wellington's Guns* (Osprey, 2013).
14. Beamish, Ludlow, *History of the King's German Legion*, Vol. 2 (London, 1832).
15. The counter-accusation is that Cotton and his escort ignored the sentry's challenge.
16. Combermere, Mary and Knolleys, William, *Memoirs and correspondence of Field Marshal Viscount Combermere* (Hurst & Blackett, 1866).

Chapter Ten: Pursuit and Garcihernández

1. Girard, Étienne-François, *Les Cahiers du Colonel Girard*, quoted by Muir.
2. Chemineau's brigade; 6th *Légère* and 76th *Ligne*.
3. Beamish, Ludlow, *History of the King's German Legion*, Vol. 2 (London, 1832).
4. Ingilby, Lieutenant, *Diary of Lieutenant Ingilby* (ed. Major Lambert) (Proceedings of the Royal Artillery Institute, Vol. 20, 1893).
5. Chauvel's brigade; 1st Hussars and 31st Chasseurs.
6. As previously stated, an English league was equal to 3 miles.
7. Browne, Thomas Henry, *The Napoleonic Journal of Captain Thomas Henry Browne, 1807–1816* (Army Records Society, 1987).
8. Blue coats were issued to the light cavalry and artillery, with the former cutting them down into jackets.
9. This pause not only allowed time for consideration of courses of action but for the army's convoys to catch up and haversacks to be filled for the first moves of the next phase of the campaign, which would limit looters looking for food.
10. The French refer to this as a 'battle' but the categorization based on the scale of the action would in British terms be an 'affair' or combat.
11. Beamish, Ludlow, *History of the King's German Legion*, Vol. 2 (London, 1832).
12. General Trelliard's cavalry division, which consisted of the 13th, 18th, 19th and 22nd dragoons and were supported by the Westphalian Lancers and the Spanish La Mancha Regiment from the Madrid garrison. Providing infantry support were Chassé's infantry brigade and parts of Palombini's Italian division, including the *Napoleone* Dragoons.
13. Dyneley, Captain, quoted in Lipscombe, *Wellington's Guns* (Osprey, 2013).
14. There is some debate over the guns. Beamish says they were the captured guns turned against the allies, but it is most probable that they were Chassé's guns.
15. A reference to Wellington's criticism that the British cavalry 'galloped at everything'.

16. Leach, Lieutenant Colonel Jonathan, *Rough Sketches of the Life of an Old Soldier: In the Campaigns from 1808–1814* ... (London, 1831).
17. These were principally replacements for Ney's Army of the South rather than Joseph's Army of the Centre.
18. A subdivision was half a company and at full strength presented a frontage of ± 12 files.
19. The Eagles of the 13th Dragoons and 51st *Ligne* were found in the Retiro, bringing the total sent to London during the 1812 campaign to four.

Regimental cap, drum and fife case of the XI Regiment of Foot.

A mounted officer of the 95th Rifles.

Index

Note: French divisions are listed under the name of their commander.

Alba de Tormes 99, 100, 117, 169, 184, 187, 203, 205–6, 211–14, 243
Aldetatejada 120, 121, 123, 128, 244, 253
Almaraz 21, 22, 25
Alten, General Victor 37, 38, 63, 64, 65, 78, 81, 88, 89, 109, 240, 253
Andaluciá 13, 19, 21, 32, 136, 234, 238
Anson, General 64, 65, 71, 73, 74, 77, 88, 90, 113, 128, 148, 161, 169, 171, 179, 181, 214, 214, 221, 239, 240, 246, 247, 252, 253
Arapiles (Greater and Lesser) 41, 112, 113, 116, 119, 121, 125, 137, 171–6, 179, 243–6
Arapiles Village 113, 117, 123, 130, 150, 153, 169, 181, 182, 212, 213, 248, 255
Arentschildt, Colonel 109, 135, 139, 145, 148, 165, 166

Badajoz 5–12, 13, 16, 17, 18, 21, 28, 99, 186, 236, 252
Baggage 4, 29, 37, 48, 73, 77, 95, 108, 110, 121, 207, 220, 229
Beresford, Martial 5, 6, 11, 12, 55, 65, 79, 80, 81, 83, 12, 122, 181, 245, 247, 251
Blanket tent 91–2
Bonet, General 37, 59, 63, 95, 112, 117, 18, 123, 125, 130, 131, 169, 170, 171, 179, 183, 184, 185, 187, 241, 252, 255
Bradford, General 31, 120, 128, 148, 149, 193, 240, 244, 245, 247
British Army
  1st Division 7, 23, 31, 52, 55, 63, 116
  3rd Division 3, 4, 7, 13, 15, 16, 18, 31, 63, 68, 100, 120, 121, 128, 129, 135, 136, 137, 140, 141, 144, 145, 146, 146, 149, 154, 157, 162, 198, 239, 243, 244, 244, 245, 255
  4th Division 18, 31, 63, 73, 77, 81, 82, 83, 85, 86, 88, 90, 111, 113, 115, 120, 123, 131, 169, 170, 171, 176, 177, 179, 181, 183, 186, 189, 193, 203, 239, 244, 245, 246, 247, 253, 255, 256

5th Division 4, 5, 7, 11, 18, 31, 38, 63, 78, 83, 86, 117, 123, 127, 131, 148–53, 155, 166, 181, 187, 197, 211, 220, 239, 244, 245, 247, 255
6th Division 5, 7, 11, 23, 31, 40, 41, 42, 45, 48, 50, 52, 63, 71, 96, 99, 100, 123, 128, 154, 169, 176, 179, 181, 182, 185, 187, 188, 189, 191, 192, 206, 209, 212, 223, 239, 245, 246, 247, 252, 254
7th Division 4, 7, 31, 35, 45, 52, 53, 58, 61, 63, 100, 103, 108, 109, 110, 112, 116, 123, 129, 159, 187, 207, 214, 224, 231, 232, 240, 244, 245, 252, 253
Light Division 2, 3, 4, 7, 11, 13, 15, 16, 18, 25, 31, 25, 37, 38, 56, 71–86, 88, 93, 94, 100, 101, 116, 127, 130, 132, 187, 199, 200, 201–6, 211, 215, 223, 232, 238, 240, 251, 252
Heavy Brigade 150–8, 246
5th Dragoon Guards 101, 154, 157, 158, 161, 163, 240
16th Light Dragoons 50, 56, 73, 101, 117, 215, 240, 252
1st Hussars KGL 13, 38, 88, 109, 165, 240, 256
1st Royal Scots 91, 147, 149, 151, 155, 220
11th Foot 25, 27, 39, 45, 48, 74, 75, 88, 139, 145, 181, 182–4, 188, 192–5, 209, 210, 215, 239, 241, 252, 255, 256
27th Inniskilling 113
32nd Foot 184, 188, 190, 191, 210, 239
40th Foot 88, 115, 116, 177–9, 239
43rd LI 4, 35, 37, 50 58, 68, 73, 75, 79, 80, 81, 82, 93, 94, 101, 176, 177, 179, 200–3, 205, 221, 240, 252
44th Foot 158, 239
51st LI 25, 58, 102, 110, 129, 233, 240, 267
68th LI 50, 51–5, 61, 95, 109, 111, 130, 231
88th Connaught Rangers 3, 10, 11, 100, 128, 135, 142, 143, 145, 146, 239, 247, 254
94th (Scotch Brigade) 68, 69, 140, 239, 247, 253

95th Rifles 4, 12, 35, 65, 66, 71, 73, 101, 145, 169, 209, 232, 240, 252
Brunswick Oels 7, 53, 103, 109, 116, 150, 169, 239, 240
Cacçadores 4, 38, 90, 110, 112, 113, 114, 130, 135, 139, 148, 151, 169, 170, 171, 176, 177, 180, 239, 240, 244, 252, 252
Browne, Lieutenant 31, 41, 86, 89, 95, 96, 103, 112, 117, 118, 120, 121, 122, 181, 200, 212, 223, 231, 232, 233, 251, 254
Buçaco Battle/ridge 1, 4, 6, 53, 132

Cabreizos Ford 58, 61, 99, 120, 243
Cafarelli, General 59, 61, 63, 67, 99, 221, 222
Calvarrasa de Ariba 61, 103, 108, 109, 125, 169, 201, 244
Castrejón vii, 63, 71, 73–91, 85, 86, 253
Castrillo 71–85, 93, 95
Charleville Musket (1777 Pattern) 103–4, 243
Ciudad Rodrigo vii, 2, 10, 11, 13, 15, 18, 21, 29, 31, 48, 99, 108, 110, 120, 123, 203, 223, 226, 238, 243, 251, 252
Clausel, General 60, 86, 87, 88, 89, 118, 123, 169, 170, 176, 177, 181, 182, 187, 214, 222, 235, 240, 256
Cole, General 73, 86, 88, 96, 111, 116, 145, 169, 174, 181, 239, 244, 245, 247
Colummn French 63, 131–3
Cooke, Lieutenant 37, 38, 50, 56, 58, 75, 76, 79, 81, 82, 85, 87, 90, 93, 201, 202, 221, 252
Costello, Rifleman 25, 25, 53
Curto, General 38, 71, 72, 103, 125, 135, 137, 143, 145, 166, 187, 215, 214, 253, 254

D'Urban, General 77, 99, 129, 135, 137, 138, 143, 148, 161, 162, 166, 223–6, 229, 231, 240, 243–5, 247, 254, 256
Deuro, Rio vii
Distraction, Policy of 23, 68
Donaldson, Private 68, 140, 144, 146, 254
Douglas, Sergeant 73, 77, 85, 91, 118, 131, 140, 145, 146, 149, 151, 153, 155, 220, 240, 247, 249
Drouet, General, Comte d'Erlon 10, 68, 237, 251
Dyneley, Captain 114, 130, 226, 227, 253, 256

Eagle, French 146, 148, 158, 159, 195, 234, 254, 257

Ersline, General 4, 11, 239
España, General Don Carlos 31, 206, 240, 245
Exploring officers 25, 27, 70, 71

Ferey, General 7, 10, 60, 108, 125, 127, 169, 187, 190, 191, 196, 197, 198, 203, 240
Foy, General 59, 70, 103, 109, 116, 123, 125, 127, 169, 187, 199, 201, 202, 203, 205, 206, 207, 214, 215, 219, 221, 240, 254, 256
French armies
  Army of Portugal vii, 1, 4, 5, 11, 21, 27, 32, 57, 63, 67, 68, 93, 107, 123, 126 153, 187, 206, 207, 214, 220, 222, 235, 237, 240
  Army of the Centre 63, 68, 99, 222, 224, 257
  Army of the North 7, 59, 63, 67, 99, 221, 243, 246
  VI Corps 2
Funtes de Oñoro 7–11

Garcihernández 211–20
Graham General Sir Thomas 28, 29, 31, 54, 55, 61
Grant, Malor Colquhoun 25, 27, 28, 251
Grattan, Lieutenant William 3, 20, 100, 128, 135, 139–47, 155, 157, 190, 192, 211, 251, 254
Great Paris Cypher 98–9
Green, Private 50–4, 95, 109, 110, 119, 130–1, 231, 233, 240
Grenville, Lieutenant Colonel 125, 151, 154, 247, 253
Guareña, Rio 71, 79, 81, 86, 93, 95
Guerrilla, Spanish 5, 7, 13, 19, 23, 25, 28, 32, 61, 63, 97, 168, 222, 234

Halket, General 45, 103, 240
Hill, General Sir Rowland 21, 22, 28, 29, 31, 32, 235, 238
Home Popham, Captain RN 23, 61
Hope, General 100, 108, 110, 169, 240, 245
Huerta, Ford 60, 96, 99, 100, 103, 187, 220, 206, 238, 243, 246
Hulse, General 45, 46, 47, 180, 181, 183, 184, 186, 188–92, 194, 197, 239

Intelligence 25–8

Index

Jones, Major RE 42–8, 252
Joseph, King 19, 20, 28, 63, 68, 99, 140, 208, 222, 223, 224, 231–4, 237, 248, 254, 257
Jourdan, Marshal 20, 32, 232

Keys of Spain 13, 18, 21
Kincaid, Lieutenant John 60, 71, 74, 75, 79, 81, 83, 107, 110, 171, 215, 224, 254
King's German Legion (KGL) 38, 45, 165, 239, 246, 253, 256

Le Marchant, General 63, 64, 78, 85, 128, 135, 151–62, 240, 245, 247, 255
Leach, Captain Jonathan 65, 66, 86, 232, 252, 257
Leith, General 31, 38, 40, 73, 117, 149, 151, 154, 244, 245, 247
Lieth Hatt, Captain 38, 39, 41, 47, 57, 111, 117, 149, 151
Lisbon 1, 29, 223
Liverpool, Lord 30, 32, 55, 65, 67
Logistics 28–30

Macune, General 41, 60, 123, 125, 129, 130, 147, 148, 150, 151, 153, 155, 157, 163, 164, 169, 187, 203, 213, 214, 253
Madrid vii, 21, 63, 68, 221, 222, 223, 224, 231–8, 256
Majadahonda 223–31
Marmont, Marshal vii, 11, 12, 13, 15, 21, 22, 28, 30, 32, 37, 46, 48, 50, 52, 55, 57, 58, 59, 60, 61, 63, 64, 68, 69, 70–1, 85, 89, 93, 95, 96, 97, 99, 100, 103, 107, 108, 109, 110, 111, 112, 113, 116, 118, 119, 120, 121, 123, 129, 130, 131, 208, 211, 221, 222, 243, 247, 251, 254, 255
Masséna 1, 2, 4, 5, 6, 7, 10, 11, 19, 98, 251, 253,
Mondego, Rio 1
Monte de Azan 123, 129, 131, 135, 137, 141
Moricos 50, 52–5, 61, 101

Napier, Major William vi, 25, 29, 73–5, 95, 101, 123, 125, 186, 201, 203, 205, 221, 251, 254, 255, 256
Napoleon 1, 5, 18, 19, 20, 21, 22, 32, 103, 141, 159, 177, 233, 251, 256
Nava del Rey 63, 64, 71, 74, 78, 223

Newman, Major 181, 182, 185, 192, 255, 266
Ney, Marshal 2, 3, 11, 199, 257
Nuestra Señorade de la Peña 103, 108, 109, 110, 130, 169, 187, 244

Pack, General 31, 63, 100, 128, 169, 171–6, 240, 244, 245, 247, 253
Packenham, General Sir Edward 99, 128, 129, 135, 137, 139, 140, 141, 142, 145, 148, 149, 155, 176, 189, 190, 191, 239, 244, 245, 247
Parquin, Captain 107, 116, 253, 254
Peñas Águeda ridge 184, 187, 192, 194, 195, 212, 213
Pico de Miranda 123, 125, 129, 135
Picton, General 3, 13, 16, 18, 31, 70, 91, 141, 244, 252
Piquets 7, 19, 38, 45, 63, 64, 65, 68, 73, 74, 75, 93, 103, 109, 155, 197, 207, 211
Pollos, Ford of 65, 69, 70, 243
Ponsonby, Colonel 50, 58, 231, 247, 248

Ross-Lewin, Captain 184, 190, 191
Ross, Major 75, 76, 82, 84, 93, 206, 214, 240, 252
Rueda 63–5, 68, 70, 71
Russia vii, 18, 32, 254, 256

San Christobal 42, 46, 50–2, 55
Santa Marta Ford 58, 61, 99, 101, 116, 169, 243
Scott Lillie, Major 112, 177, 179
Siera Guadarama 223, 224
Skirmish 40, 52, 53, 55, 58, 60, 95, 104, 108–10, 121–3, 130, 132, 133, 139, 140 150, 151, 169, 192, 198, 200–4, 207, 226
Stanhope, Captain 55, 57, 60, 61, 252
Stapelton Cotton, General Sir 7, 31, 39 55, 63, 64, 65, 71, 74, 77, 78, 154, 207, 208, 245, 246, 247, 255
Sympher, Major 86, 113, 114, 240
Synge, Captain 171–76

Tagus, Rio 1, 11, 21, 22, 28, 29, 98, 235
Talavera 1
Teso del Judio 123, 169, 183
Thomières, General 119–21, 123, 125, 130, 131, 135–7, 139, 140–3, 145, 148, 153, 158, 164, 176, 191, 241, 254

Tomkinson, Lieutenant 39, 40 50, 52, 55, 59, 63, 64, 73–5, 79, 101, 117, 146, 215, 252
Tordasillas 28, 29, 63, 64, 65, 69, 71, 222, 238
Tores Vedras, Lines of 1, 2, 4
Tormes, Rio 39, 41, 42, 60, 61, 96, 99, 100, 101, 103, 107, 117, 120, 129, 169, 184, 187, 202, 203, 205, 206, 211, 213, 214, 220, 238, 243, 244, 246,
Toro 29, 50, 55, 63, 65, 67, 69, 70, 71, 77, 90
Torrecilla de la Orden 78, 83, 85
Trabacanos, Rio 63, 71, 73, 75, 81, 86, 253

Valmusa, Riva de 37, 38, 40
Vere, Colonel 88, 169, 176, 177, 179, 189, 197, 253, 255

Wallace, Colonel 135, 139, 140–3, 146, 148, 155, 239, 247
Warre, Captain William 69, 181, 252
Wheeler, Private 58, 61, 102, 110, 129, 232